A Propertius Reader

ℬℭ LATIN Readers
Series Editor:
Ronnie Ancona, Hunter College and CUNY Graduate Center

These readers provide well annotated Latin selections written by experts in the field, to be used as authoritative introductions to Latin authors, genres, topics, or themes for intermediate or advanced college Latin study. Their relatively small size (approximately 600 lines) makes them ideal to use in combination. Each volume includes a comprehensive introduction, bibliography for further reading, Latin text with notes at the back, and complete vocabulary. Nineteen volumes are currently scheduled for publication. Check our website for updates: www.BOLCHAZY.com.

A Propertius Reader
Eleven Selected Elegies

P. Lowell Bowditch

Bolchazy-Carducci Publishers, Inc.
Mundelein, Illinois USA

Series Editor: Ronnie Ancona
Volume Editor: Laurie Haight Keenan
Design & Layout: Adam Phillip Velez
Maps: Mapping Specialists, Inc.

A Propertius Reader
Eleven Selected Elegies

P. Lowell Bowditch

© 2014 Bolchazy-Carducci Publishers, Inc.
All rights reserved.

Bolchazy-Carducci Publishers, Inc.
1570 Baskin Road
Mundelein, Illinois 60060
www.bolchazy.com

Printed in the United States of America
2014
by United Graphics

ISBN 978-0-86516-723-0

Library of Congress Cataloging-in-Publication Data

Propertius, Sextus, author.
 [Elegiae. Selections]
 A Propertius reader : eleven selected elegies / P. Lowell Bowditch.
   pages cm -- (BC Latin readers)
 ISBN 978-0-86516-723-0 (pbk. : alk. paper) 1. Propertius, Sextus. Elegiae. I. Bowditch, Phebe Lowell, 1961- II. Title. III. Series: BC Latin readers.
 PA6644.A3 2014
 874'.01--dc23

2014024910

Contents

List of Illustrations vii

Preface ix

Introduction xi

Latin Text 1
  Elegy 1.1 2
      1.3 3
      2.1 5
      2.10 8
      2.16 9
      2.31 11
      2.32 12
      3.3 14
      3.11 16
      4.8 19
      4.9 22

Commentary 25
  Elegy 1.1 25
      1.3 32
      2.1 42
      2.10 57
      2.16 64

2.31 73
2.32 79
3.3 92
3.11 103
4.8 121
4.9 136

Appendix: Maps
Map of the ancient Mediterranean. 150

Map of Rome. 151

Complete Vocabulary. 153

List of Illustrations

1. Perseus and Andromeda 33
2. Sleeping Maenad. 38
3. Danaid hermsculpture 74
4. "Apollo Barberini". 78
5. Apollo fighting with Hercules over the
   Delphic tripod. 82

Preface

When the Roman orator Quintilian discusses Augustan love elegy in his work on rhetoric he famously ranks Tibullus before the others, citing his polish and elegance, but concedes that "there are those who prefer Propertius" (*sunt qui malint Propertium*). Although I am not one to rank or give out blue ribbons to the ancients, I would have to include myself in that latter group. As a result, I have found it an immense pleasure to write this commentary—wrestling with Propertius's difficult syntax, shedding light on his wide-ranging use of myth, and interpreting his frequently novel use of diction. It is these very qualities that make Propertius both an appealing and fascinating author and one not generally taught until at least the third year of Latin at the undergraduate level and often beyond. It is my hope that this commentary will make Propertius accessible to more students, to those newer to the Latin language as well as to the more advanced. His elegies will reward reading and rereading, with diverse pleasures for different audiences: as a love poet, Propertius offers a unique perspective on how the idea of passion evolved in the Western literary tradition; as an Augustan author, he brings insight to a momentous time in history—the transition from the Roman republic to the rule of empire; as a poet who experiments with language he delights with the sheer materiality of his words.

In writing this commentary I have benefited enormously from several people. I am truly grateful to Ronnie Ancona, the series editor, for inviting me to undertake this project as well as for her unflagging support and sage advice at every turn. The two anonymous referees for the press offered excellent suggestions that have strengthened many of the notes and the overall presentation of the volume. I am also indebted to Laurie Haight Keenan, the volume editor at Bolchazy-Carducci, for her cheerful responsiveness to all my queries, her careful editing, her sense of audience, and her attention to all matters of production. Many thanks are owed as well to Joshua Hainy, who assisted in the preparation of the vocabulary with his customary professionalism, and to all the students in my upper-division Propertius class in the fall 2011 who provided me the opportunity for a trial run of the first draft. Finally, I owe probably the greatest debt of gratitude to those authors of previous commentaries—for highlighting alternate interpretations, for drawing my attention to textual issues I may have neglected, and for having guided my own appreciation of Propertius for so many years.

I dedicate this volume to Florence Verducci, my professor at UC Berkeley, who first introduced me to the thrill of Propertius.

P. LOWELL BOWDICH

Introduction

༄ *Propertius: Background and literary works*

"Cynthia first, with her eyes, caught wretched me—one never previously infected by passion" (**1.1.1–2**). At one time scholars did not hesitate to read Propertius's elegies as the sincere outpouring of the poet's anguish over his relationship with a flesh-and-blood mistress. Such biographical interpretation of his verse went hand-in-hand with a willingness to construct his life and background from details provided by the poems. Although Propertian scholarship of the past few decades by and large now draws a distinction between the first-person narrator of the poems and the poet as author, it is not so easy when it comes to information that seems conveyed to the reader in the spirit of a biographical sketch. Unlike his contemporaries Horace and Vergil, Propertius is not included in Suetonius's *Lives of the Ancient Poets*. Of course, several grains of salt should accompany any reading of Suetonius who, in some instances, appears to derive his material from the poetry of his subjects. Regardless, for Propertius, aside from some archaeological and epigraphical evidence and brief mention in later authors (e.g., Ovid *Tr.* 4.10.44–45; Mart. 8.73.5), the poems are our only source about the poet's background.

What do they tell us? In keeping with the convention of the *sphragis*—the last poem that provides a "seal" to a poetry book and gives information about a poet's background—the final brief elegy of Propertius's first collection puts his birthplace in the region of Umbria, in the plains below the city of Perusia (now Perugia, about two hundred kilometers north of Rome). Addressing his friend and patron, Tullus, the speaker claims he lost his kinsman in the aftermath of the siege of that city, one of the battles that ensued in the civil conflict unleashed—or reignited—by the murder of Julius Caesar. In just a few lines, the poet not only identifies his origins, but also, more ambiguously, raises the haunting specter of an unburied relative and the gruesome episode of the Perusine war, where sources claim Octavian systematically murdered three hundred of the city's knights and senators after it fell to his besieging army in 40 BCE. Although the kinsman does not appear as one of those immediate victims, the poem implies that Propertius began his writing career at a time of deep division and trauma in his country and that his family suffered—directly or indirectly—at the hands of the man who ultimately became Rome's supreme leader and patron of the arts.

It is not until the fourth and last collection of Propertius's poems that we learn more about his family background. Here, in addition to the speaker's claims (4.1.63–66), an astrologer confirms Propertius's Umbrian origins, further specifying the town of Assisi, whose great walls will become—he asserts—more famous from the poet's genius (4.1.121–26). Although Propertius may well be teasing us by having an astrologer—a notoriously unreliable ilk—give us such facts, the mention of Assisi's ramparts coupled with inscriptional evidence of a family of *Propertii* as members of the "wall-building elite" (Cairns 2006.9) lends credibility to the stargazer's assertions. We learn, as well, that Propertius lost his father at a young age, that his family suffered from the loss of its landed wealth—probably in the expropriations following the battle of Philippi in 42 BCE—and that as soon as he came of age he turned to poetry and eschewed a legal or political career (4.1.127–34), the more usual path for well-heeled youth of the time. Propertius's "bio" here resembles in certain key points the early, formative years of other Augustan poets: Vergil, Horace, and Tibullus also appear to have lost ancestral estates to the land confiscations carried out by the second triumvirate—Octavian, Antony, and Lepidus—to provide recompense to discharged soldiers (cf. Verg. *Ecl.* 1, 9; Hor. *Epist.* 2.2.51–52; Tib. 1.1.19, 21–22, 33), particularly those who had earlier fought for Julius Caesar. And Ovid, half a generation later, similarly asserts his early renunciation of a career in law. That such information for these poets often comes across in their verse has varied implications. On the one hand, the political turbulence of the 40s and 30s left a permanent scar, visible in these apparently autobiographical statements as well as in such pastoral figures as Vergil's Tityrus, the shepherd who, in the first eclogue, narrates the loss and subsequent restoration of his land and thus provides grist for scholars seeking to construct the author's life. For the elegists, in particular, the repeated allusion to the loss of their ancestral estate and patrimony throws light on their speakers' turn to the elegiac mistress as an alternative *domus*, a "household" that substitutes for the institution of the elite family that has fallen victim to the ravages of war (Gardner 2010). On the other hand, for all that these snapshot bios appeal to and secure the reader's sympathy, they also underscore elegy as a stylized posture of the self, pointing to autobiography as a trope—that is, as a convention of the genre where the details at once serve the rhetorical interests of the poems themselves and communicate about the authors' lives.

Such a trope indeed lends verisimilitude to the Propertian poet's account of emotional turmoil, but in general outside historical forces impinge rarely or obliquely on the self-absorbed world of his first collection of elegies, often called the *Monobiblos*, published around 30–28 BCE. Aside from the reference to Perusia and the civil wars in the two final poems, these elegies tend to explore the shifting attitudes and psychological stances of a first-person speaker, an elegiac lover-poet as the Propertian "I," who writes poems that theatrically expose and flaunt the evolution of his passion for a woman named Cynthia (see p. xxii below). The various addressees of these poems, however, comprise not just the mistress herself, but an entire circle of male companions—friends whose aid he seeks, erotic and literary rivals, those he would instruct about the condition of elegiac love, and his initial patron, Volcacius Tullus, to whom no fewer than four elegies of the *Monobiblos* are addressed (**1.1**, 1.6, 1.14, and 1.22). Other historical personages include Cornelius Gallus, the first prefect of Egypt after Rome's annexation of it as a province, and the poet credited with the origins of Roman love elegy (see pp. xxx–xxxi below), who also receives the honor of four poems (1.5, 1.10, 1.13 and 1.20). The inevitable political resonance of such prominent figures lends a historical backdrop to the lover-poet's otherwise insular condition. Thus, while the Propertian speaker's erotic malaise dominates as the book's overarching focus, the homosocial relations implicit in the circle of these addressees provide an underlying political and social counterpoint, a subtle historical framework that only comes to the fore with the concluding elegies.

The term "patron" here, as elsewhere, needs qualification, since Propertius held equestrian status and—even despite the loss of ancestral estates—likely did not depend on a benefactor so much for material support as for the less tangible goods of an audience, venue, subject matter, and social connections. As a character within the poems Tullus provides a foil for the speaker's amorous condition of elegiac lassitude and stasis in Rome: he is the normative aristocratic male embarked on a military career that will take him abroad to Asia, a journey the speaker declines on account of his ties to Cynthia at home (1.6). But Tullus also constitutes an actual historical figure, the scion of a high-ranking senatorial family, the Volcacii, that had enjoyed close ties with Julius Caesar and that maintained similar relations with his great-nephew and adoptive son, Octavian (Cairns 2006.44–47). Indeed, historians have identified three eminent members of this family: L. Volcacius Tullus, who attained consular office in 66 BCE; his son, or perhaps nephew, C. Volcacius Tullus, who served as an officer in Caesar's army in the Gallic wars and remained loyal to him in the subsequent civil wars with Pompey; and a third distinguished personage, L. Volcacius L. f. Tullus, the uncle of Propertius's initial patron, who shared the consulship with Octavian in 33 BCE before becoming governor of Asia, a post that may well have been the reward for loyalty to the triumvir's cause. It is in the retinue of this uncle that the younger Tullus goes abroad in 30–29 BCE—an "after which" event (*terminus postquem*) used to date the *Monobiblos*—while the Propertian speaker languishes in Rome. Regardless, with the publication and immediate success of the *Monobiblos*, connections with the Volcacii presumably served the poet well. Whether his three subsequent books of poetry were published as individual volumes (at approximate dates determined from the poet's mention of historical events) or altogether as a *tribiblos* (Butrica 2006.29–30), they clearly demonstrate an increasing familiarity with the Augustan regime.

Indeed, although Tullus does not appear in Propertius's second collection of elegies, dated to 28–26 BCE, the specific addressees of Maecenas, as the dedicatee of the volume in **2.1**, and Augustus Caesar, in **2.10**, reveal the poet's social ascent and inclusion in the prestigious literary circle around the emperor and his confidante. The use of the title "Augustus" in fact allows us to date the publication of the volume after 27 BCE, when Octavian changed his name. As for Gaius Maecenas, descended from Etruscan royalty, he was the most trusted political advisor to Augustus during the 30s and 20s BCE, and he exerted his influence as a powerful patron of letters, lending his support and recognition to the poets Vergil, Horace, and Propertius, among others. Propertius's greater proximity to the pulse of political life can be felt beginning with this second book, where public, historical themes seem to compete with the speaker's avowed preference to write about the private affairs of the heart. This opposition between a political and a personal focus extends into his third book of elegies, dated to 22 BCE, but the justification of love elegy as a genre that repudiates the grand scale becomes more programmatic in this collection, which implicitly and explicitly invokes the work of Callimachus as a predecessor (see 3.1.1–4, **3.3.13–26,** and pp. xxiv–xxvi below). With his fourth and last book of verse, published around 16 BCE, Propertius more fully embraces the public, historical sphere, writing a novel form of aetiological elegy that explores the origins of Roman rites, buildings, and customs, even as it often incorporates the love themes of traditional Roman elegy. The poet's mistress Cynthia, decisively renounced at the end of the third book, reappears in two poems in the fourth—first as a ghost (4.7) and then as a powerful mistress demanding the surrender of her philandering lover-poet (**4.8**).

⁂ *Propertian elegy and the Augustan regime*

As the temporal sweep of Propertius's four books indicates, his work significantly coincides with the first Roman emperor Augustus's rise to power and the transformation of political structures that occurred as the republic gave way to the principate. This volume aims to introduce students to the major themes of Propertian verse in a way that captures how closely intertwined his elegies are with these momentous political and historical changes. With the exception of **1.1**, **1.3**, and **4.8**, all the selections explicitly engage—however paradoxically—this greater political dimension. The verse selected from the *Monobiblos* (**1.1, 1.3**), by establishing the speaker's erotic and poetic relations with Cynthia, sets the stage for the subsequent dialectic between private and public themes in the poems that follow. While this dialectic often takes place within one poem it also occurs at the level of the arrangement in the poetry book itself. Thus, the comic **4.8**, with its focus on a personal episode of mutual betrayal by the two lovers, balances the mytho-historical, if parodic, focus of **4.9** on the figure of Hercules in early Rome. By including selections from each of Propertius's four books, I have tried to give a sense of the evolution of his poetry as it responded to the radical transformations in the ancient world that was Augustan Rome.

Historians often date Augustus's unrivalled supremacy to his victory over Antony and Cleopatra at the battle of Actium, off the coast of Greece, in 31 BCE. With this conquest Octavian, the adopted son of Julius Caesar, put an end to the internecine civil strife that had plagued Roman society for generations. However, peace came at a price: from the political perspective of systems of government, it was the following decade and a half that saw unprecedented, if at times subtle, changes that paved the way for the increasing concentration of power in the hands of a single ruler. In 27 BCE, although Octavian made a show of restoring republican powers to the Roman Senate, that body unanimously conferred on him the symbolic name of Augustus (Dio Cass. 53.16.8; Suet. *Aug.* 7.2), harking back to the augury of Romulus, the first king of Rome, who founded the city based on his reading or "divination" (*augurium*) of the signs marked by bird flight. In addition to such symbolic gestures, the Senate also allowed Augustus to continue to hold the consulate, an annually elected office during the republic. Such consular *imperium* may have justified the Senate's approval of his continuous control over several provinces—the Iberian peninsula, Gaul, Syria, Egypt, and Cyprus—for a ten-year period that would be renewed. Whether or not construed at the time as "proconsular authority," the command of provincial legions gave Augustus dominance over the military establishment abroad in addition to his consular powers in Rome (Eder 2005.24–25; Gruen 2005.34). Four years later, in 23 BCE, Augustus resigned his consulship (Dio 53.32.3), and yet the Senate not only permitted him to keep and even increased his military authority but it also granted him the powers of a tribune of the people (*tribunicia potestas*). Since only a member of the *plebs* could serve as tribune, Augustus did not hold the actual office but rather exercised its right to convene an assembly as well as the Senate and to introduce legislation (Eder 2005.26). And five years after this second major restructuring of the government, in 18 BCE, Augustus effectively passed the *Lex Iulia de ordinibus maritandis* and the *Lex Iulia de adulteriis*, laws intended to curb the perceived sexual profligacy of the upper classes by offering rewards for marriage, regulating it in relation to status, and prosecuting and severely penalizing adultery in a permanent court. Although these laws were both unpopular and largely unsuccessful in practice, their passage reflects the increasing control exercised by the *princeps* over the civil state, in addition to his military powers.

Propertius's elegiac poems respond in a paradoxical fashion to this rapidly changing urban and imperial environment. Rather than directly engage the public, military dimension of Augustus's swift ascent to political preeminence the Propertian narrator fashions himself as a lover-poet choosing to write about private, erotic themes, because his talent does not permit him to undertake epic or even lyric *encomia* ("praise poems"). And yet, in the very gesture of renunciation, the speaker often highlights events or themes of the public, imperial world that he seemingly eschews. This type of poem has earned the critical name of the *recusatio* or "refusal poem," since it generally addresses a patron or other public figure, such as Augustus himself, and implies—or pretends—that the addressee has requested poetry celebrating his accomplishments. However, aside from Suetonius's claim that Augustus solicited Horace's fourth book of *Odes* and commissioned the *Carmen Saeculare*, we do not know whether patrons in fact asked for poems and if such requests lie behind the convention of the *recusatio*. Many scholars incline to view the elegist's posture of refusal as a literary conceit, but the socioeconomic relationship of patronage serves, all the same, to draw the greater, imperial world and its concerns into the narrow sphere of the speaker's elegiac love.

In Propertius's case, the poems addressed to the figures of Tullus, Maecenas, and Augustus conspicuously feature the public world of empire. So, for example, the first poem of Propertius's second book (**2.1**), a *recusatio* to Maecenas, includes a brief description of Octavian's triple triumph in 29 BCE, celebrating his defeat of Antony and Cleopatra at Actium, the annexation of Egypt, and victory in Illyria. Allusions to other major battles of the civil wars—all mentioned as material the speaker declines to write about—provide a public dimension of Italy's suffering as the backdrop to the speaker's private passion. But when Propertius alludes to the public world he does not focus exclusively on the trauma of the past. The tenth elegy of the second book (**2.10**), for example, addresses Augustus and sketches out a vista of imperial possibility: Hispania, Parthia, India, Britannia, and Arabia crowd into the poem as either partially achieved or potential victories of the future. Even elegies to Cynthia, or to an unspecified addressee, can engage the themes and imagery that follow from such geographic expansion: not only the ritual of military triumph but also the material goods of military booty and maritime trade, and the transformed urban environment of Augustan Rome itself. Cynthia's dalliance with a wealthy praetor, returned from the provinces in **2.16**, highlights the luxury goods that Rome's territories abroad produce for an acquisitive metropolitan market at the imperial center. In turn, the ekphrasis (a verbal description of a visual work of art) describing Augustus's temple to Apollo on the Palatine, **2.31**, draws attention to the expensive foreign marble imported from

Africa after Egypt became a province. Indeed, for all that this poem avoids overt politics, the focus on the aesthetic aspects of the temple, a building first vowed to celebrate the naval defeat of Sextus Pompey but increasingly associated with the victory at Actium, points up the very mechanics of the elegiac genre. Similar to the temple, the aesthetics of elegy operate through indirection: in the elegiac speaker's gestures eschewing grand, public issues, the poems in fact communicate the idea of empire and the dominance of Rome.

By the time Propertius writes his fourth book of elegies Augustus's power is well established and the Roman republic a nostalgically cultivated idea and ideal of the past. However, it is precisely that past—the mythic origins, transformative events, and military glory of Rome before the Augustan principate—that Propertius explores in many of the poems of this book. The absence of Maecenas as an addressee, coupled with the arguably propagandistic or at least nationalistic tone of the book, has suggested to some scholars the heightened presence of Augustus as a patronal force, a phenomenon that certainly parallels what Suetonius asserts about Horace's fourth book of *Odes*, published a few years later in 13 BCE. And yet, Propertius's treatment of patriotic themes is so ambiguous, often verging on parody as in 4.6 on the origins of the temple to Apollo on the Palatine or **4.9** on Hercules and the *Ara Maxima*, that the role of Propertian elegy in relation to the regime eludes any simple analysis. To be sure, the scope of the elegies in Book 4 has dramatically increased from the narrowly obsessive passion of the speaker in the *Monobiblos* to the history of the city and its monuments, but the genre remains, in Propertius's hands, a *fallax opus* ("tricky business," "deceptive endeavor"), as the astrologer Horus calls it in 4.1.135. The connotations of *fallax* are many, of course, but the adjective has particular resonance for the relationship between public and private concerns in elegy: in the first three books, the lover-poet often occupies a marginal position—one alienated from Roman masculine norms that nonetheless get articulated in gestures of refusal; the fourth book, by contrast, tends to undercut its avowed new directions—historical, aetiological, urban, public—by sporadically reverting to the theme of private, erotic love.

⁘ Gender and genre in Propertius

Roman love elegy, and Propertian elegy in particular, may constitute a *fallax opus*, but the genre displays identifiable conventions that distinguish it from other literary forms. With the exception of the handful of poems that have come down to us from Sulpicia, the niece of Messalla Corvinus, the first-person speaker of Roman love elegy is male and—aside from Tibullus's poems for Marathus—suffers from an excruciating passion for a mistress who often remains inaccessible. The elegies give voice to his feelings and so the speaker self-identifies not just as a lover but also as a poet. This double identity of lover-poet or poet-lover sustained throughout the first three books of Propertius's poems makes it tempting to conflate the speaker with the author, particularly when the poems are mined for biographical information (see pp. xi–xiii above). However, in recognizing that Propertius adopts a constructed persona, the reader of elegy more readily perceives the behavior and attitudes of the speaker as a convention of the genre. So, for example, we see the "slavery of love" or *servitium amoris* when the lover-poet of **1.1** declares his willingness to suffer cauterizing fire and iron, if only he could regain the *libertas* of his freeborn status (27–28). Similarly, the wish for an exclusive relationship and fidelity until death with his mistress, Cynthia, (**2.1.47–48**) points to the speaker's adoption of traits often characterized by the Romans as "feminine." Here we see an ironic endorsement of the values of the *mos maiorum*, the "ways of the ancestors," that Augustus championed and attempted to restore, eventually passing the marriage and adultery laws of 18 BCE (almost a decade after the publication of Propertius's second book): the elegiac lover-poet declares his desire for marital virtues but in the context of an extramarital and possibly adulterous liaison.

Moreover, to complement the departure from Roman gender norms on the speaker's part, we see the mistress frequently constructed in "masculine" terms, exercising the power in the relationship. Thus, the common designation *domina*, applied to Cynthia in **1.1.21** and **1.3.17**, draws on its connotations outside of elegy: in the context of the Roman household, a *domina* refers to the mistress of slaves—the female counterpart to a *dominus*, the master of the house. Indeed, despite the feminine gender of *domina* as a morphological form, as a cognate the term evokes masculine authority—the power of the *paterfamilias* over all the members of his *domus*, all those living under his roof or on his estate—and the status of a *dominus* in particular, with ultimate control over his slaves. In this way, the term *domina* contributes to elegy's metaphor of *servitium amoris*, "the slavery of love." But we also see the mistress take on masculine roles in the closely aligned trope of *militia amoris*, "the soldiery of love." Such military rhetoric appears at the end of **4.8** where Cynthia, successful in routing her rivals, plays the role of victorious general, exacting the terms of a treaty. Similarly, at the end of 2.7, the speaker declares his preference to follow in the camp of his girl as leader, rather than in the retinue of Augustus.

Scholars have advanced several theories for the inversion of gender roles in elegy, ranging from a kind of "proto-feminism" on Propertius's part, to his experimentation with alternative distributions of social power, to the genre's erotic relations as a historical metaphor for the political impotence of the aristocratic male under the Augustan principate. Indeed, the erosion of *libertas*, particularly in regards to political free speech, increasingly characterized the Roman senate's relationship to Augustus and the later emperors. From a literary-historical perspective, elegy also reacts to the expansion of Rome as a military power over the preceding two hundred years: the lover-poet as a soft voluptuary, marked by his *mollitia* ("softness," "effeminacy"), has a striking kinship with those soldiers who, according to Sallust (*Cat.* 11–14), became corrupted during campaigns in Asia and brought back not only vast amounts of military spoil—including slaves—but also a propensity to indulge. Whatever the influences shaping the non-normative gender relations of elegy, recent feminist scholarship is quick to point out that the higher status of the mistress constitutes a literary fantasy on the part of both poet and speaker. And whereas, in the actual world beyond elegy, the mistress would remain on the margins, excluded from politics as a female and of low status as a courtesan, the lover-poet as a freeborn male in fact possesses all the privileges and status of Roman citizenship.

But just who was Cynthia? Was she in fact a high-priced *meretrix* ("prostitute," "courtesan")? Or, alternatively, a prominent *matrona*? Readers have often tried to fashion a historical identity for Propertius's mistress, influenced, in part, by her literary predecessor Lesbia, the woman who dominates the speaker's emotional life in Catullus's love poetry. And yet, although scholars tend to concur that Clodia Metelli, the sister of Publius Clodius, furnished the historical model for Lesbia, a conclusion based on Apuleius's identification and on the portrait in Cicero's *Pro Caelio*, there is little evidence for Propertius's Cynthia. To be sure, Apuleius (*Apol.* 10) also identified her with an actual woman, Hostia, the descendant of an epic poet, Hostius, but beyond this little is known. Moreover, the poetry offers its readers conflicting images of Cynthia—as a woman living alone without husband or guardian (**1.3**), as a *meretrix* who seeks expensive goods from her lovers and clients (**2.16**), as the jealously guarded wife of a man she must outwit (4.7). Such inconsistency in her portrayal suggests Cynthia as a variable construct, a figure cast according to the dramatic demands of the poem. Even within a single poem, moreover, the fiction of the mistress as a character in the speaker's drama becomes problematic. The aesthetics of realism begin to break down when Cynthia's attributes also convey qualities of poetry and the mistress becomes a metaphor for verse. Even Cynthia's name, derived from the cult name for Apollo of Mt. Cynthos, identifies her with the god of the lyre and the poetic domain over which he presides. Indeed, after the publication of the *Monobiblos* the volume became known as the *Cynthia*, in keeping with the Greco-Roman convention of referring to literary works by their opening word. Cynthia's promiscuity—all about Rome—thus becomes a trope for the fame of Propertius's poetry (cf. 2.5).

Moreover, the "masculine" mistress and her "feminine" or effeminate lover derive their gendered characteristics in part from epithets that have broader stylistic implications. In the *recusatio* to Maecenas, for example, the speaker imagines his patron weeping over the poet's tomb and ascribing his death to a *dura puella* ("hard girl," **2.1.78**). The adjective *dura* resonates with military connotations and evokes the epic genre, as appears earlier in the poem when the speaker claims that his poetic powers are not suited to tracing, in "hard verse," the name of Caesar back to Phyrgian ancestors (**2.1.41-42**)—a nod to Vergil's *Aeneid*. Similarly, the corresponding antonym *mollis*, meaning "soft," not only implies the effeminacy of the lover-poet but also characterizes the elegiac verse he chooses to write (**2.1.2**). The opposition established by these terms in relation to gender and genre pervades all the Roman love elegists, but the polarities can be confusing and are by no means stable. Why would the elegiac mistress be associated with the militarism of epic values? At one level, this dovetails with the elegiac trope of *militia amoris*, the "soldiery of love," wherein the speaker's avowed preference for a life of passion and poetry parallels, competes with, and appropriates the military sphere he rejects: life under his mistress can be as exacting as a military excursion abroad. At another level, the mistress with her insatiable appetite for foreign goods embodies the very spirit of Roman imperial expansion and economic exploitation. And yet, when the lover-poet casts off his *mollitia* and threatens or in fact engages in violence against his mistress (Prop. 2.15; Ovid *Am.* 1.7), his behavior in fact inscribes epic masculine force in an elegiac context. The mistress, in turn, though *dura* in her interactions with the elegiac lover, takes on the characteristics of *mollitia* as soon as she becomes identified with elegy itself: Cynthia's soft Coan silks, her dexterous lyre-playing, and the delicacy of her eyelashes all metonymically elide with the *mollis liber* that she inspires in **2.1**. Coan fabric, in particular, connotes the poetic style of Philitas of Cos as well as the actual material for a fancy edition of elegiac poems (1.2.2; **2.1.5-6**). Literary style conflates with the mistress again in **2.16**: when the speaker laments that she sends him across the Mediterranean to seek pearls from the Indian Ocean and fabric from Tyre, the image of *recherché* luxuries suggests the elegance of Hellenistic verse—the arcane mythological allusion of the Alexandrian tradition. Such learned allusions and the appeal to oblique or less well-known versions of a myth comprise, in part, the refined and delicate style embraced by the Hellenistic poet Callimachus.

∾ *Callimachus and the Hellenistic influence on Propertian elegy*

Both scholar and poet, Callimachus worked in the vast library at Alexandria and composed verse under the patronage of the Ptolemaic court of the third century BCE. The library culture of the royal court created a heady atmosphere of esoteric learning, and the literature produced during this period, in association with the Egyptian metropolis, shows distinct characteristics. A familiarity with myth and the more obscure variants of a story, a polished and mellifluous style, psychological acuity, an interest in brevity, and, above all, showy erudition all constitute elements of "Alexandrianism" or the Alexandrian tradition. Since Callimachus often pronounced on stylistic issues in his poetry, these literary qualities also became associated specifically with his work and the poetics he programmatically espoused. Although only six hymns, approximately sixty epigrams, and some fragments now survive of his reputed eight hundred works, his influence on Roman poetry and love elegy in particular was profound.

His *Aetia*, a collection of elegiac poems on the origins of Greek cults, ceremonies, and cities, served as a model for Propertius's experimental fourth book of elegies, but Callimachean poetics is evident from the very start of the *Monobiblos*. Here, the speaker's statement that *Amor* does not remember to travel along familiar ways (*nec meminit notas . . . ire vias*, **1.1.17**) serves as a trope for the recondite use of myth and alludes to a passage in the prologue to Callimachus's *Aetia* where Apollo tells the poet to fatten his sacrifices but to keep his Muse lean and to journey on unworn paths (21–30). Propertius **3.3** also recalls this scene and conflates it with an allusion to another Callimachean passage from the *Hymn to Apollo*, where the god contrasts the powerful Assyrian river that carries mud and debris with the delicate and pure stream from a sacred spring (108–112). By evoking these Callimachean passages Propertius too makes a statement of aesthetics—endorsing verse that is refined in its arcane and allusive learning, polished and precise in its language, and of small compass, a poetry distinguished from the grand themes and large scale of epic. And yet, despite such programmatic distinctions in genre, Propertian and Roman love elegy in general thrives on the paradoxical inclusion of elements of the genre it eschews: not only does elegy appropriate the rhetoric of epic warfare as the overarching trope for erotic love but it also, as discussed above, includes direct references to the imperial, public world. Such appropriation of epic imagery in the context of love goes all the way back to Sappho of course, but Callimachus himself also sets a precedent: for example, his poem the "Lock of Berenice," of which we have a few extant fragments as well as a translation by Catullus, refers to Ptolemy III's departure for war with the Assyrians, after lovemaking with his young wife, and carrying off "sweet traces of their nighttime tussle, which he had waged for the maiden's spoils" (Cat. 66.13-14).

The Alexandrian influence on Propertius and love elegy goes well beyond the author of the *Aetia*, however. Legend had it that Callimachus's vehement rejection of the epic genre derived, in part, from an intense rivalry with his student Apollonius of Rhodes, author of the *Argonautica*. Whether or not there is any truth to this, the *Argonautica* in fact exhibits aesthetic features espoused by Callimachus—it is short for an epic poem and studied in its allusive antiquarianism. Woven into the narrative fabric of the quest for the golden fleece are aetiological digressions on Greek cult and ritual. Moreover, the treatment of Medea's passion for Jason in the third book displays a nuanced attention to psychological states that prefigures the extended explorations of the speaker's moods in elegy. Although the mixed-narrative and dialogue form of Apollonius's work lacks the compelling immediacy of elegy's first-person meditations, their similar psychology of erotic attachment suggests the Hellenistic epic's influence on the later genre. And earlier than either Callimachus or Apollonius is Philitas of Cos, to whom the Propertian speaker alludes in his reference to Cynthia's Coan silks (**2.1.5–6**) and whom he mentions explicitly in his third book, imagining the Muse anointing him with water from Philitas's sacred spring (**3.3.52**). Indeed, in the opening lines of Propertius's programmatic 3.1, he links Philitas with the poet of the *Aetia* when he hails the two as his poetic models. The first figure to be called "scholar and poet," Philitas also had a connection to the great library at Alexandria and wrote both hexameter verse and elegy. Only fragments of his work survive, but his elegiac verse appears to have included both erotic and mythological subjects, his most famous poem addressing Demeter's search for the lost Persephone.

ᴄᴡ *Other influences on Propertius and Augustan elegy*

As the elegiac poetry of Callimachus and Philitas attests, elegy before the Augustan poets embraced a wide variety of content. Strictly speaking, the form was defined merely by its metrical scheme as a sequence of elegiac couplets—a dactylic hexameter followed by an elegiac pentameter (see pp. xxxv–xxxvii below). The first known instances of poems in the elegiac meter date to the archaic period of Greece, in the seventh century BCE, by the poet Archilochus, who wrote elegies on topics as diverse as war, politics, banquets, and lamentation. His elegiac fragments mourning men who drowned at sea point to the possible origins of the meter in relation to songs for the dead. The popular etymology of the Greek word *elegos* as deriving from *e e legein*, ("to cry woe, woe") and the widespread use of elegiac couplets as memorial epitaphs reinforce this possible connection with funereal poetry. We see this association between elegy and death often in Propertius—in the penultimate poem of the *Monobiblos*, where the poet's supposed kinsman speaks out as he is dying, a victim of civil conflict; or in the lover-poet's frequent imagination of his own death and tombstone, as in **2.1**; or in the instructions for his funeral in 2.13, including his own epitaph. Tibullus's elegiac lover similarly imagines his funeral rites, when sick and wasting away on the island of Scheria, unable to continue on a military expedition with his patron, Messalla (1.3). Even Ovid's elegiac collection, *Tristia*, expresses his exile to the Black Sea in 8 CE as a metaphorical death.

In addition to funereal and other themes, some early Greek elegy features extended mythological narrative in connection with a single woman. Antimachus of Colophon, categorized by Propertius as an epic poet in 2.34.45, also wrote elegies narrating tragic myths about love and he gave his collection the title *Lyde*, after the death of his beloved. A far cry from the autobiographical pose of the Augustan elegist, lamenting the inaccessibility of his own mistress, Antimachus's work nonetheless displays the literary nexus of elements that also figure in Roman love elegy. Moreover, by calling his collected volume of poems after his beloved (a convention possibly initiated by Mimnermus before him), Antimachus anticipates not only Propertius's *Monobiblos* known as "Cynthia" but also the general conflation of mistress and verse so common in the Augustan elegists.

It is not until Catullus, writing during the late republic a few decades before the elegists, that we see the elegiac meter used for an extended first-person meditation, interwoven with mythological *exempla*, on the speaker's emotional and erotic life. Catullus 68, in particular, is viewed either as "proto-elegy" or the first Roman love elegy, for its discursive rumination on the speaker's relationship with Lesbia set in the context of the myth of Laodamia and Protesilaus. The associative and often seemingly discontinuous leaps of thought that convey the sense of subjective interiority in this and other Catullan poems also characterize the later elegists, particularly the verse of Tibullus and Propertius. But as a first-person reflection on an adulterous liaison in an extended poem of elegiac couplets, Catullus 68 is unique in the corpus for its particular blend of the common ingredients of love elegy. A similar meditation on the theme of betrayal, with specific mention of Lesbia as a prototype for Cynthia, Propertius 2.32, alludes to Catullus 68 as an intertext, signaling its importance as an antecedent.

The Augustan elegists also inherit from Catullus a complex vision of love. The Catullan speaker theatrically flaunts a degraded, even masochistic passion, with all its contradictions and nuances, before his readers. Erotic self-abasement anticipates elegy's *servitium amoris*, but influential too is Catullus's emphasis on the value system of patronage and the homosocial relations between men. The patron-client relationship permeated Roman society, creating hierarchies of dependency and networks of attachment between men of varying levels of socioeconomic status. In one sense, slavery as an institution merely occupied the far end of the spectrum of patronage, given that a manumitted slave would generally become the freedman client of his former master. At the upper reaches of society, among the senatorial and equestrian orders, Romans referred to patronal relations among themselves as "friendship," or *amicitia*, as a way of softening the inevitable status distinctions between the two parties. Regardless of such euphemism, political patronage in ancient Rome consisted of an enduring relationship between individuals of unequal status, who would exchange goods and services of different kinds. Such exchange occurred in an ideological context of interpersonal moral values—*fides* ("loyalty," "good faith," "trustworthiness"), *pietas* ("dutiful respect"), *constantia* ("perseverance," "steadfastness")—that bound citizens together. All these concepts associated with upright behavior in the Roman homosocial fabric become redeployed in Catullus's view of ideal erotic relationships: thus, invoking the gods to secure the success of his affair with Lesbia, the Catullan speaker asks for "a lifelong pact of sacred friendship" (*aeternum . . . sanctae foedus amicitiae*, 109.6); in turn, reviewing the affair's demise, he wistfully holds out his own *fides* as he takes solace in his *pietas* despite Lesbia's betrayals (76.3; 87.3). The Augustan elegists recall the Catullan speaker's invocation of these concepts in their own desire for *fides* (cf. **2.1.47–48**) and for reciprocation of their attentive service, duties (*officia*), and good deeds (*bene facta*; cf. Cat. 76.1; Prop. **1.1.16**). In such longing these love poets metaphorically inhabit the subordinate position of the client, implicitly viewing their mistress as a *patronus*, and expressing an ironic nostalgia for the *mos maiorum*, or "ancestral values," in an adulterous or extramarital context.

And yet, despite the metaphor of patron-client and homosocial relations between men, it is paradoxically with a female position that the Catullan *ego* (or his love) often identifies. This is less of a paradox when we consider that the client's—and the slave's—own subordinate status partially aligns him with women in relation to powerful men. We see the Catullan "woman" when the speaker projects himself as Laodamia in the intensity of her passion and loss in 68; he takes on the persona of Sappho herself, dying from jealousy, in Catullus 51; and his *amor* is construed as a flower at the edge of a field in 11. All these identifications highlight Greco-Roman ideas about women as less able to control their emotions and thus more vulnerable to the passions than men—an intemperance that also marks the character of the slave. Although the Catullan *ego* certainly adopts a masculine persona in his invective poetry, his struggle with and surrender to the turbulence of his feelings in the Lesbia poems display a feminine identity that prefigures the inversion of Roman gender roles in elegy. Of course, such postures are ultimately a rhetorical conceit, since the actual male gender of the freeborn poet assures him the higher status of a citizen in relation to the politically disenfranchised position of his mistress. Regardless, for the elegists as for Catullus, playing the subordinate role—whether of the client, slave, or woman—becomes a distinctive, if rhetorical, feature of their poems.

Adding to the feminized vision of the elegiac lover-poet is the idea of love as a pathological disease or madness—a trope pronounced in both Catullus and Lucretius but ultimately traceable to Sappho. In Catullus 76, love is a *pestem* ("affliction," 20), *perniciem* ("curse," 20), *taetrum ... morbum* ("foul disease," 25), and *torpor* ("numbness," 21) that creeps through the speaker's deepest marrow, the last a physical symptom recalling Sappho's description of desire as a kind of collapse or breakdown of defective senses. For Lucretius, the madness of passion described in the fourth book of *De Rerum Natura* disturbs the ideal equilibrium of Epicurean *ataraxia* ("equanimity," "lack of disturbance"), with the lover experiencing an obsessive inability to satisfy himself—he stands in the midst of a river, drinking, but cannot quench his thirst (4.1097–1104). We see similar metaphors of disease and madness in Propertius **1.1**, where the speaker once infected (*contactum*) has suffered from *furor* for a year, seeks aid for his *non sani pectoris* ("diseased heart"), and is willing to undergo the surgeon's knife. Propertius **2.1**, in turn, lists famous mythological doctors and their patients—Machaon and Philoctetes, Chiron and Phoenix, Asclepius and Androgeon—only to conclude that there is no cure for love. Such rhetoric of disease only reinforces the marginalized position that the elegiac lover-poet occupies in his rejection of the social norms of Roman masculinity.

Finally, the triangulated dramatic structure or cast of characters in elegy draws from the plots of Roman new comedy (with its storylines based on those of Menander and other Greek practitioners of the genre). In his resistance to the social norms of development for the Roman male—marriage and a public career—the lover-poet looks back to the lovesick *adulescens* ("youth") who is out of step with his family's wishes in a typical comic plot. In addition, the stock character of the braggart soldier (see Plautus's *Miles Gloriosus*) appears in various guises in elegy—sometimes as an actual warrior returned from battle (e.g., Ovid *Am.* 3.8), at others as a wealthy *praetor* departing for or returning from a post abroad (1.8; **2.16**). Such characters, with ample financial resources, function as rivals and pose a threat to the lover-poet who, whether sincerely or not, professes poverty. Another blocking figure from New Comedy, the *lena* or "procuress," similarly plays a role in elegy, offering her advice to the mistress—that she open her door to the rich alone (Tib. 1.5, 2.6; Prop. 4.5; Ovid *Am.* 1.8). In turn, the extortionate courtesan of comedy provides the model for the elegiac *puella* who, though accused of greed by her lover, must support herself with gifts. Thus, for all that Augustan elegy emerges at a particular time and place, these comic prototypes reveal the degree to which elements from previous genres commingle and recombine to fashion its unique form and content.

Probably the most profound influence on the love elegies of Propertius, Tibullus, and Ovid is also the most mysterious in that we know the least about it—namely, the elegy of Cornelius Gallus, the first governor—literally *praefectus*—of Egypt when it came under Roman authority in 30 BCE, after its annexation. Gallus's tenure in Egypt was short-lived, since his independent behavior as a *praefectus* threatened Augustus, who had him recalled to Rome where he subsequently committed suicide in 26 BCE. Although we are hard-pressed to judge the precise nature of Gallus's impact, since we only possess ten lines of his poetry, ancient authors held his work in high regard, with Ovid (*Trist.* 4.51–54) listing him as the "first" to write in the genre (not counting the prototype of Catullus 68) and thus the inventor of Roman love elegy. He wrote four books of poems addressed to a woman with the name "Lycoris," thought to be a pseudonym for his actual mistress. In addition to the erotic content and autobiographical posture of Gallus's verse, we can deduce from Vergil's tenth eclogue that his elegies likely displayed the arcane and refined mythological learning typical of Alexandrian style. All the same, Quintilian's judgement that the verse of Gallus was *durior* ("rather harsh") has an ironic resonance for the programmatic opposition, so pronounced in Propertius, between "soft" or *mollis* elegy and *durus* epic.

↜ *Propertian style*

Students approaching Propertius for the first time may consider his own poetry *durior* or "rather hard"—not, of course, from the perspective of ancient aesthetics but simply in terms of the initial difficulty they will encounter reading his work. To some degree this can be attributed to various characteristics of his style and his Callimachean poetics discussed above. In particular, Propertius's fondness for mythological *exempla* to illuminate, elaborate, and amplify his chosen topic makes commentaries and dictionaries of myth indispensable as reading tools for his poems. And that he does not always illustrate with a well-known story but rather with an arcane variant compounds the difficulty of his allusions. Moreover, Propertius makes lavish and abundant use of Greek loan-words, further displaying his erudition and lending a cosmopolitan polish to the sonorous impact of his elegies. Nevertheless, although daunting for the uninitiated, Propertius's refined style, with its *recherché* myths, would have appealed to and flattered ancient readers by establishing between them and the author a kind of community of educated elite.

Other difficulties posed by Propertius's poems are not so easily explained by Alexandrian erudition. Complex syntax, shifting and fluctuating addressees within the same poem, unusual uses of diction, and logical inconsistencies add to the challenge—or frustration—of a first-time reader. Scholars have variously attributed these characteristics to the representation of subjectivity in first-person poetic narrative, to a crisis in the ideology of Roman masculinity under the Augustan principate, to Propertius's poetic experimentation, and to lacunose or discrepant manuscripts. Certainly a genre that aims to convey the psychological complexity of first-person meditations on love, art, and politics will demonstrate contradiction and even, at times, a surface incoherence as a kind of reality effect that imitates processes of thought. Moreover, from a historical perspective, one that views generic conventions as rooted in the conditions of a particular time and place, such aesthetic effects of first-person "subjective" elegy indeed derive, at some level, from the breakdown of ideological systems of the republic and their inadequacy in the transformed Rome of Augustus.

In addition, Propertius as a poet tends to push language beyond its conventional meanings and to use words in novel ways. For his own time and place he exemplifies the poetic manifesto propounded by Ezra Pound in the early twentieth century—"make it new!" No wonder that Pound was particularly drawn to the elegist, loosely translating and arranging select poems in *Homage to Sextus Propertius,* a brilliant work that captures his quality of *logopoeia,* the modernist poet's term for the ironical and rhetorical play of poetic language. Specifically, *logopoeia* refers to how words can bring all their connotations from normative linguistic contexts into a poem where they are redeployed in novel ways. Thus, when the speaker of Propertius 2.1 refers to Maecenas's loyalty to Augustus "in both wartime and peace" (*et sumpta et posita pace,* 36), the Latin *sumere et ponere pacem* is an ironic distortion of the usual phrases, *sumere arma* and *ponere arma* ("to take up" and "to lay down arms"), and points to the violence underwriting the Augustan settlement. Such departures from normative phrasing (and contexts) can be challenging for readers of Propertius.

All the same, there is no denying the particularly corrupt manuscript tradition for Propertius's poems and the manifold conjectures and emendations that editors have made as a result—a situation that led to the quip by J. S. Phillimore in his 1901 OCT edition, *quot editores, tot Propertii* ("However many editors, so many texts of Propertius are there"). The almost 150 surviving manuscripts of Propertius all derive from a single lost archetype, with the earliest extant copy dating to approximately 1200. Scholars have concluded that the

Propertian archetype was gravely flawed, with scribal errors ranging from miscopying, to faulty incorporation of glosses and corrections, to wrongful divisions of poems (Butrica 2006: 31). Although much of the twentieth century produced conservative editions of Propertius, the last few decades have witnessed a return to a more skeptical and interventionist approach to editing his poems. In making their emendations the "skeptics"—those distrustful of the poems as transmitted—often refer to the discrepancy between ancient assessments of Propertius's style, as in Ovid's reference to *blandi . . . Propertius oris* ("smooth-tongued Propertius," *Tr.* 5.1.17), and the manuscript tradition of a difficult and often opaque text. For my own selection of poems I have opted to use Barber's more conservative 1960 edition of the OCT, although in a few places I do depart and print the emendations of Heyworth's 2007 OCT or those of others (see p. 1, Latin Text). I believe that Barber's edition offers poems that are easier and less confusing for the undergraduate student to read, precisely because there are fewer proposed line transpositions and lacunae than printed in Heyworth's 2007 OCT.

Manuscript tradition aside, there are certain forms, constructions of syntax, and stylistic tendencies that appear often in Propertius and that the first-time reader of this difficult but rewarding author should anticipate. I do not pretend to be comprehensive in the following brief list but single out some of those features that occur frequently.

1. Propertius will shift addressees in the middle of the poem and signals such changes with an *apostrophe* (lit. "turning away" to address those absent) that is often but not always accompanied by the vocative case. Cf. **1.1.19, 1.1.25, 3.11.37–38**.
2. To succinctly express complex ideas Propertius often uses ablative absolutes that can be difficult to translate without careful attention to the nuances of context. Cf. **2.16.38**, *damnatis . . . militibus*, where Marc Antony's flight effectively dooms his soldiers, so that he fills the Actian waters with their useless cries.

3. *Hyperbaton*, the departure from conventional word order and thus, for inflected languages, the separation of modifier and noun, is common in Propertius—and all the Augustan poets—for poetic and metrical effect. Cf. **1.1.4**, *et caput impositis pressit Amor pedibus*, where the separation of participle from noun in the absolute seems to reinforce the extent of Amor's domination. Similarly, in **1.3.24**, *nunc furtiva cauis poma dabam manibus*, the adjectives preceding their nouns accentuate the stealthy tenuousness of the action. In this last example, the *hyperbaton* produces *synchysis*, or interlocking word order in the form of ABAB: here, two noun-adjective phrases are arranged so that the first modifier is followed by the second, followed by their nouns in similar alternation. Cf. **1.1.30** and **1.1.34** for further examples of *synchysis*.

4. Postpositive conjunctions and prepositions similarly depart from expected word order in Propertius (cf. **3.11.46**: *statuas inter et arma Mari*).

5. Syncopated verb forms appear as accomodations to the meter (cf. **1.1.30**: *norit* for *nouerit*; **1.3.27**: *duxti* for *duxisti*; **2.16.25**: *peccarim* instead of *peccauerim*).

6. Masculine and feminine *i*-stem nouns and adjectives regularly have -*īs* for the accusative plural.

7. The alternative ending -*ēre* is often used in place of -*ērunt* in the third person plural perfect active indicative (cf. **2.32.53**: *fluxere*).

8. The alternative endings of -*āre*, -*ēre*, -*bēre* are used in place of -*āris*, -*ēris*, and -*bēris*, in the passive forms of the second person singular present indicative, present subjunctive, and future indicative (cf. **2.32.7**: *spatiere*; **3.3.39**: *uectabere*; **3.11.1**: *mirare*).

All these alternative forms allow the poet greater flexibility in meeting the metrical demands of the elegiac couplet.

✧ *Elegiac couplet*

Ancient elegy is simply any verse composed in elegiac couplets, a meter in which a pentameter line follows a line of dactylic hexameter. The meter of Homeric epic and epic poetry in general, dactylic hexameter is the oldest known Greco-Roman poetic form. Although the metrical name indicates six feet of dactyls (defined as one long syllable followed by two shorts, $-\cup\cup$), the last foot always consists of either a spondee (two long syllables, $--$), or a trochee (a long syllable followed by a short, $-\cup$). The elegiac pentameter, in turn, consists of the duplication of the first two and a half feet of a hexameter—that is, a pattern that repeats the sequence of two dactyls followed by the initial longum of the third foot ($-\cup\cup-\cup\cup-$).

Both the hexameter and the pentameter allow for the substitution of two short syllables by one long syllable in certain positions as diagrammed below:

$$-\underline{\cup\cup}-\underline{\cup\cup}-\underline{\cup\cup}-\underline{\cup\cup}-\cup\cup-\cup$$
$$-\underline{\cup\cup}-\underline{\cup\cup}-|-\cup\cup-\cup\cup-$$

Thus, one or more of the first four feet of dactyls in the hexameter may regularly be resolved into spondees (but the fifth foot rarely so). Similarly, one or both of the dactyls of the first half of the pentameter may also be resolved into spondees, so that, in the case of double resolution, the initial half line can consist of five long syllables. However, there is never resolution in the second half of the pentameter. Consider the pentameter of the opening couplet of **1.1**, *contactum nullis ante cupidinibus*, where the spondees of the first half of the line give way to the dactyls of the second half.

The natural pause that occurs in reading a line of poetry is called a *caesura*, translated as "cutting," because it refers to the breaking of a line after a word within a foot. In the hexameter, the pause after the first syllable of the third foot is called the main *caesura*. Because the elegiac pentameter replicates the hexameter line up to its main *caesura* the pentameter also contains this strong break between its two halves. Such pauses not only allow the meter to reinforce groups of words as units of sense but also give rise to internal rhyme. Often nouns and their modifiers, though separated in *hyperbaton*, produce such rhymes between the word before the *caesura* and the word at the end of the line. Consider **1.1.11–12**, where both the hexameter and the pentameter exhibit internal rhymes:

> *nam modo Partheniis amens errabat in antris*
> *ibat et hirsutas ille videre feras.*

From a stylistic perspective, the elegiac couplet tends, in the Roman love elegists, to be "end-stopped," meaning that the syntax of the sentence or clause and the thought contained within it conclude at the end of the pentameter. This creates a certain terse and epigrammatic elegance, particularly in the enumeration or development of *exempla* that flesh out the speaker's "thesis" or contention. Moreover, since the dactylic hexameter is the meter of epic poetry, the following pentameter becomes identified specifically as the *elegiac pentameter* and the thematic opposition between epic and elegy that love elegy explores on the level of content frequently plays out on the level of the couplet itself. Thus, in **2.10.25–6**, the hexameter refers to the epic source that Propertius fails to reach, whereas the pentameter identifies the stream that inspires his elegy:

> *Nondum etiam Ascraeos norunt mea carmina fontis,*
> *Sed modo Permessi flumine lauit Amor.*

Similarly, in **3.11.19–20**, the hexameter evokes Hercules's epic feats as memorialized in the vanquished world at peace, whereas the pentameter depicts the hero in a "soft" and elegiac light:

> *ut qui pacato statuisset in orbe columnas*
> *tam dura traheret mollia pensa manu.*

Scanning and reading aloud the poems will bring alive this thematic use of the couplet.

For further discussion of scansion and the rules of Latin meter, including what makes syllables long or short, the reader should consult Califf 2002; Halporn, Ostwald, and Rosenmeyer 1994.

ॐ *Suggested reading*
General

Ancona, R., and E. Greene, eds. *Gendered Dynamics in Latin Love Poetry*. Baltimore, 2005.

Baker, R. J. "*Laus in amore mori*: Love and Death in Propertius." *Latomus* 29 (1970) 670–98.

Cairns, F. *Sextus Propertius. The Augustan Elegist*. Cambridge, 2006.

De Brohun, J. *Roman Propertius and the Reinvention of Elegy*. Ann Arbor, 2003.

Fear, T. "The Poet as Pimp. Elegiac Seduction in the Time of Augustus." *Arethusa* 33.2 (2000) 217–40.

Fredrick, D. "Reading Broken Skin: Violence in Roman Elegy." In *Roman Sexualities*, edited by J. P. Hallett and M. B. Skinner, 172–93. Princeton, 1997.

Gardner, H. *Gendering Time in Augustan Love Elegy*. Oxford, 2013.

———. "The Elegiac *Domus* in the Early Augustan Principate." *American Journal of Philology* 131.3 (2010) 453–93.

Gold, B., ed. *The Blackwell Companion to Roman Love Elegy*. Oxford, 2012.

———. "The Natural and Unnatural Silence of Women in the Elegies of Propertius." *Antichthon* 41 (2007) 54–72.

———. "'But Ariadne was Never There in the First Place': Finding the Female in Roman Poetry." In *Feminist Theory and the Classics*, edited by N. Rabinowitz and A. Richlin, 75–101. New York, 1993.

Greene, E. *The Erotics of Domination*. Baltimore, 1998.

Günther, H-C. *Brill's Companion to Propertius*. Leiden, 2006.

Hallett, J., and M. Skinner, eds. *Roman Sexualities*. Princeton, 1997.

Heyworth, S. J. "Propertius, patronage, and politics." *Bulletin of the Institute of Classical Studies of the University of London* 50 (2007) 93–128.

Hubbard, M. *Propertius*. New York, 1975.

James, S. *Learned Girls and Male Persuasion. Gender and Reading in Roman Love Elegy*. Berkeley and Los Angeles, 2003.

Janan, M. *The Politics of Desire. Propertius IV*. Berkeley and Los Angeles, 2001.

Johnson, W. R. *A Latin Lover in Ancient Rome: Readings in Propertius and his Genre*. Columbus, 2009.

Keith, A. *Propertius, Poet of Love and Leisure*. London, 2008.

Kennedy, D. *The Arts of Love: Five Studies in the Discourse of Roman Love Elegy*. Cambridge, 1992.

King, J. K. "Propertius' Programmatic Poetry and the Unity of the Monobiblos." *Classical Journal* 71.2 (1976) 108–24.

Luck, G. *The Latin Love Elegy*. 2nd ed. London, 1969.

McCoskey, D. "Reading Cynthia and Sexual Difference in the Poems of Propertius." *Ramus* 28.1 (1999) 16–39.

Miller, P. A. *Subjecting Verses*. Princeton, 2004.

Papanghelis, T. D. *Propertius: a Hellenistic Poet on love and death*. Cambridge, 1987.

Ramsby, T. *Textual Permanence. Roman Elegists and the Epigraphic Tradition*. London, 2007.

Shackleton Bailey, D. R. *Propertiana*. Cambridge, 1956.

Sharrock, A. "Constructing Characters in Propertius." *Arethusa* 33.2 (2000) 263–84.

Stahl, H-P. *Propertius, "Love" and "War": Individual and State under Augustus*. Berkeley and Los Angeles, 1985.

Sullivan, J. P. *Propertius: A Critical Introduction*. Cambridge, 1976.

Veyne, P. *Roman Erotic Elegy*. Trans. D. Pellauer. Chicago, 1988.

Welch, T. *The Elegiac Cityscape: Propertius and the Meaning of Roman Monuments*. Columbus, 2005.

Wyke, M. *The Roman Mistress*. Oxford, 2002.

Elegy 1.1

Ahl, F. "Propertius 1.1." *Wiener Studien* 87.8 (1974) 80–98.

Booth, J. "Problems and programmatics in Propertius 1.1." *Hermes* 129.1 (2001) 63–74.

Fratantuono, L. "'*Velocem potuit domuisse puellam*': Propertius, Catullus, and Atalanta's Race." *Latomus* 67.2 (2008) 342–52.

Gardner, H. "Taming the *velox puella*: Temporal Propriety in Propertius 1.1." *Phoenix* 65.12 (2011) 100–124.

Parca, M. "*Tardus Amor* and *Tardus Apollo* in Propertius' Monobiblos." *Latomus* 41 (1982) 584–88.

Elegy 1.3

Breed, B. W. "Portrait of a Lady: Propertius 1.3 and Ecphrasis." *Classical Journal* 99.1 (2003) 35–56.

Greene, E. "Elegiac Woman: Fantasy, *Materia* and Male Desire in Propertius 1.3 and 1.11." *American Journal of Philology* 116.2 (1995) 303–18.

Harrison, S. J. "Drink, suspicion and comedy in Propertius 1.3." *Proceedings of the Cambridge Philological Society* 40 (1994) 18–26.

Kaufhold, S. "Propertius 1.3: Cynthia Rescripted." *Illinois Classical Studies* 22 (1997) 87–98.

Tatham, G. "'Just as Ariadne Lay . . .': Images of Sleep in Propertius 1.3." *Scholia* 9 (2000) 43–53.

Valladares, H. "The Lover as a Model Viewer: Gendered Dynamics in Propertius 1.3." In *Gendered Dynamics in Latin Love Poetry*, edited by R. Ancona and E. Greene, 206–42. Baltimore, 2005.

Elegy 2.1

Colaizzi, R. "A New Voice in Roman Elegy: The Poeta of Propertius 2.1." *Rheinisches Museum für Philologie* 136.2 (1993) 126–43.

Greene, E. "Gender Identity and the Elegiac Hero in Propertius 2.1." *Arethusa* 33.2 (2000) 241–62.

Herrera, G. R. "Propertius 2.1.71–78 and the Latin Epitaphs." *Mnemosyne* 52 (1999) 194–97.

Wiggers, N. "Reconsideration of Propertius II. 1." *Classical Journal* 72.4 (1977) 334–41.

Elegy 2.10

Bowditch, L. "Propertius 2.10 and the Eros of Empire." In *Being There Together: Essays in Honor of Michael C. J. Putnam on the Occasion of his Seventieth Birthday*, edited by H. Haskell and P. Thibodeau, 163–180. Afton, MN, 2003.

Lyne, R. O. A. M. "Propertius 2.10 and 11 and the Structure of Books '2A' and '2B.'" *Journal of Roman Studies* 88 (1998) 21–36.

Nethercut, W. "Propertius, Elegy 2.10." *Symbolae Osloenses* 47 (1972) 79–94.

Tatum, W. J. "Aspirations and Divagations: The Poetics of Place in Propertius 2.10." *Transactions of the American Philological Association* 130 (2000) 393–410.

Elegy 2.16

Bowdith, L. "Propertius and the Gendered Rhetoric of Luxury and Empire: A Reading of 2.16." *Comparative Literature Studies* 43.3 (2006) 306–25.

Dzino, D. "The 'Praetor' of Propertius 1.8 and 2.16 and the Origins of the Province of Illyricum." *Classical Quarterly* 58.2 (2008) 699–703.

Griffin, J. "Propertius and Antony." *Journal of Roman Studies* 67 (1977) 17–26.

Elegy 2.31/2.32

Barchiesi, A. 2005. "Learned Eyes: Poets, Viewers, Image Makers." In *The Cambridge Companion to the Age of Augustus*, edited by K. Galinsky, 281–305. Cambridge, 2005.

Batinski, E. "*In Cynthiam* / *Pro Cynthia* (Propertius 2,32)." *Latomus* 62.3 (2003) 616–26.

Bowditch, L. "Palatine Apollo and the Imperial Gaze: Propertius 2.31 and 2.32." *American Journal of Philology* 130.3 (2009) 401–38.

Hubbard, T. "Art and Vision in Propertius 2.31/32." *Transactions of the American Philological Association* 114 (1984) 281–97.

Kuttner, A. 1999. "Culture and History at Pompey's Museum." *Transactions of the American Philological Association* 129 (1999) 343–73.

Elegy 3.3

Cairns, F. "Propertius the Historian (3.3.1–12)?" In *Clio and the poets: Augustan poetry and the traditions of ancient historiography*, edited by D. Levene and D. Nelis, 25–44. Boston, 2002.

Frost, C. "Propertius 3.3.45–46: Don't Go Near the Water." *American Journal of Philology* 112 (1991) 251–59.

Miller, J. "Ennius and the Elegists." *Illinois Classical Studies* 8 (1993) 277–83.

Elegy 3.11

Baker, R. "Propertius, Cleopatra and Actium." *Antichthon* 10 (1976) 56–62.

Butrica, J. "Propertius 3.11.33–38 and the Death of Pompey." *Classical Quarterly* 43.1 (1993) 342.

Mader, G. "Heroism and Hallucination: Cleopatra in Horace c. 1.37 and Propertius 3.11." *Grazer Beiträge. Zeitschrift für die klassische Altertumswissenschaft* 16 (1989) 183–201.

Nethercut W. R. "Propertius 3.11." *Transactions of the American Philological Association* 102 (1971) 411–43.

Tronson, A. "What the Poet Saw: Octavian's Triple Triumph, 29 B.C. Jeremiah Markland's Conjectures at Propertius 3.11.52–53." *Acta Classica* 42 (1999) 171–86.

Elegy 4.8

Currie, H. MacL. "Propertius IV. 8—A Reading." *Latomus* 32 (1973) 616–22.

Dee, J. H. "Elegy 4.8: A Propertian Comedy." *Transactions of the American Philological Association* 108 (1978) 41–53.

Kiss, D. "How did Propertius 4.8 begin?" *Acta Antiqua Academiae Scientiarum Hungaricae* 49.2 (2009) 157–62.

Walin, D. "Cynthia Serpens: A Reading of Propertius 4.8." *Classical Journal* 105.2 (2009/10) 137–51.

Warden, J. "The dead and the quick: structural correspondences and thematic relationships in Propertius 4.7 and 4.8." *Phoenix* 50.2 (1996) 118–29.

Elegy 4.9

Berry, M. "Political Poetics : the Bona Dea Episode in Propertius 4, 9." *Latomus* 70.2 (2011) 391–404.

Davies, M. "Thirsty work for Hecules: Propertius IV.9 and the folk tale." *Bulletin of the Institute of Classical Studies of the University of London* 49 (2006) 105–30.

Fox, M. "Propertius 4.9 and the Toils of Historicism." *Materiali e Discussioni per l'analisi dei testi classici* 43 (1999) 157–76.

Janan, M. "Refashioning Hercules: Propertius 4.9" *Helios* 25.1 (1998) 65–78.

Lindheim, S. "Hercules cross-dressed, Hercules undressed: unmasking the construction of the Propertian *amator* in elegy 4.9." *American Journal of Philology* 119.1 (1998) 43–66.

Spencer, D. "Propertius, Hercules, and the Dynamics of Roman Mythic Space in Elegy 4.9." *Arethusa* 34.3 (2001) 259–84.

Welch, T. "Masculinity and Monuments in Propertius 4.9." *American Journal of Philology* 125.1 (2004) 61–90.

On the manuscript tradition of Propertius

Butrica, J. "On the transmission of the text of Propertius," In *Brill's Companion to Propertius*, edited by H.-C. Günther, 25–44. Leiden, 2006.

Housman, A. E. "The Manuscripts of Propertius," In *The Classical Papers of A. E. Housman*, Volume 1, 1882-1897, edited by J. Diggle and F.R.D Goodyear, 314-47. Cambridge, 1972.

Commentaries and translations in English

Butler H. E., and E. A. Barber, eds. *The Elegies of Propertius*. With intro. and comm. Oxford, 1933.

Buttimore, R. A., and R. I. V. Hodge, eds. *Propertius: Elegies Book I*. London, 2002.

Camps, W. A., ed. *Propertius. Elegies. Book I*. London, 1977 (1961).

———. *Propertius. Elegies. Book II*. Cambridge, 1997 (1966).

———. *Propertius. Elegies. Book III*. Cambridge, 1985 (1966).

———. *Propertius. Elegies. Book IV*. Cambridge, 2001 (1965).

Goold, G. P., ed. and trans. *Propertius. Elegies*. Cambridge, MA, 1990.

Heyworth, S. J. *Cynthia: A Companion to the Text of Propertius*. Oxford, 2009.

Heyworth, S. J., and J. H. W. Morwood, eds. *A Commentary on Propertius, Book III*. Oxford, 2011.

Hutchinson, G., ed. *Propertius. Elegies, Book IV*. Cambridge, 2006.

Miller, P. A., ed. *Latin Erotic Elegy*. London, 2002.

Lee, G., trans., and O. Lyne, ed. *Propertius. The Poems*. Oxford, 2009.

Richardson, L., ed. *Propertius: Elegies I–IV*. Norman. OK, 1977.

Slavitt, D. R., trans., and M. Santirocco, ed. *Propertius in Love: The Elegies*. Berkeley and Los Angeles, 2002.

Historical background

Eder, W. "Augustus and the Power of Tradition." In *The Cambridge Companion to the Age of Augustus*, edited by K. Galinsky, 13–32. Cambridge, 2005.

Gruen, E. "Augustus and the Making of the Principate." In *The Cambridge Companion to the Age of Augustus,* edited by K. Galinsky, 33–52. Cambridge, 2005.

———. "The Expansion of Empire Under Augustus." In *The Cambridge Ancient History, 2nd edition, vol. 10*, edited by A. K. Bowman, E. Champion, and A. Lintott, 147–97, Cambridge, 1996.

Galinsky, K., ed. *The Cambridge Companion to the Age of Augustus.* Cambridge, 2005.

———. *Augustan Culture. An Interpretive Introduction*. Princeton, 1996.

Raaflaub, K., and M. Toher, eds. *Between Republic and Empire: Interpretations of Augustus and His Principate*. Berkeley, 1990.

Wallace-Hadrill, A. *Rome's Cultural Revolution*. Cambridge, 2008.

Books on Latin meter

Califf, D. 2002. *A Guide to Latin Meter and Verse Composition*. London.

Halporn, J. W., M. Ostwald, and T. Rosenmeyer. *The Meters of Greek and Latin Poetry*. Indianapolis, 1994.

Latin Text

- Note that intervocalic *u* rather than consonantal *v* is used throughout.
- Barber's 1960 OCT is used throughout except for the following specific divergences from his text and punctuation:

2.1.5	**uidi** for **cogis**
2.10.22	**his** for **haec**
2.32.33–40	follow Heyworth's 2007 OCT
2.32.33	**quamuis** for **fertur** and comma for semi-colon after **Martis**
2.32.34	**non minus** for **nec minus** and period for comma after **fuit**
2.32.35	**deam** for **Parim**
2.32.36	comma for semi-colon after **deam**
2.32.38	comma for semi-colon after **chori**
2.32.39	no comma after **antro**
3.11.49	**cane** for **cape**
3.11.61–63	semi-colons at the end of each line
4.8.19–20	transposed after 4.8.1–2
4.8.5	**hic** for **qua**
4.8.39	semi-colon after **Phyllis** as proper name
4.8.40	**et** for **haec**
4.8.45	**secundam** for **secundos**
4.9.5	**quaque** for **quoque**
4.9.65–66	transposed to follow a lacuna after 4.9.41

༄ *Elegy 1.1*

Cynthia prima suis miserum me cepit ocellis,
   contactum nullis ante cupidinibus.
tum mihi constantis deiecit lumina fastus
   et caput impositis pressit Amor pedibus,
5 donec me docuit castas odisse puellas
   improbus, et nullo uiuere consilio.
et mihi iam toto furor hic non deficit anno,
   cum tamen aduersos cogor habere deos.
Milanion nullos fugiendo, Tulle, labores
10   saeuitiam durae contudit Iasidos.
nam modo Partheniis amens errabat in antris,
   ibat et hirsutas ille uidere feras;
ille etiam Hylaei percussus uulnere rami
   saucius Arcadiis rupibus ingemuit.
15 ergo uelocem potuit domuisse puellam:
   tantum in amore preces et bene facta ualent.
in me tardus Amor non ullas cogitat artis,
   nec meminit notas, ut prius, ire uias.
at uos, deductae quibus est fallacia lunae
20   et labor in magicis sacra piare focis,
en agedum dominae mentem conuertite nostrae,
   et facite illa meo palleat ore magis!
tunc ego crediderim uobis et sidera et amnis
   posse Cytaeines ducere carminibus.
25 et uos, qui sero lapsum reuocatis, amici,
   quaerite non sani pectoris auxilia.

fortiter et ferrum saeuos patiemur et ignis,
  sit modo libertas quae uelit ira loqui.
ferte per extremas gentis et ferte per undas,
30   qua non ulla meum femina norit iter:
uos remanete, quibus facili deus annuit aure,
  sitis et in tuto semper amore pares.
in me nostra Venus noctes exercet amaras,
  et nullo uacuus tempore defit Amor.
35 hoc, moneo, uitate malum: sua quemque moretur
  cura, neque assueto mutet amore locum.
quod si quis monitis tardas aduerterit auris,
  heu referet quanta uerba dolore mea!

ॐ *Elegy 1.3*

Qualis Thesea iacuit cedente carina
  languida desertis Cnosia litoribus;
qualis et accubuit primo Cepheia somno
  libera iam duris cotibus Andromede;
5 nec minus assiduis Edonis fessa choreis
  qualis in herboso concidit Apidano:
talis uisa mihi mollem spirare quietem
  Cynthia non certis nixa caput manibus,
ebria cum multo traherem uestigia Baccho,
10   et quaterent sera nocte facem pueri.
hanc ego, nondum etiam sensus deperditus omnis,
  molliter impresso conor adire toro;

et quamuis duplici correptum ardore iuberent
   hac Amor hac Liber, durus uterque deus,
15 subiecto leuiter positam temptare lacerto
   osculaque admota sumere et arma manu,
non tamen ausus eram dominae turbare quietem,
   expertae metuens iurgia saeuitiae;
sed sic intentis haerebam fixus ocellis,
20   Argus ut ignotis cornibus Inachidos.
et modo soluebam nostra de fronte corollas
   ponebamque tuis, Cynthia, temporibus;
et modo gaudebam lapsos formare capillos;
   nunc furtiua cauis poma dabam manibus;
25 omniaque ingrato largibar munera somno,
   munera de prono saepe uoluta sinu;
et quotiens raro duxti suspiria motu,
   obstupui uano credulus auspicio,
ne qua tibi insolitos portarent uisa timores,
30   neue quis inuitam cogeret esse suam:
donec diuersas praecurrens luna fenestras,
   luna moraturis sedula luminibus,
compositos leuibus radiis patefecit ocellos.
   sic ait in molli fixa toro cubitum:
35 'tandem te nostro referens iniuria lecto
   alterius clausis expulit e foribus?
namque ubi longa meae consumpsti tempora noctis,
   languidus exactis, ei mihi, sideribus?
o utinam talis perducas, improbe, noctes,
40   me miseram qualis semper habere iubes!

nam modo purpureo fallebam stamine somnum,
  rursus et Orpheae carmine, fessa, lyrae,
interdum leuiter mecum deserta querebar
  externo longas saepe in amore moras:
45 dum me iucundis lapsam sopor impulit alis.
  illa fuit lacrimis ultima cura meis.'

ᚼ *Elegy 2.1*

Quaeritis, unde mihi totiens scribantur amores,
  unde meus ueniat mollis in ora liber.
non haec Calliope, non haec mihi cantat Apollo.
  ingenium nobis ipsa puella facit.
5 siue illam Cois fulgentem incedere uidi,
  hac totum e Coa ueste uolumen erit;
seu uidi ad frontem sparsos errare capillos,
  gaudet laudatis ire superba comis;
siue lyrae carmen digitis percussit eburnis,
10 miramur, facilis ut premat arte manus;
seu cum poscentis somnum declinat ocellos,
  inuenio causas mille poeta nouas;
seu nuda erepto mecum luctatur amictu,
  tum uero longas condimus Iliadas;
15 seu quidquid fecit siue est quodcumque locuta,
  maxima de nihilo nascitur historia.
quod mihi si tantum, Maecenas, fata dedissent,
  ut possem heroas ducere in arma manus,
non ego Titanas canerem, non Ossan Olympo
20 impositam, ut caeli Pelion esset iter,

nec ueteres Thebas, nec Pergama nomen Homeri,
    Xerxis et imperio bina coisse uada,
regnaue prima Remi aut animos Carthaginis altae,
    Cimbrorumque minas et bene facta Mari:
25 bellaque resque tui memorarem Caesaris, et tu
    Caesare sub magno cura secunda fores.
nam quotiens Mutinam aut ciuilia busta Philippos
    aut canerem Siculae classica bella fugae,
euersosque focos antiquae gentis Etruscae,
30   et Ptolemaeei litora capta Phari,
aut canerem Aegyptum et Nilum, cum attractus in urbem
    septem captiuis debilis ibat aquis,
aut regum auratis circumdata colla catenis,
    Actiaque in Sacra currere rostra Via;
35 te mea Musa illis semper contexeret armis,
    et sumpta et posita pace fidele caput:
Theseus infernis, superis testatur Achilles,
    hic Ixioniden, ille Menoetiaden.

                    *   *   *

sed neque Phlegraeos Iouis Enceladique tumultus
40   intonet angusto pectore Callimachus,
nec mea conueniunt duro praecordia uersu
    Caesaris in Phrygios condere nomen auos.
nauita de uentis, de tauris narrat arator,
    enumerat miles uulnera, pastor ouis;
45 nos contra angusto uersantes proelia lecto:
    qua pote quisque, in ea conterat arte diem.

laus in amore mori: laus altera, si datur uno
　　posse frui: fruar o solus amore meo!
si memini, solet illa leuis culpare puellas,
50　et totam ex Helena non probat Iliada.
seu mihi sunt tangenda nouercae pocula Phaedrae,
　　pocula priuigno non nocitura suo,
seu mihi Circaeo pereundum est gramine, siue
　　Colchis Iolciacis urat aena focis,
55　una meos quoniam praedata est femina sensus,
　　ex hac ducentur funera nostra domo.
omnis humanos sanat medicina dolores:
　　solus amor morbi non amat artificem.
tarda Philoctetae sanauit crura Machaon,
60　Phoenicis Chiron lumina Phillyrides,
et deus exstinctum Cressis Epidaurius herbis
　　restituit patriis Androgeona focis,
Mysus et Haemonia iuuenis qua cuspide uulnus
　　senserat, hac ipsa cuspide sensit opem.
65　hoc si quis uitium poterit mihi demere, solus
　　Tantaleae poterit tradere poma manu;
dolia uirgineis idem ille repleuerit urnis,
　　ne tenera assidua colla grauentur aqua;
idem Caucasia soluet de rupe Promethei
70　bracchia et a medio pectore pellet auem.
quandocumque igitur uitam mea fata reposcent,
　　et breue in exiguo marmore nomen ero,

Maecenas, nostrae spes inuidiosa iuuentae,
    et uitae et morti gloria iusta meae,
75 si te forte meo ducet uia proxima busto,
    esseda caelatis siste Britanna iugis,
talique illacrimans mutae iace uerba fauillae:
    'Huic misero fatum dura puella fuit.'

∾ *Elegy 2.10*

Sed tempus lustrare aliis Helicona choreis,
    et campum Haemonio iam dare tempus equo.
iam libet et fortis memorare ad proelia turmas
    et Romana mei dicere castra ducis.
5 quod si deficiant uires, audacia certe
    laus erit: in magnis et uoluisse sat est.
aetas prima canat Veneres, extrema tumultus:
    bella canam, quando scripta puella mea est.
nunc uolo subducto grauior procedere uultu,
10   nunc aliam citharam me mea Musa docet.
surge, anime, ex humili; iam, carmina, sumite uires;
    Pierides, magni nunc erit oris opus.
iam negat Euphrates equitem post terga tueri
    Parthorum et Crassos se tenuisse dolet:
15 India quin, Auguste, tuo dat colla triumpho,
    et domus intactae te tremit Arabiae;
et si qua extremis tellus se subtrahit oris,
    sentiat illa tuas postmodo capta manus!
haec ego castra sequar; uates tua castra canendo
20   magnus ero: seruent hunc mihi fata diem!

at caput in magnis ubi non est tangere signis,
   ponitur his imos ante corona pedes;
sic nos nunc, inopes laudis conscendere carmen,
   pauperibus sacris uilia tura damus.
25 nondum etiam Ascraeos norunt mea carmina fontis,
   sed modo Permessi flumine lauit Amor.

∾ *Elegy 2.16*

Praetor ab Illyricis uenit modo, Cynthia, terris,
   maxima praeda tibi, maxima cura mihi.
non potuit saxo uitam posuisse Cerauno?
   a, Neptune, tibi qualia dona darem!
5 nunc sine me plena fiunt conuiuia mensa,
   nunc sine me tota ianua nocte patet.
quare, si sapis, oblatas ne desere messis
   et stolidum pleno uellere carpe pecus;
deinde, ubi consumpto restabit munere pauper,
10   dic alias iterum nauiget Illyrias!
Cynthia non sequitur fascis nec curat honores,
   semper amatorum ponderat una sinus.
at tu nunc nostro, Venus, o succurre dolori,
   rumpat ut assiduis membra libidinibus!
15 ergo muneribus quiuis mercatur amorem?
   Iuppiter, indigna merce puella perit.
semper in Oceanum mittit me quaerere gemmas,
   et iubet ex ipsa tollere dona Tyro.
atque utinam Romae nemo esset diues, et ipse
20   straminea posset dux habitare casa!

numquam uenales essent ad munus amicae,
   atque una fieret cana puella domo;
numquam septenas noctes seiuncta cubares,
   candida tam foedo bracchia fusa uiro;
25 non quia peccarim (testor te), sed quia uulgo
   formosis leuitas semper amica fuit.
barbarus exclusis agitat uestigia lumbis–
   et subito felix nunc mea regna tenet!
aspice quid donis Eriphyla inuenit amaris,
30   arserit et quantis nupta Creusa malis.
nullane sedabit nostros iniuria fletus?
   an dolor hic uitiis nescit abesse tuis?
tot iam abiere dies, cum me nec cura theatri
   nec tetigit Campi, nec mea mensa iuuat.
35 at pudeat certe, pudeat!–nisi forte, quod aiunt,
   turpis amor surdis auribus esse solet.
cerne ducem, modo qui fremitu compleuit inani
   Actia damnatis aequora militibus:
hunc infamis amor uersis dare terga carinis
40   iussit et extremo quaerere in orbe fugam.
Caesaris haec uirtus et gloria Caesaris haec est:
   illa, qua uicit, condidit arma manu.
sed quascumque tibi uestis, quoscumque smaragdos,
   quosue dedit flauo lumine chrysolithos,
45 haec uideam rapidas in uanum ferre procellas:
   quae tibi terra, uelim, quae tibi fiat aqua.
non semper placidus periuros ridet amantis
   Iuppiter et surda neglegit aure preces.

uidistis toto sonitus percurrere caelo,
50   fulminaque aetheria desiluisse domo:
  non haec Pleiades faciunt neque aquosus Orion,
    nec sic de nihilo fulminis ira cadit;
  periuras tunc ille solet punire puellas,
    deceptus quoniam fleuit et ipse deus.
55 quare ne tibi sit tanti Sidonia uestis,
    ut timeas, quotiens nubilus Auster erit.

ᛋ *Elegy 2.31*

  Quaeris, cur ueniam tibi tardior? aurea Phoebi
    porticus a magno Caesare aperta fuit.
  tantam erat in speciem Poenis digesta columnis,
    inter quas Danai femina turba senis.
5 †hic equidem Phoebo† uisus mihi pulchrior ipso
    marmoreus tacita carmen hiare lyra;
  atque aram circum steterant armenta Myronis,
    quattuor artificis, uiuida signa, boues.
  tum medium claro surgebat marmore templum,
10   et patria Phoebo carius Ortygia:
  in quo Solis erat supra fastigia currus,
    et ualuae, Libyci nobile dentis opus;
  altera deiectos Parnasi uertice Gallos,
    altera maerebat funera Tantalidos.
15 deinde inter matrem deus ipse interque sororem
    Pythius in longa carmina ueste sonat.

ᴄ⋗ *Elegy 2.32*

Qui uidet, is peccat: qui te non uiderit ergo,
    non cupiet: facti lumina crimen habent.
nam quid Praenesti dubias, o Cynthia, sortis,
    quid petis Aeaei moenia Telegoni?
5 cur ita te Herculeum deportant esseda Tibur?
    Appia cur totiens te uia Lanuuium?
hoc utinam spatiere loco, quodcumque uacabis,
    Cynthia! sed tibi me credere turba uetat,
cum uidet accensis deuotam currere taedis
10 in nemus et Triuiae lumina ferre deae.
scilicet umbrosis sordet Pompeia columnis
    porticus, aulaeis nobilis Attalicis,
et platanis creber pariter surgentibus ordo,
    flumina sopito quaeque Marone cadunt,
15 et leuiter nymphis tota crepitantibus urbe
    cum subito Triton ore recondit aquam.
falleris, ista tui furtum uia monstrat amoris:
    non urbem, demens, lumina nostra fugis!
nil agis, insidias in me componis inanis,
20 tendis iners docto retia nota mihi.
sed de me minus est: famae iactura pudicae
    tanta tibi miserae, quanta meretur, erit.
nuper enim de te nostras me laedit ad auris
    rumor, et in tota non bonus urbe fuit.
25 sed tu non debes inimicae credere linguae:
    semper formosis fabula poena fuit.

non tua deprenso damnata est fama ueneno:
    testis eris puras, Phoebe, uidere manus.
sin autem longo nox una aut altera lusu
30   consumpta est, non me crimina parua mouent.
Tyndaris externo patriam mutauit amore,
    et sine decreto uiua reducta domum est.
ipsa Venus, quamuis corrupta libidine Martis,
    non minus in caelo semper honesta fuit.
35 quamuis Ida deam pastorem dicat amasse
    atque inter pecudes accubuisse deam,
hoc et Hamadryadum spectauit turba sororum
    Silenique senes et pater ipse chori,
cum quibus Idaeo legisti poma sub antro
40   supposita excipiens, Nai, caduca manu.
an quisquam in tanto stuprorum examine quaerit
    'Cur haec tam diues? quis dedit? unde dedit?'
o nimium nostro felicem tempore Romam,
    si contra mores una puella facit!
45 haec eadem ante illam iam impune et Lesbia fecit:
    quae sequitur, certe est inuidiosa minus.
qui quaerit Tatios ueteres durosque Sabinos,
    hic posuit nostra nuper in urbe pedem.
tu prius et fluctus poteris siccare marinos,
50   altaque mortali deligere astra manu,
quam facere, ut nostrae nolint peccare puellae:
    hic mos Saturno regna tenente fuit;
at cum Deucalionis aquae fluxere per orbem,
    et post antiquas Deucalionis aquas,

55 dic mihi, quis potuit lectum seruare pudicum,
   quae dea cum solo uiuere sola deo?
uxorem quondam magni Minois, ut aiunt,
   corrupit torui candida forma bouis;
nec minus aerato Danae circumdata muro
60 non potuit magno casta negare Ioui.
quod si tu Graias es tuque imitata Latinas,
   semper uiue meo libera iudicio!

ᛋ *Elegy 3.3*

Visus eram molli recubans Heliconis in umbra,
   Bellerophontei qua fluit umor equi,
reges, Alba, tuos et regum facta tuorum,
   tantum operis, neruis hiscere posse meis;
5 paruaque tam magnis admoram fontibus ora,
   unde pater sitiens Ennius ante bibit;
et cecinit Curios fratres et Horatia pila,
   regiaque Aemilia uecta tropaea rate,
uictricesque moras Fabii pugnamque sinistram
10 Cannensem et uersos ad pia uota deos,
Hannibalemque Lares Romana sede fugantis,
   anseris et tutum uoce fuisse Iouem:
cum me Castalia speculans ex arbore Phoebus
   sic ait aurata nixus ad antra lyra;
15 'Quid tibi cum tali, demens, est flumine? quis te
   carminis heroi tangere iussit opus?
non hic ulla tibi speranda est fama, Properti:
   mollia sunt paruis prata terenda rotis;

ut tuus in scamno iactetur saepe libellus,
20   quem legat exspectans sola puella uirum.
cur tua praescriptos euecta est pagina gyros?
   non est ingenii cumba grauanda tui.
alter remus aquas alter tibi radat harenas,
   tutus eris: medio maxima turba mari est.'
25 dixerat, et plectro sedem mihi monstrat eburno,
   quo noua muscoso semita facta solo est.
hic erat affixis uiridis spelunca lapillis,
   pendebantque cauis tympana pumicibus,
orgia Musarum et Sileni patris imago
30   fictilis et calami, Pan Tegeaee, tui;
et Veneris dominae uolucres, mea turba, columbae
   tingunt Gorgoneo punica rostra lacu;
diuersaeque nouem sortitae iura Puellae
   exercent teneras in sua dona manus:
35 haec hederas legit in thyrsos, haec carmina neruis
   aptat, at illa manu texit utraque rosam.
e quarum numero me contigit una dearum
   (ut reor a facie, Calliopea fuit):
'Contentus niueis semper uectabere cycnis,
40   nec te fortis equi ducet ad arma sonus.
nil tibi sit rauco praeconia classica cornu
   flare, nec Aonium tingere Marte nemus;
aut quibus in campis Mariano proelia signo
   stent et Teutonicas Roma refringat opes,
45 barbarus aut Sueuo perfusus sanguine Rhenus
   saucia maerenti corpora uectet aqua.

quippe coronatos alienum ad limen amantis
    nocturnaeque canes ebria signa fugae,
ut per te clausas sciat excantare puellas,
50   qui uolet austeros arte ferire uiros.'
talia Calliope, lymphisque a fonte petitis
    ora Philitea nostra rigauit aqua.

ᛋ *Elegy 3.11*

Quid mirare, meam si uersat femina uitam
    et trahit addictum sub sua iura uirum,
criminaque ignaui capitis mihi turpia fingis,
    quod nequeam fracto rumpere uincla iugo?
5 uenturam melius praesagit nauita mortem,
    uulneribus didicit miles habere metum.
ista ego praeterita iactaui uerba iuuenta:
    tu nunc exemplo disce timere meo.
Colchis flagrantis adamantina sub iuga tauros
10   egit et armigera proelia seuit humo,
custodisque feros clausit serpentis hiatus,
    iret ut Aesonias aurea lana domos.
ausa ferox ab equo quondam oppugnare sagittis
    Maeotis Danaum Penthesilea ratis;
15 aurea cui postquam nudauit cassida frontem,
    uicit uictorem candida forma uirum.
Omphale in tantum formae processit honorem,
    Lydia Gygaeo tincta puella lacu,
ut, qui pacato statuisset in orbe columnas,
20   tam dura traheret mollia pensa manu.

Persarum statuit Babylona Semiramis urbem,
    ut solidum cocto tolleret aggere opus,
et duo in aduersum mitti per moenia currus
    nec possent tacto stringere ab axe latus;
25 duxit et Euphraten medium, quam condidit, arcis,
    iussit et imperio subdere Bactra caput.
nam quid ego heroas, quid raptem in crimina diuos?
    Iuppiter infamat seque suamque domum.
quid, modo quae nostris opprobria uexerit armis,
30   et famulos inter femina trita suos?
coniugi obsceni pretium Romana poposcit
    moenia et addictos in sua regna Patres.
noxia Alexandria dolis aptissima tellus,
    et totiens nostro Memphi cruenta malo,
35 tris ubi Pompeio detraxit harena triumphos!
    tollet nulla dies hanc tibi, Roma, notam.
issent Phlegraeo melius tibi funera campo,
    uel tua si socero colla daturus eras.
scilicet incesti meretrix regina Canopi,
40   una Philippeo sanguine adusta nota,
ausa Ioui nostro latrantem opponere Anubim,
    et Tiberim Nili cogere ferre minas,
Romanamque tubam crepitanti pellere sistro,
    baridos et contis rostra Liburna sequi,
45 foedaque Tarpeio conopia tendere saxo,
    iura dare et statuas inter et arma Mari!
quid nunc Tarquinii fractas iuuat esse securis,
    nomine quem simili uita superba notat,

si mulier patienda fuit? cane, Roma, triumphum
50 et longum Augusto salua precare diem!
    fugisti tamen in timidi uaga flumina Nili:
        accepere tuae Romula uincla manus.
    bracchia spectaui sacris admorsa colubris,
        et trahere occultum membra soporis iter.
55 'Non hoc, Roma, fui tanto tibi ciue uerenda!'
        dixit et assiduo lingua sepulta mero.
    septem urbs alta iugis, toto quae praesidet orbi,
58   femineo timuit territa Marte minas.
67 nunc ubi Scipiadae classes, ubi signa Camilli,
68   aut modo Pompeia, Bospore, capta manu?
59 Hannibalis spolia et uicti †monumenta† Syphacis,
60   et Pyrrhi ad nostros gloria fracta pedes?
    Curtius expletis statuit monumenta lacunis;
        at Decius misso proelia rupit equo;
    Coclitis abscissos testatur semita pontis;
        est cui cognomen coruus habere dedit:
65 haec di condiderant, haec di quoque moenia seruant:
66   uix timeat saluo Caesare Roma Iouem.
69 Leucadius uersas acies memorabit Apollo:
70   tantum operis belli sustulit una dies.
    at tu, siue petes portus seu, nauita, linques,
        Caesaris in toto sis memor Ionio.

ᴄᴧ *Elegy 4.8*

Disce, quid Esquilias hac nocte fugarit aquosas,
  cum uicina nouis turba cucurrit agris.
19 turpis in arcana sonuit cum rixa taberna;
20   si sine me, famae non sine labe meae.
Lanuuium annosi uetus est tutela draconis,
  hic ubi tam rarae non perit hora morae;
5 hic sacer abripitur caeco descensus hiatu,
  qua penetrat (uirgo, tale iter omne caue!)
ieiuni serpentis honos, cum pabula poscit
  annua et ex ima sibila torquet humo.
talia demissae pallent ad sacra puellae,
10 cum temere anguino creditur ore manus.
ille sibi admotas a uirgine corripit escas:
  uirginis in palmis ipsa canistra tremunt.
si fuerint castae, redeunt in colla parentum,
  clamantque agricolae 'Fertilis annus erit.'
15 huc mea detonsis auecta est Cynthia mannis:
  causa fuit Iuno, sed mage causa Venus.
Appia, dic quaeso, quantum te teste triumphum
  egerit effusis per tua saxa rotis!
  <..>
20 <..>
spectaclum ipsa sedens primo temone pependit,
  ausa per impuros frena mouere locos.
serica nam taceo uulsi carpenta nepotis
  atque armillatos colla Molossa canis,

qui dabit immundae uenalia fata saginae,
    uincet ubi erasas barba pudenda genas.
cum fieret nostro totiens iniuria lecto,
    mutato uolui castra mouere toro.
Phyllis Auentinae quaedam est uicina Dianae,
    sobria grata parum: cum bibit, omne decet.
altera Tarpeios est inter Teia lucos,
    candida, sed potae non satis unus erit.
his ego constitui noctem lenire uocatis,
    et Venere ignota furta nouare mea.
unus erat tribus in secreta lectulus herba.
    quaeris concubitus? inter utramque fui.
Lygdamus ad cyathos, uitrique aestiua supellex
    et Methymnaei Graeca saliua meri.
Nile, tuus tibicen erat, crotalistria †Phyllis†;
    et facilis spargi munda sine arte rosa,
nanus et ipse suos breuiter concretus in artus
    iactabat truncas ad caua buxa manus.
sed neque suppletis constabat flamma lucernis,
    reccidit inque suos mensa supina pedes.
me quoque per talos Venerem quaerente secundam
    semper damnosi subsiluere canes.
cantabant surdo, nudabant pectora caeco:
    Lanuuii ad portas, ei mihi, solus eram;
cum subito rauci sonuerunt cardine postes,
    et leuia ad primos murmura facta Laris.
nec mora, cum totas resupinat Cynthia ualuas,
    non operosa comis, sed furibunda decens.

pocula mi digitos inter cecidere remissos,
   palluerantque ipso labra soluta mero.
55 fulminat illa oculis et quantum femina saeuit,
   spectaclum capta nec minus urbe fuit.
Phyllidos iratos in uultum conicit unguis:
   territa uicinas Teia clamat aquas.
lumina sopitos turbant elata Quiritis,
60   omnis et insana semita nocte sonat.
illas direptisque comis tunicisque solutis
   excipit obscurae prima taberna uiae.
Cynthia gaudet in exuuiis uictrixque recurrit
   et mea peruersa sauciat ora manu,
65 imponitque notam collo morsuque cruentat,
   praecipueque oculos, qui meruere, ferit.
atque ubi iam nostris lassauit bracchia plagis,
   Lygdamus ad plutei fulcra sinistra latens
eruitur, geniumque meum protractus adorat.
70 Lygdame, nil potui: tecum ego captus eram.
supplicibus palmis tum demum ad foedera ueni,
   cum uix tangendos praebuit illa pedes,
atque ait 'Admissae si uis me ignoscere culpae,
   accipe, quae nostrae formula legis erit.
75 tu neque Pompeia spatiabere cultus in umbra,
   nec cum lasciuum sternet harena Forum.
colla caue inflectas ad summum obliqua theatrum
   aut lectica tuae se det aperta morae.
Lygdamus in primis, omnis mihi causa querelae,
80   ueneat et pedibus uincula bina trahat.'

indixit leges: respondi ego 'Legibus utar.'
   riserat imperio facta superba dato.
dein quemcumque locum externae tetigere puellae,
   suffiit, at pura limina tergit aqua,
85 imperat et totas iterum mutare lucernas,
   terque meum tetigit sulpuris igne caput.
atque ita mutato per singula pallia lecto
   respondi, et toto soluimus arma toro.

ᴏ *Elegy 4.9*

Amphitryoniades qua tempestate iuuencos
   egerat a stabulis, o Erythea, tuis,
uenit ad inuictos pecorosa Palatia montis,
   et statuit fessos fessus et ipse boues,
5 qua Velabra suo stagnabant flumine quaque
   nauta per urbanas uelificabat aquas.
sed non infido manserunt hospite Caco
   incolumes: furto polluit ille Iouem.
incola Cacus erat, metuendo raptor ab antro,
10   per tria partitos qui dabat ora sonos.
hic, ne certa forent manifestae signa rapinae,
   auersos cauda traxit in antra boues,
nec sine teste deo: furem sonuere iuuenci,
   furis et implacidas diruit ira fores.
15 Maenalio iacuit pulsus tria tempora ramo
   Cacus, et Alcides sic ait: 'Ite boues,
Herculis ite boues, nostrae labor ultime clauae,
   bis mihi quaesitae, bis mea praeda, boues,

aruaque mugitu sancite Bouaria longo:
20   nobile erit Romae Pascua uestra Forum.'
dixerat, et sicco torquet sitis ora palato,
   terraque non ullas feta ministrat aquas.
sed procul inclusas audit ridere puellas,
   lucus ubi umbroso fecerat orbe nemus,
25 femineae loca clausa deae fontisque piandos,
   impune et nullis sacra retecta uiris.
deuia puniceae uelabant limina uittae,
   putris odorato luxerat igne casa,
populus et longis ornabat frondibus aedem,
30   multaque cantantis umbra tegebat auis.
huc ruit in siccam congesta puluere barbam,
   et iacit ante fores uerba minora deo:
'Vos precor, o luci sacro quae luditis antro,
   pandite defessis hospita fana uiris.
35 fontis egens erro circaque sonantia lymphis;
   et caua succepto flumine palma sat est.
audistisne aliquem, tergo qui sustulit orbem?
   ille ego sum: Alciden terra recepta uocat.
quis facta Herculeae non audit fortia clauae
40   et numquam ad uastas irrita tela feras,
atque uni Stygias homini luxisse tenebras?

   <..>
65 Angulus hic mundi nunc me mea fata trahentem
66   accipit: haec fesso uix mihi terra patet.
43 quodsi Iunoni sacrum faceretis amarae,
   non clausisset aquas ipsa nouerca suas.

45 sin aliquem uultusque meus saetaeque leonis
　　terrent et Libyco sole perusta coma,
　idem ego Sidonia feci seruilia palla
　　officia et Lydo pensa diurna colo,
　mollis et hirsutum cepit mihi fascia pectus,
50　et manibus duris apta puella fui.'
　talibus Alcides; at talibus alma sacerdos,
　　puniceo canas stamine uincta comas:
　'Parce oculis, hospes, lucoque abscede uerendo;
　　cede agedum et tuta limina linque fuga.
55 interdicta uiris metuenda lege piatur
　　quae se summota uindicat ara casa.
　magno Tiresias aspexit Pallada uates,
　　fortia dum posita Gorgone membra lauat.
　di tibi dent alios fontis: haec lympha puellis
60　auia secreti limitis unda fluit.'
　sic anus: ille umeris postis concussit opacos,
　　nec tulit iratam ianua clausa sitim.
　at postquam exhausto iam flumine uicerat aestum,
64　ponit uix siccis tristia iura labris:
67 'Maxima quae gregibus deuota est Ara repertis,
　　ara per has' inquit 'maxima facta manus,
　haec nullis umquam pateat ueneranda puellis,
70　Herculis aeternum ne sit inulta sitis.'
73 hunc, quoniam manibus purgatum sanxerat orbem,
74　sic Sanctum Tatiae composuere Cures.
71 Sancte pater salue, cui iam fauet aspera Iuno:
72 Sancte, uelis libro dexter inesse meo.

Commentary

℘ *Elegy 1.1*

This programmatic poem to Propertius's first book of elegies, the *Monobiblos*, introduces the poet's mistress Cynthia, the inception of their affair, and the condition of elegiac love. The speaker bemoans his condition as marked by suffering and hardship, and compares it figuratively to madness and disease. He appeals to his friends for a cure, but considers himself past help. One of these friends is (C. Volcacius) Tullus, the addressee of the poem and Propertius's patron at the time of the poet's first volume. From a prestigious senatorial family, the Volcacii, the young Tullus brings to the speaker's subjective musings the historical dimension of patronage networks and elite readership. The recipient of three other poems in the *Monobiblos* (1.6, 1.14, and 1.22), as well as 3.22, Tullus serves as a foil for the Propertian lover-poet's withdrawal from the more usual public roles of a young elite male. This contrast between the two men is already visible in the implicit inclusion of Tullus among those who attempt to bring the speaker back to his senses (25).

The speaker's amorous state also serves as a metaphor for his activity as a writer: in the description of Love's treatment of him, where Amor goes on "unfamiliar paths," the speaker alludes to the Callimachean aesthetic value of arcane erudition. Hence, this poem also illustrates Propertius's novel use of mythological analogy and the expectations that his erudite allusions to less well-known versions of a myth place on the reader.

The poem has four major sections: the speaker's current predicament and its evolution (1–8); a mythological *exemplum* intended to explain the usual course of *amor* and the speaker's exceptional case (9–18); appeals to outside parties for assistance (19–30); and a warning to others to avoid his own condition (31–38).

1 **Cynthia** The name of the speaker's beloved is the very first word of the poetry book and became synonymous with the collection itself. Such metonymic identification of the elegiac mistress with the poetry is a common trope in elegy. Her name also serves to identify her with Apollo, god of lyric poetry, and his sister Diana, both of whom had cult names deriving from Mount Cynthos on the island of Delos, where they were born (see Introduction, p. xxii).

me cepit ocellis The idea of the eyes as erotic weapons, wounding the recipient with their gaze, had a long tradition in Greco-Roman literature. Cf. Pind., fr.123 S.-M.

2 **contactum** expresses the metaphor of love as a disease (see Introduction, p. xxix; cf. Lucr. 4.1097–1104; Catul. 76.20–23, 25), but the sense of "hit" by a missile is also present (*OLD* sv *contingo* 3, 6).

3 **lumina** "gaze" here

constantis ... fastus gen. of quality or description

4 **impositis ... pedibus** abl. absolute; the image of Amor holding down the speaker's head implies military domination but there is also a pun in that Amor has imposed the elegiac meter ("feet"). Cf. Ovid *Am.* 1.1.

5 **castas ... puellas** an ambiguous phrase; the speaker has either learned to hate women like Cynthia, who do not succumb to his desires (at least in this poem and as often in love elegy), or he hates women of his own aristocratic status, for whom the norm is chastity, because he is now in love with a courtesan.

Commentary 1.1

6 **nullo ... consilio** abl. of manner; the emphasis is on the speaker's loss of self-control and departure from Roman norms of masculinity.

7 **toto ... anno** abl. of time within which

8 **cum** is here concessive, as *tamen* implies; the implication is that the speaker's suffering should have earned him the gods' favor by now.

9–18 Propertius introduces a mythological *exemplum* that he uses to illustrate the elegiac topos of the lover's subservience or *seruitium amoris*, "the slavery of love," which is an effective strategy for Milanion but—ironically—not for the speaker. Such use of mythology is a common device in Propertius, where the emphasis is often on a less well-known version of a myth or on a fragmentary detail that evokes the whole story for the audience. Here, Milanion breaks down the resistance of Atalanta, daughter of Iasus, by enduring trials, confronting wild beasts, and even suffering a wound at the hands of the centaur Hylaeus, who has attacked the virgin huntress (Ovid *Ars Am*. 2.185–92; cf. Apollod. 3.9.2, where it is Atalanta who kills Hylaeus and his centaur companion Rhoeteus). With the adj. *uelocem* (15), however, Propertius evokes the more popular myth associated with Atalanta, where she challenges all her suitors to a footrace that she inevitably wins, until Hippomenes succeeds by distracting her with three golden apples tossed in her way as they compete (Ovid *Met*. 10.560–707). Note that the figure of the *uelocem ... puellam* ("swift girl") conquered, or tamed, in love, also resonates with the speaker himself as interrupted in the temporal trajectory of his life by *tardus Amor* (17) and forced to live without a plan (*nullo ... consilio*, 6), implicitly forsaking the *cursus ... honorum* ("sequence of public offices") typically pursued by an elite Roman in the course of masculine development.

9 **fugiendo** gerund; abl. of means

Tulle the nephew of the consul L. Volcacius and one of several male addressees in the *Monobiblos* who exemplify the high status and male gender of the poet's notional audience; see the introductory remarks to 1.1 above and the Introduction, p. xiv.

10 **saeuitiam** "cruelty" but also "savagery," recalling that Atalanta was exposed as an infant and nursed by a she-bear in the wilderness

durae "hard" in the sense of inaccessible and unyielding to suitors but also "hardy" in physical endurance and prowess. The adj. is applied to the elegiac mistress (cf. **2.1.78**) and contrasts with the lover's *mollitia*, in keeping with the gender inversion that characterizes elegy (see the Introduction, pp. xx–xxi).

Iasidos "daughter of Iasus"—i.e., Atalanta; Greek gen. of the patronymic, a form that defines a person in reference to the father

11 **modo** "sometimes," here without another corresponding *modo* or other correlative

Partheniis adj. referring to Mt. Parthenius in Arcadia. Propertius here shows off his geographical knowledge and expects a similarly educated reader. The adj. may also connote the Greek word *parthenos* ("maiden") and thus the Muses (cf. Pind. *I*. 8.127) as well as the Greek first-century–BCE poet and scholar Parthenius who wrote both elegiac verse and a prose collection, *Erotika Pathemata*, summarizing the love stories of earlier writers. These he dedicated to Cornelius, the poet recognized as the first to compose Roman love elegy (see Introduction, pp. xiii, xx–xxi).

12 **et** The conj. here is postpositive, coming after *ibat* for metrical reasons.

uidere infinitive of purpose after *ibat*

13–14 **uulnere ... saucius ... ingemuit** Milanion experiences an actual wound, but the vocabulary describing his condition also evokes the pain of elegiac love.

16 **bene facta** "good deeds," referring back to the intervention on Atalanta's behalf that is implied in Milanion's wound. The phrase also suggests Roman patronage, the social relations of which often appear in the rhetoric of elegiac love and in Catullus's love poetry (see Introduction, pp. xxvii–xxviii).

17 **non ullas cogitat artis** "contrives no devices." The language here points as much if not more to the suppressed myth associated with Atalanta—specifically, the "device" or *ars* by which Hippomenes won the foot race—as to Milanion's *labores* and struggle with the centaur. The phrase also echoes *nullo uiuere consilio* (6).

artis the alternative *-īs* 3rd decl. acc. pl. ending is common in the Augustan poets and frequently used by Propertius. Note the following instances in this poem: *amnis* (23) *ignis* (27), *gentis* (29), *auris* (37).

18 In the speaker's case, Amor does not behave in any predictable fashion. Since the experience of elegiac love often acts as a metaphor for the writing of love elegy, the departure from *notas . . . uias* ("familiar paths") also alludes to the novelty of the Roman genre and to the aesthetics of the Alexandrian poet, Callimachus, who famously advocated the difficult and less-traveled route (*Aet.* fr. 1.25–8; see Introduction, pp. xxiv–xxvi).

19-24 The speaker now turns to the magic arts and those who practice them for assistance. The figure of the witch and her capacity to perform *adunata* ("impossibilities") appear often in elegy (cf. Tib. 1.2.43–44). Here, until she casts a spell on Cynthia, inducing the pallor that indicates lovesickness, the speaker will not believe in the witches' reputed feats.

19 **quibus** dat. of possession with *est fallacia*

deductae . . . lunae gen. of apposition dependent on *fallacia*, "the trick of the drawn-down moon," a conventional skill attributed to the witch

20 **piare** predicate infinitive after *est* (supplied from line 19), with *labor* as subject and *sacra* as an internal or "cognate"

acc.: "and whose task it is to perform sacred rites." *piare* suggests the expiation of some offence that incurs the anger of the gods. Propertius ironically employs religious language in an amorous, extramarital context.

22 **facite [ut]** introduces a substantive clause of result, with verb in the subjunctive (Bennett sec. 297).

meo ... ore abl. of comparison

palleat The speaker wishes that Cynthia turn more pale than his own countenance. In the Roman pathology of passion, such a symptom would clearly indicate her amorous condition.

23 **crediderim** potential subjunctive; pf. tense with pres. meaning, implying the belief of the witch's claims

uobis dat. with *credere* but supply *uos* as the implied subject-acc. of *posse* as an infinitive in indirect discourse, in line 24, also introduced by *crediderim*.

23–24 **sidera et amnis ... ducere** "to draw [down] the stars" and "to lead [back] rivers" (in the sense of "causing to flow backwards") are further feats; *ducere* depends on *posse* and serves almost as a *zeugma* here—see **1.3.16** and accompanying note for a definition.

24 **Cytaeines** Greek gen. sing., "of the woman from Cytae," a town in Colchis, referring to the birthplace of Medea, the famous sorceress who assisted Jason of the Argonauts in acquiring the Golden Fleece (cf. **2.1.54, 2.16.30, 3.11.9–12**, and accompanying notes)

25–28 The speaker now addresses his friends, *amici*, with the request that his cohort bring aid to his ailing heart. He professes his willingness to suffer both surgical cuts (*ferrum*, "knife") and cauterizing fire, if only he regain his *libertas* (28), the republican freedom of speech appropriate to his freeborn status. He likens his experience of love not only to being sick but implicitly to being enslaved—a condition identified by the critical term *seruitium amoris* and suggested here by his loss of *libertas* and the connotative associations of fire and metal to brand slaves.

26 **non sani pectoris** objective gen. (Bennett sec. 200). The image of the *amator*'s ailing heart, suffering as though from a disease, recalls his earlier statement that prior to Cynthia's debilitating gaze, he had been immune to passion (see lines 1–2 and note). As well as physical illness, *non sani pectoris* suggests mental madness—love as a condition of "insanity" that afflicts those who are its victims. A variant of this view of passion goes back to Greek tragedy but it appears distinctly in Roman literature for the first time in New Comedy (cf. Ter. *Eun.* I.1.5–22).

28 **sit modo** subjunctive verb in a clause of proviso, "provided that there be . . . " (Bennett sec. 310)

quae uelit rel. clause of characteristic (Bennett sec. 283) with *ira* as a subject and *quae* as the acc. rel. pron. with a suppressed *ea* as antecedent: " . . . the things which anger wishes"

loqui infinitive dependent on *libertas*, as though on the adj. *liber* implicit in the noun

29-30 In asking his friends to transport him across the sea to distant lands, where no woman will know to find him, the speaker also alludes to the Callimachean aesthetic of the arcane, less-traveled territory, referred to in line 18. Echoes of Catullus (11.1–4; 101) are also present.

29 **ferte** Supply *me* as object.

30 Although not technically a golden line, the interlocking word order here separates the two adjectives in the first hemistich (or half-line of the pentameter) from the nouns they agree with in the second hemistich. Note the similar structure of line 34.

norit syncopated fut. pf. in place of the full form *nouerit*

31-34 The speaker draws a distinction between those to whom the god nods approval (*annuit*), heeding their prayers with receptive ear (*facili . . . aure*), and his own plight of solitary and bitter nights.

32 **sitis et** optative subjunctive with postpositive *et*

33 **in me** a phrase with the acc., "against me," or with the abl., "in my case"

34	**uacuus ... Amor** an ambiguous phrase. The line can mean either (a) "at no time is love idle" or (b) "at no time is idle love absent." In both readings, the speaker is in torment, but in the second case "idleness" constitutes a defining quality or attribute of elegiac *amor*, in keeping with the speaker's avowed life of "no purpose" (*nullo ... consilio*) at the poem's outset.
35	**hoc ... malum** "this affliction," in reference to the speaker's condition
35–36	**moretur ... mutet** jussive subjunctives
36	**cura** means "beloved" here (*OLD* sv 8). Cf. **2.16.2** where it means "anxiety."
	assueto ... amore abl. absolute or abl. of separation
37–38	future-more-vivid condition; the exclamatory clause introduced by the interr. adj. phrase *quanto ... dolore* provides the apodosis.

nostra Venus refers to the Venus who governs all those who, like the speaker, experience an unrequited love.

᷈ *Elegy 1.3*

This justly famous poem describes the poet's response to his sleeping mistress, after he stumbles in from a night of drunken revelry. In a dream-like reverie the speaker, at the beginning, compares the sleeping Cynthia to mythological figures in three sexually suggestive and highly visual vignettes that were popular topics for ancient wall-painting. The poem has prompted debate among feminist critics as it raises the issue of Cynthia's subjectivity, asking whether she is more than a constructed textual figure onto which the speaker projects his fantasies. The inclusion of Cynthia's own voice, after she has awoken, and her perspective highlighting the potential infidelity of the speaker as an *exclusus amator* ("locked-out lover") from another woman's home, suggest the poet's interest in exploring the status of the elegiac mistress not only as an object but also as a "subject"—an individual with her own thoughts and feelings.

The poem may be divided into three major sections: lines 1–10 focus on the speaker's initial perception of Cynthia and set the stage for lines 11–30 on his inebriated calculations, vacillating between rape fantasy, awe, and fearful paralysis, before her sleeping body; the final lines, 31–47, feature the awakened Cynthia's recriminations and lament.

Fig. 1. Perseus and Andromeda. First century CE fresco from Pompeii, Dioscuri House. Wikimedia Commons.

1-6 The speaker compares the sleeping Cynthia to three mythological figures in the opening six lines: to Ariadne, daughter of Pasiphae and King Minos, who fell in love with but was later abandoned by Theseus on the island of Naxos—the two had sailed here from Crete after he had slain the Minotaur and escaped from the labyrinth with a woolen thread she provided (Cat. 64.50–264ff; Ovid *Her.* 10); to Andromeda released by Perseus from the rock where she had been fastened by her father, Cepheus, the king of the Ethiopians, as a sacrifice to a sea-monster sent to punish her mother's arrogance for claiming that she, Cassiopeia, surpassed the Nereids in beauty (Apollod. 2.4.3–5); and to a bacchante, a female devotee of the wine-god Bacchus, known for her wild dancing and participation in his orgiastic rituals. Each vignette suggestively implies a sexual encounter just preceding the moment captured in the mythological "narrative." The image of the Edonian woman, a bacchante, spent on the grass, also looks back to the figure of Ariadne: after Theseus departs, Bacchus appears as Ariadne's savior and takes her as his wife. The speaker's mythological fantasies about Cynthia indicate both desire and fear—his own wish to make sexual advances, as he soon contemplates doing, and his anxiety that she has been with someone else (revealed as well in what he imagines her dreaming later in line 30). The figures in all three scenes were popular subjects for painting, as murals from Pompeii reveal (see the illustrations on pp. 33, 38; frescoes of Ariadne and Theseus decorated the House of the Vettii, the House of L. Caecilius Jucundus, the House of the Coloured Capitals, and the Caupona of Sotericus, among others. Some of these are now displayed in the Naples National Archaeological Museum). The projection of the speaker's fantasies onto Cynthia points up her status as an aesthetic object to be shaped by the poet, but contrasts with the inclusion of her accusing voice at the end of the poem.

1 **qualis**, repeated in 3 and 6, correlates with *talis*, 7, and introduces each of the three mythological vignettes.

Thesea abl. agreeing with the abl. absolute *cedente . . . carina*

2 **languida** implies sexual exhaustion.

Cnosia refers to Ariadne, from Knossos, the palace-complex on Crete.

3 **primo . . . somno** dat. with the compound verb *accubuit*, which has erotic meaning in Propertius

Cepheia agrees with *Andromede*, "daughter of Cepheus," the king of Ethiopia.

4 **duris cotibus** abl. of separation with *libera*

5 **nec minus** "and"

Edonis nom. sing., "an Edonian woman," from the Edoni who lived in Thrace, an area known for its worship of Bacchus, so that *Edonis* suggests a bacchante

assiduis . . . choreis abl. of cause with *fessa*

6 **in herboso . . . Apidano** refers to the Apidanus, a tributary of the river Peneius in Thessaly. Presumably it ran dry in the summer or perhaps the bacchante drops on its grassy banks.

7 **uisa** Supply *est*.

mollem spirare quietem literally, "to breathe soft rest"; the phrase emphasizes both the rhythmic breathing of Cynthia and the vision of repose that she embodies.

8 **caput** acc. object of *nixa*, functioning as a Greek middle (Bennett sec. 175.2.d); also known as Greek acc. of respect

non certis . . . manibus suggests that Cynthia's hands may not continue to support her head.

9–10 **cum . . . traherem . . . quaterent** circumstantial *cum* clause in secondary sequence. The slave-boys, *pueri*, shake torches to keep them going in the late night; the murky light combined with the speaker's drunken state accounts for his "triple" vision at the poem's outset.

11 **hanc** refers to Cynthia and is the object of the infinitive *adire* in line 12.

nondum etiam is used by Propertius as the equivalent of *nondum*.

sensus acc. object of *deperditus*, functioning as a Greek middle (Bennett sec.175.2d). Although the following lines emphasize the sense of touch, it is the speaker's vision that has dominated to this point.

12 **impresso ... toro** abl. of place where

13 **correptum** agrees with an unexpressed *me*, the subject-acc. of the infinitives *temptare* in line 15 and *sumere* in line 16.

iuberent is in the subjunctive in an adversative clause with *quamuis* (Bennett sec. 309) and introduces the infinitives of indirect discourse in lines 15 and 16.

14 **hac ... hac** "on one side ... on the other"

Liber another name for Bacchus because of the liberating effects of wine, freeing those who indulge from inhibitions

15 **positam** refers to Cynthia.

subiecto ... lacerto abl. of means

16 **sumere** here functions as a *zeugma*, a word—and usually a verb—that "yokes together" or governs two different but parallel phrases or clauses in a way that changes the sense of the yoking word; *sumere oscula* is used literally but *sumere ... arma*, "to take up arms," is slang for making a sexual advance, in keeping with the elegiac trope of *militia amoris* ("the soldiery of love") and with *arma* as a metaphor for penis.

17 **ausus eram** use of the plpf. for the impf.

18 **expertae ... saeuitiae** gen. of quality; the speaker has experienced Cynthia's temper and does not wish to provoke it. Translate *expertae* passively, although *experior* is a deponent verb.

19–20 Having lost his nerve to make an assault, the speaker stands transfixed, comparing himself to the mythological Argus, the guardian of a hundred eyes set by Juno to watch over Inachus's daughter, Io, after Jupiter had seduced and then transformed her into a cow (cf. Apollod. 2.1.3–4; Aesch. *PV* 561–886; Ovid *Met.* 1.583–750). Like the opening mythological vignettes, the transformation of Io was a popular subject for painting and the comparison again emphasizes how much Cynthia herself is an aesthetic object to be transfigured by the poet. At the same time, Cynthia's beauty has a reciprocal, paralyzing effect on the speaker.

19 **intentis ... ocellis** abl. of specification

20 **ignotis cornibus** dat. or abl. with *haerebam*; Io's horns are "strange" and "wondrous" because never before seen on her.

21-26 The lover-poet now acts the part of devotee making offerings—*corollas, poma, munera*—to his goddess; in the process, he arranges her hair—*lapsos formare capillos*—and places his gifts as though composing a still life, again suggesting the artist's process of shaping his material.

21 **corollas** a poetic pl.; such a "garland" of flowers would be worn at parties and is often left by the *amator* at his mistress's doorstep, as a token gift, when he is "locked-out" (cf. Ovid *Am.*1.6.67–68; Prop. **3.3.47**). The garland is also a symbol of poetic practice (cf. 3.1.19); that the lover-poet here places his own wreath on Cynthia's brow may imply that he is "authorizing" her to speak in the second half of the poem. That is, he bestows on her the symbol of his own status as elegiac lover-poet, an identity that Cynthia later invokes for herself when she laments his absence in song and describes herself as wretched, wishing that he experience such nights as he forces on her (39–44).

24 **cauis ... manibus** abl. of means, referring to the speaker's hands curved around the fruit he offers

25 **ingrato ... munera somno** Her sleep lacks the gratitude that she would, presumably, display if awake. Again, the elegiac relationship employs the language of patronage, with the lover-poet here giving little gifts that nonetheless recall the more substantial *bene facta* of Milanion in **1.1.16**.

largibar an alternative form in place of *largiebar*

27 **duxti** a syncopated 2nd sing. pf. act. indicative in place of *duxisti*

raro ... motu abl. of manner

29-30 **ne ... neue** introduce parallel clauses of fearing in secondary sequence, technically dependent on *obstupui* ("I froze in fear"), a response stirred by *uano ... auspicio* ("the empty omen"). The speaker's anxious projections about the content of Cynthia's dreams (*qua ... uisa*), look back to the opening sequence of mythological analogues, all of which feature women in various states of post-sexual exhaustion.

30 **inuitam** modifies an implied *te* both as the object of *cogeret* and as the subject-acc. of *esse*, which is followed by *suam* as a predicate nom. (on *cogo* with acc. and infinitive, see Bennett sec. 331, VI).

Fig. 2. Sleeping Maenad. First century CE fresco from Pompeii, House of the Citharist. De Agostini Picture Library / A. Dagli Orti / The Bridgeman Art Library.

suam is a reflex. poss. pron. that refers back to the subject *quis*, the abstract someone who, in the speaker's rape fantasy, would force Cynthia to be "his."

31-33 **donec ... patefecit** introduces a temporal clause that is subordinate to *obstupui* in line 28.

31 **diuersas ... fenestras** The image of the moon passing by Cynthia's windows and illuminating her from different angles again echoes the opening sequence of mythological comparisons.

praecurrens "passing before"; *prae-* substitutes here for *praeter-*.

luna As the celestial body identified with Diana, sister of Apollo, the moon suggestively mirrors Cynthia herself: both god and goddess, twins, were born on the island of Delos, at Mount Cynthos, from which they each took cult names (see Introduction, p. xxii).

32 **moraturis ... luminibus** abl. of specification; the fut. act. pple. of *moror* here suggests an inclination—the busy moon's "beams inclined to linger" or "lingering light."

34 **cubitum** acc. object of *fixa*, functioning as a Greek middle (Bennett 1752d).

35-46 Cynthia wakes up and chastises Propertius for his late—early morning—arrival at her bed. She mirrors his anxiety about her infidelity with accusations about his own betrayal with another. The inclusion of her voice in the poem contrasts with all the earlier images emphasizing the mistress as fantasy and object-to-be-fashioned by the poet. Nonetheless, Cynthia too knows how to manipulate myth and stereotype to her advantage—she paints herself as a faithful Penelope or Roman Lucretia weaving at her loom into the long hours of the night.

35-36 **iniuria** It is unclear whether Propertius is the perpetrator or the victim of injurious conduct and, if the perpetrator, which is more likely, whether Cynthia refers to the offense committed against her by his infidelity or to some insult to another woman that has resulted in his being thrown out of her house, making him a "locked-out lover" or *exclusus amator*. In the latter case, *alterius* is an objective gen. dependent on *iniuria* as well as gen. of possession dependent on *clausis ... foribus*.

37-38 **meae ... noctis** gen. of the whole, dependent on *tempora*; Cynthia conceives the night as belonging to her but Propertius has "spent" or "consumed" it on someone else, arriving home *languidus*, in the same spent condition as he imagines the bacchante in line 5.

37 **consumpsisti** 2nd sing. pf. act. indicative

38 **exactis ... sideribus** abl. absolute expressing time when and referring to the fading stars at dawn

39-40 **utinam** introduces an optative subjunctive.

talis ... noctes ... qualis "such nights ... as ..." Note the alternative *-is* ending for the acc. pl. As **1.1.33-34** makes clear, the Propertian lover-poet does in fact experience such nights as Cynthia wishes him to have. The correlatives here also echo those in lines 1-6, underscoring how Cynthia's speech structurally complements the speaker's fantasies, all the while juxtaposing her "actual voice" to his mythologizing, erotically tinged visions.

40 **me** subject-acc. of *habere* following *iubes*; understand *qualis* (*noctes*) as the acc. object of the infinitive.

41-42 The image of Cynthia "deceiving" (*fallebam*)—i.e., fending off—sleep by weaving evokes Homer's Penelope faithfully awaiting Odysseus, while craftily evading the suitors: claiming she would pick one as her next husband when she finished her shroud for Laertes, Odysseus's father, she in fact unravels her work at night and keeps the suitors at bay indefinitely. The weaving woman as a symbol of chastity also resonates specifically in the Roman cultural imagination by conjuring the figure of Lucretia, whose rape in Livy's account was the catalyst for Rome's transition from the monarchic rule of the Tarquins to the republic. The wife of Collatinus, who served in the army of the Tarquin royal family, Lucretia exhibited model behavior when a group of soldiers vyed with each other, each claiming his wife as the most virtuous. When the men made a surprise visit to their spouses to prove such claims, they found all the other women engaged in banqueting except Lucretia, who was at her loom, surrounded by her handmaids. The vision ignited such a passionate lust in Sextus Tarquinius, the nephew of the king, that he secretly returned to the home of Lucretia a few weeks later, burst into her bedroom, and compelled her to have sex with him by threatening to kill her and a slave, so that their corpses would falsely suggest an even more transgressive and shameful adultery. After Lucretia informed her husband and father of her rape, a group of men, led by Iunius Brutus, took revenge on the Tarquins, eventually deposing them and ushering in republican rule. Lucretia herself committed suicide to preserve the image of her chastity (cf. Livy 1.57.658). In Propertius's poem, the image of Cynthia at the loom serves to align the speaker not only with the male kin wishing to defend Lucretia's chastity, but also, given the *amator*'s unannounced visit and desire to assault his sleeping girlfriend, with Sextus Tarquinius himself.

42 **Orpheae** adj. modifying *lyrae*; in classical mythology Orpheus was the preeminently gifted poet and musician whose lyre playing charmed both the animate and inanimate worlds, causing even rocks to move. In the fourth georgic Vergil recounts the story of Orpheus descending to the underworld to lead back Eurydice (4.453–527). His fateful backward glance, however, causes him to lose her and he suffers his subsequent demise at the hands of maenads, angry that he spurns them and their god. Cynthia's reference to the ill-fated lyricist in her choice of modifiers seems vaguely menacing, particularly given the speaker's own initial comparison of her to an "Edonian woman"—or maenad from Thrace (5)—a likeness reinforced by the echo of *fessa* in this line.

43-44 Following the image of her Orphic skill on the lyre, Cynthia's plaint (*querebar*) to herself (*mecum*) conjures the role of elegiac poet: abandoned (*deserta*), she laments Propertius's long delay in another's embrace (*externo . . . amore*), thus mimicking the elegist's usual anguish and frustrated desire. Note that *deserta* recall the *desertis . . . litoribus* of Ariadne.

45 **lapsam** a proleptic past pple., describing the effect of winged sleep's visitation

iucundis . . . alis abl. of means or accompaniment

46 **illa . . . ultima cura** either refers to Propertius's other mistress or *illa* has been corrupted from *ille*, so that *cura*, as predicate nom., refers to *sopor*, sleep, as a cure for Cynthia's tears.

↬ *Elegy 2.1*

This programmatic poem to Propertius's second book of elegies, 2.1, addresses the poet's new patron, Maecenas, and justifies the writing of elegy as a poetic form distinguished from, but parallel to, the genre of epic. The opening of the poem celebrates the choice to write elegy by playing on the ambiguity between Cynthia as a real mistress and alternately as a metaphor for elegiac poetry. Characterized as a *recusatio*, a "refusal poem" in which the speaker declares his talents insufficient for the high-style, 2.1 exhibits the usual incorporation of elements from the disavowed genre. In this case, the speaker lists significant battles of the recent civil wars—Mutina, Philippi, Naulochus, Perusia, Actium—and arguably displays his unsuitability for celebrating Augustus's epic deeds by emphasizing the dead: the focus on citizen-tombs (*ciuilia busta*, 27) at Philippi and the overthrown hearths (*euersos . . . focos*, 29) of Perusia underscores the human cost of Augustus's bloody victories. This poem would be profitably read against other examples of the *recusatio*, not only in Propertius (**3.3** in this volume; 3.9), but in Vergil (*Ecl.* 6) and Horace (*Carm.* 1.6; 2.1) as well. A variation on the motif, the first poem of Horace's second lyric book, *Odes* 2.1, echoes Propertius's flirtation with the topic of civil war in the form of a lamentation or dirge for the dead (see notes on lines 27–29, below).

COMMENTARY 2.1 43

The Propertian lover-poet's shifts of thought divide the poem into seven sections: the first sixteen lines assert Cynthia and her beguiling ways as the poet's inspiration; lines 17–26 list all the subjects the poet would *not* write about if he had the talent—since Augustus and Maecenas would be his chief concern; lines 27–38 ennumerate Augustus's conquests; lines 39–46 justify the poet's incapacity to celebrate them; lines 47–56 take up his exclusive devotion to Cynthia; lines 57–70 elaborate the theme of passion as an incurable disease; and lines 71–76 imagine Maecenas stopping to read the brief epitaph on the poet's tombstone.

1–2 **quaeritis** The poet addresses Maecenas and, as the pl. implies, a more general audience of friends and readers who are interested in the inspiration for his poetry; the verb introduces two parallel indirect questions that are governed by *unde* and take the subjunctive. Translate *unde* as "why," with the secondary, literal sense of "whence," as in "from what source."

1 **amores** refers to poems about love (cf. Ovid's *Amores*) as well as to the experiences that make up the content of the verse.

mihi dat. of agent with passive verb, common in poetry

2 **mollis** a highly charged and programmatic word in love elegy: its basic sense of "soft" takes on various connotations of "unmanly," "feminine," "voluptuous," "languorous," depending on the context (see Introduction, p. xxiii). Here, the adj. can be taken predicatively, referring to the stylistic sensuous quality of Propertian verse, "soft on the lips" (*mollis in ora*), but it also functions attributively to describe the contents of the poet's *liber*, so the question becomes "What makes your voluptuous love elegies so popular?" or "Why is everybody talking about them?" Propertius programmatically establishes his *mollis liber* in contrast to the *durus uersus* (2.1.41), or epic, that he is unable to write.

3 **Calliope ... Apollo** The traditional sources of a poet's inspiration, either the Muses or the god of poetry himself, do not inspire him but rather the "girl herself" is responsible for his

	genius. This line contributes to the drama of control that is played out over the course of the Propertian corpus, culminating in 4.7.77–78, where Cynthia's ghost demands that the poet burn the verses that he composed about her.
5–16	A sequence of vignettes that capture Cynthia's fascination for the poet even as the fragmentation of her body (clothing, hair, fingers, hands, eyes) points up the elusiveness of the elegiac mistress as a literary character: these discrete glimpses emphasize not the person but rather the transfiguration of Cynthia into verse, underscoring the mistress as both metaphor and metonym for elegiac poetics (see Introduction, pp. xxii–xxiii).
5–7	**siue . . . seu** The choice of form for the conj. that introduces each successive couplet depends on the meter; translate "if . . . or if," except for *seu cum* (line 11), "or when," indicating the shift from hypothetical gestures or actions to an actual repeated occurrence.
5	**uidi** a fifteenth-century manuscript variant on the more authoritative but impossible-to-construe *cogis*; *illam* is the subject-acc. of *incedere*.
5–6	**Cois . . . Coa ueste** a sheer silky fabric from the island of Cos; its seductive transparency made it a favorite dress of prostitutes, although it also signaled refinement and luxury. Here, the production of verse from Coan cloth may be both metaphorical, evoking Philitas of Cos (see Introduction, pp. xxv–xxvi), and literal, suggesting a fancy volume of verse with an expensive silken cover.
7	**ad frontem . . . errare** "stray across (her) brow"
8	**gaudet** with infinitive *ire*, "rejoices in going"
	laudatis . . . comis abl. of specification or cause with *superba*
9–10	The image of the lyre-playing elegiac mistress draws from the Greek courtesan, conventionally accomplished in the arts of song, dance, and poetry.
9	**digitis . . . eburnis** abl. of means

COMMENTARY 2.1 45

10 **miramur ... ut** introduces an indirect question with the subjunctive.

facilis ... premat arte manus literally, "presses nimble hands with skill," but the image refers in fact to pressing the strings of the lyre with one hand, creating chords, while the other would "pluck" (*percussit*) the notes of the melody; *facilis* is acc. pl.

11 **poscentis** acc. pl. with *ocellos* and taking *somnum* as object

12 **causas** "themes," as some interpret (*OLD* sv 15); or "reasons" for composing poetry, referring back to the question of "source" or "whence," *unde*, in the first couplet 13–14

The speaker's erotic tussles with his mistress inspire elegy that rivals the epic genre. In this couplet, the trope of *militia amoris*, the "soldiery of love," extends even to the metaphorical use of the *Iliad*—the seminal epic of warfare—to describe elegiac verse.

13 **erepto ... amictu** abl. absolute; the image of clothing "snatched away" or "ripped from" the mistress points to the undercurrent of actual violence that periodically surfaces in elegy (see Introduction, p. xxiii, and cf. Prop. 2.15.18–21; Tib. 1.4; Ovid *Am.* 1.7)

15 **quidquid ... quodcumque** indef. pronouns with the value of *quiduis* or *quidlibet*

16 **maxima de nihilo ... historia** the shift from epic (14) to history anticipates the progression of topics renounced by the poet in lines 19–34. The distinction, however, was not firm. On the one hand, for the Romans, the epic genre before Vergil's *Aeneid* dealt with historical events—cf. the *Annales* of Ennius—while early legend itself was considered history. On the other, *historia* can mean simply "story" (*OLD* sv 4), without necessarily implying either a grand narrative or a document of the past. All the same, by claiming that "the greatest history [or story] is born from nothing," the poet elevates his elegies and their seeming emphasis on quotidian, private

life to a higher status in the hierarchy of genres. Note that *de nihilo* recalls line 4, where the speaker claims that *ipsa puella* ("the girl herself")—the raw material of his verse— drives his genius.

17-38 Here begins the *recusatio* ("refusal") proper, but with a twist: the poet first recounts all the epic topics that he would *not* write about, if he had the talent, before stating that recent, contemporary history would be his subject. In keeping with the convention, the list of themes evokes and even recreates in miniature—in elegy—the very genres the poet renounces: the chronological movement from Hesiod to the battle of Actium constitutes an epic sweep from the world's mythic origins to the present. An extended mixed contrary-to-fact condition structures lines 17–26, with a past protasis, *si . . . dedissent* (17), and a present negative apodosis, *non . . . canerem* (19), that concludes with *bene facta Mari* in line 24. This is followed by a second positive—if ironic—apodosis, *memorarem* (25), stating what the speaker would sing about if he could. The same contrary-to-fact structure governs lines 27–36, with *quotiens* (27) . . . *canerem* (28, 31) functioning as the protasis and *mea Musa . . . contexeret* (35) as the apodosis.

17 **quod . . . si tantum** "But if only"; alternatively, *tantum* may be taken as the object of *dedissent*, indicating "such great talent" and introducing the result clause of line 18.

Maecenas Gaius Maecenas, patron of Propertius as well as close friend and political advisor to Octavian, later Augustus, until the late 20s BCE.

18 **ut possem . . . ducere in arma manus** a substantive result clause (Bennett 297.1) dependent on *si . . . dedissent*; here the military imagery most likely serves as a metaphor for writing epic or history about such events, although Propertius does emphasize elsewhere his renunciation of a political, military career (cf. 3.4).

19–20 **Titanas . . . Ossan Olympo . . . Pelion esset iter** This couplet refers to two separate intergenerational conflicts: Hesiod, *Theogony*, 629–720, recounts the battle between the Titans and the younger Olympian gods; the *Odyssey*, 11.315, refers to the giants Otus and Ephialtes, sons of Poseidon, who piled Ossa on Olympus and Pelion on Ossa in an attempt to scale heaven and carry off Hera and Artemis. Although Propertius here distinguishes these mythic intergenerational conflicts from the events of recent contemporary history in lines 25–34, such myth serves as allegory for the civil wars in other poets (e.g., Hor. *Carm.* 3.4).

19 **Olympo** dat. with the compound *impositam*

20 **caeli** objective gen. dependent on *iter*

ut . . . esset purpose clause: "so that Pelion might be a path to heaven"

21 **ueteres Thebas** refers to an epic cycle about the conflict between the sons of Oedipus, Eteocles, and Polyneices, over the throne of Thebes.

Pergama Troy

nomen "glory," i.e., "source of fame"

22 **bina coisse uada** subject-acc. and infinitive in indirect statement dependent on *canerem* (19); in 484 BCE the Greek king Xerxes cut a canal across the isthmus behind Mt. Athos, thus joining two bodies of water and avoiding a trip around the promontory where the fleet of his father, Darius, had been wrecked (Hdt. 7.22–24).

23 **regna . . . prima Remi** as a poetic plural refers either to the chosen realm of Romulus's brother Remus before their conflict (the Aventine Hill, where Remus wished to found Rome) or, as some commentators argue on account of metrical reasons, to the rule of Romulus himself after Remus's death (cf. Catul. 58.5 *magnanimi Remi nepotes*). However, intergenerational conflict, fratricide, and civil war thematically

combine to define many of the mythic and historical subjects renounced in lines 19–34, making a reference to the "first realm" of Remus entirely appropriate.

animos Carthaginis altae "the fierce spirit of lofty Carthage"—a reference to the Punic Wars, treated in the early Roman historical epics of Naevius and Ennius

24 **Cimbrorumque minas** The *Cimbri* were a German tribe that, emboldened by many military successes, invaded northern Italy and threatened the Roman republic, only to be defeated at the Raudine plain, in Cisalpine Gaul, by Marius in 101 BCE.

bene facta Treat as one word—"feats" or "accomplishments"—but there is also the sense of "service" provided to the republic by averting the danger of invasion (cf. **1.1.16**).

25 **tui . . . Caesaris** The use of the possessive *tui* emphasizes Maecenas's close relationship to Augustus, a theme picked up again in lines 37–39.

26 **Caesare sub magno** "after great Caesar"; the repetition of the honorific "Caesar" pays tribute even as it ironically contrasts with the lines that follow.

fores an alternative form for *esses*

27–34 The prominent battles of the triumviral period all receive mention in a contrary-to-fact clause dependent on *quotiens* (27). These were the *bellaque resque* (25) of Augustus to date and parallel the historical list found in Suetonius, *Aug.* 9. Nonetheless, the phrase *ciuilia busta* (27), "civil-war tombs," leaves no ambiguity about the shameful nature of these conflicts and the mention of them may well have discomfited the *princeps*.

27 **Mutinam** After the assassination of Julius Caesar in 44 BCE, his great-nephew and adopted son, Octavian, won over the loyalty of Caesar's troops and took steps to secure the favor of the Roman public and to avenge his great-uncle. The Roman senate predominantly sided with Octavian rather than Marc Antony, the consul at the time, who initially advocated a compromise with the assassins. However, after Cicero scathingly attacked

Antony in defamatory speeches, the *Philippics,* he pursued and besieged Decimus Brutus, one of the conspirators (to be distinguished from the more famous Marcus Brutus) and the rightful governor of Cisalpine Gaul, at Mutina (modern Modena). In 43 BCE Octavian joined forces with the then consuls Hirtius and Pansa, at the head of a consular army, and defeated the troops of Marc Antony in his siege. The two consuls were killed in the conflict but Brutus survived and fled Italy.

Philippos in apposition to *ciuilia busta*; the syntax reduces the location to a graveyard for the Roman dead. It was at Phillippi, on the coast of Macedonia, that the forces of Octavian and Marc Antony—now allied in the second triumvirate—decisively defeated in 42 BCE the army of Marcus Brutus and Gaius Cassius. The two main assassins of Julius Caesar committed suicide.

28   **canerem** To sing about the tombs of Roman citizens suggests a form of dirge or lamentation; cf. Hor. *Carm.* 2.1.

Siculae ... fugae a gen. of apposition, giving specific information about *classica bella* ("naval battles"). The "Sicilian flight" or "rout off Sicily" refers to the defeat of Sextus Pompey, son of Pompey the Great, at Naulochus, in 36 BCE. It was after this victory—accomplished by his admiral, Marcus Agrippa—that Octavian vowed to erect in commemoration the temple to Apollo on the Palatine Hill, which was completed in 28 BCE and subsequently became more associated with the battle of Actium (see **2.31**).

29   **euersosque focos ... gentis Etruscae** refers to the siege and subsequent destruction of the ancient Etruscan city of Perusia in 41–40 BCE. This was arguably Octavian's bloodiest chapter of the civil wars: according to Appian (*B Civ.* 5.48.203) he had all but one of the city's officials executed to exact revenge for Perusia having harbored Lucius Antonius, Marc Antony's brother, at a period of renewed hostilities among the triumvirs. 1.22, the "autobiographical" seal poem for the *Monobiblos,* reveals that the poet lost a relative in the Perusine conflict (see Introduction, pp. xi–xii).

    focos an emotionally powerful term, serving as metonymy for *domos*

30 **Ptolemaeei ... Phari** the island of Pharos, off the coast of Alexandria, which was captured by the Romans in 30 BCE after the defeat of Antony and Cleopatra at Actium (31 BCE); the island was famous for its lighthouse, one of the "Seven Wonders of the Ancient World." The Ptolemaic royal family ruled Egypt until the fall of Cleopatra.

31-34 In 29 BCE Octavian celebrated a "triple triumph" commemorating his victories in Illyricum (35 BCE), at the naval battle of Actium (31 BCE), and over Egypt (30 BCE). At such events, effigies and pictorial representations of countries, rivers, and cities would be borne, together with captives and material spoils, down the *Via Sacra*, as the triumphal procession made its way through the Roman Forum and ascended the Capitoline Hill. According to Dio Cassius (51.21.8) an effigy of Cleopatra herself was carried in Octavian's triumph. Cf. **3.11.49–56**.

31 **Nilum ... attractus in urbem** The river "dragged" through the city streets suggests a perversion of nature, a form of *adunaton* ("impossibility").

32 **septem captiuis ... aquis** refers to the streams comprising the Nile delta; abl. of accompaniment.

33 **auratis ... catenis** abl. of means; "gilded" chains signified the royal status of the captive kings.

34 **Actia ... currere rostra** indirect discourse dependent on *canerem* (31); the prows or "beaks" of ships captured at the battle of Actium formed part of the triumphal display.

35 **contexeret** impf. subjunctive in a contrary-to-fact clause that concludes the statement introduced by *quotiens* in line 27 ("As often as I would sing..., my Muse would weave..."); weaving was a common metaphor for poetic composition, but juxtaposed with *illis ... armis* (dat. with a compound verb) it creates a startling image.

COMMENTARY 2.1

36 **et sumpta et posita pace** abl. absolute, "in both wartime and peace"; Propertius here distorts the usual phrases, *sumere arma* and *ponere arma*, "to take up . . ." and "to set down arms." The ironic distortion implies the violence underwriting the Augustan peace (see Introduction, p. xxxii).

fidele caput "loyal friend" or "chief ally," in apposition to *te*

37-38 This couplet compliments Maecenas by comparing his relationship with Augustus to two famous mythological friendships between men, with the following implicit logic: just as any poems celebrating Augustus's victories would also lend glory to Maecenas, so the storied fame of Theseus and Achilles keeps alive the memory of their close companions Pirithous and Patroclus. The use of Greek patronymics in the acc., referring to Pirithous as "son of Ixion" (*Ixioniden*, 37) and Patroclus as "son of Menoetios" (*Menoetiaden*, 37), lends epic texture to the elegiac pentameter.

37 **infernis, supernis** locative abl., "the world below" and "the world above." Theseus traveled to the underworld with Pirithous, when the latter wished to carry back Persephone as a wife for himself. In the *Iliad*, Patroclus wears Achilles' armor into battle and is killed by Hektor, a turning-point of the epic that transforms Achilles's wrath—from anger at the Greeks for dishonoring him to sorrow-driven rage at the Trojans—and draws him back into the fighting.

testatur "testifies to [the glory of]" and thus "makes known"

39-46 After listing what he would sing about had he the power, Propertius compares himself to the third-century Alexandrian poet, Callimachus, whose *Aetia* advocates a refined style that eschews the grand subject matter of epic (see Introduction, pp. xxiv–xxv).

39 **Phlegraeos . . . tumultus** The battle between the Olympians and the Giants, in which Zeus struck down Encaladus with a lightning bolt, took place on the Phlegraean plain, located in Macedonia or, as Strabo (5.4.4) claims, in Campania in Italy.

40 **intonet** refers to the thunderous style of epic, as Callimachus describes it (*Aet.* 1.20)

angusto pectore abl. of means, although the sense of "origin" or "place from which" is also present. Literally, the image refers to small lung capacity but the concept of a "narrow chest" metaphorically expresses the "slender," compressed Callimachean style.

41 **praecordia** literally, "diaphragm"—Propertius continues the image of the poet's physical capacity for volume as determining the choice of genre; the implication is that he considers himself unsuited for writing epic.

duro . . . uersu abl. of place where; *durus* here contrasts to *mollis* elegy and evokes both a heavy, even oppressive style and the masculine content of military, historical epic. In his "Homage to Sextus Propertius" Pound memorably renders this and the following line as "And my ventricles to not palpitate to Caesarial *ore/ rotundos*, . . ."

42 **Phrygios . . . auos** Augustus claimed to descend from Phyrgian Aeneas, a genealogy explored in Book 6 of the *Aeneid*.

condere a complementary infinitive (also known as an object infinitive; cf. Bennett sec. 328) dependent on *conueniunt* in line 41; translate here as "to trace back," but the verb literally refers to the act of writing—i.e., "to compose"—as well as to founding a race, people, or city.

43–46 The verb *narrat* should be supplied after *nauita* and *enumerat* after *pastor*. Each person recounts what he knows best and the poet is no different: understand *uersantes* as nom., with *proelia* as the direct object both of the pple. and of an understood *enumeramus*. The verb *uersare* here metaphorically conflates the act of love with writing poetry, as frequently in elegy. "Battles in a narrow bed" suggests both the theme of *militia amoris* ("soldiery of love") and the Callimachean aesthetic of refined and "slender" verse in contrast to the grand style of epic (cf. *angusto . . . pectore* in line 40).

46 **qua** interr. adj. agreeing with *arte*

pote an alternative form for *potest*

conterat a jussive subjunctive

47-48 These lines demonstrate the close tie between the speaker's passion and death as well as elegy's typical inversion of gender roles: the *amator* embraces for himself the feminine virtue of fidelity and devotion to a single person, Cynthia, but can only hope for such loyalty in his mistress (see Introduction, pp. xx–xxi).

48 **posse frui** subject of *datur* (47) with the second infinitive as complementary with *posse*

fruar optative subjunctive

49-50 **leuis ... puellas** an ironic transposition of elegiac and epic values: Cynthia, a mistress elsewhere described as *leuis* (1.18.11; 2.5.28) and conflated with a genre similarly characterized and noted for its fickle, inconstant women, rejects the entire *Iliad* on account of Helen's *leuitas* (cf. **2.16.26**).

51-56 Magic charms will never alter Propertius's devoted passion to Cynthia—i.e., no other woman will be able to seduce him. Three parallel conditional clauses, *seu ... seu ... siue*, introduce mythological exempla: Phaedra, wife of Theseus, fell in love with her stepson Hippolytus and, in a version of the myth no longer extant, attempts to seduce him through *pocula*, draughts of love-potions. Circe transforms Odysseus's men into pigs in the tenth book of the *Odyssey*. After leaving her home in Colchis, Medea sails with Jason to Iolcus, where she promises to rejuvenate his uncle Pelias but in fact murders him in a boiling cauldron. In Ovid's telling of the story (*Meta.* 7.297–349), it is Aeson, Jason's father, whom she boils but successfully restores to youth. Note that these three powerful mythological women were all related as descendants of Helios. Moreover, just as Cynthia also represents love elegy, so each of these women may represent the rejected genres of epic and tragedy.

51	**mihi** dat. of agent with pass. periphrastic, parallel to the construction in line 53
52	**nocitura** fut. act. pple.
54	**Colchis** nom. f. sing. noun referring to Medea by her place of origin, "the woman from Colchis"
	Iolciacis adj. referring to Iolcus and agreeing with *focis*
	urat subjunctive in a future-less-vivid protasis (and parallel to the two other clauses introduced by *seu*, lines 51 and 53, which have their verbs in the indicative); line 56, with its verb in the fut. indicative, provides the apodosis to this mixed condition.
	aena n. pl. of *aenum*
56	The funereal imagery of the poet's bier departing from Cynthia's house here serves as a metaphor for his unwavering attachment to her but also anticipates lines 71–78. The motifs of death and passion are frequently interwoven in Propertius's poetry.
57–64	These lines feature a series of medical success stories in the form of mythological *exempla* that point the contrast to the disease of love, an illness that resists all cure.
58	**artificem** here, one who practices the "art" of medicine and is thus a "craftsman of disease," with *morbi* as an objective gen.
59	**Machaon** son of the healing god Asclepius and surgeon for the Greek army at Troy; in the "Little Iliad" (frag. 1) Machaon cures Philoctetes of a poisonous snake-bite he received on the island of Lemnos (an alternative legend has him poisoned accidentally by one of Hercules's arrows).
60	**Phillyrides** nom. sing., "son of Philyra," i.e., the centaur Chiron, a legendary healer who cured Phoenix of the blindness inflicted by his father after a quarrel (Apollod. 3.13.8). Philyra was an Oceanid, a nymph loved by Saturn. When his wife Rhea discovered their amorous relations he turned himself and Philyra into horses, a metamorphosis that occasioned Chiron's birth as a centaur (Apollod. 1.2.4; schol. *ad* Ap. Rhod. *Argon.* 1.554; Verg. *G.* 3.92). As in line 37, the Greek patronymic lends epic texture to the pentameter.

COMMENTARY 2.1

61 **deus ... Epidaurius** the healing god Asclepius, who had an important shrine at Epidaurus

Cressis ... herbis abl. of means

62 **Androgeona** acc. sing.; Minos and Pasiphae, king and queen of Crete, sent their son Androgeos to Athens to compete in the Panathenaic games. His success angered the Athenians and brought on his death, in one myth by the Marathonian bull and in another version by rival athletes (Apollod. 3.15.7).

63 **Mysus ... iuuenis** refers to Telephus, king of Mysia, who suffered a spear-wound from Achilles and subsequently was healed by rust from the same weapon (Hyg. *Fab.* 101).

Haemonia the ancient name for Thessaly; as an adj. here it agrees with *cuspide* and refers to Achilles's spear.

63-64 **qua cuspide ... hac ipsa cuspide** The rel. clause precedes the independent clause and incorporates the antecedent within it (Bennett 251.4a).

65-70 The speaker's illness is beyond cure—anyone who can help him will perform an impossible feat, or *adunaton*, and would alone be capable of bringing relief to legendary figures fated to suffer eternal punishment in the underworld. Cf. **1.1.19, 23-24** where the lover-poet appeals to the sorcery of witches, those who reputedly carry out *adunata*, in order to secure Cynthia's passion for him.

65 **mihi** dat. of separation with *demere*

66 **Tantaleae ... manu** dat. sing.; Tantalus killed his son Pelops and secretly offered him as a meal to the gods. For punishment he was confined to a pool of water that receded whenever he tried to drink from it, even as fruit suspended over his head continuously eluded his grasp (*Od.* 11.583ff.; Pind. *Ol.* 1.55-66).

67-68 All but one of the Danaids killed their bridegroom-cousins on their wedding night. As their eternal punishment they had to continually carry water in vessels on their shoulders to storage jars, *dolia*, that leaked and never filled (Aesch. *Supp.*; Hor. *Carm.* 3.11; Ovid *Her.* 14; see Prop. **2.31.4** and note).

67	**uirgineis ... urnis** abl. of means
68	**ne ... grauentur** negative purpose clause
69–70	For his theft of fire from the gods Prometheus was chained to a rock in the underworld, where a bird endlessly devoured his liver.
71–78	In these final lines Propertius takes the theme of the disease of *eros* to its logical and fatal conclusion: he imagines his tomb and the short statement, uttered by Maecenas in passing, that holds Cynthia responsible for the poet's death. The previous *exempla* of underworld suffering, as analogue to love's torment, provide an associative transition from the image of the poet's funeral in line 56 to the tombstone, inscription, and epitaphic remembrance of his friend and patron.
72	The short inscription fantasized by the speaker here not only points to his refusal of a public life, and thus of any civic or military offices and honors, but it also has thematic resonance for elegy as a genre characterized by a Callimachean aesthetic of small compass and exacting style: *breue* and *exiguo* recall *angusto* in lines 40 and 45.
73	**nostrae spes inuidiosa iuuentae** a typically compressed Propertian phrase that can be taken several ways: as referring to the poet's own youth and the hopes he pinned on Maecenas as a future patron; or, alternatively, to all the young writers with similar aspirations. A third interpretation understands *iuuentae* as the *iuuenes* of equestrian rank, who see in Maecenas a symbol of political success, a man who rose high in the new imperial order despite his refusal of senatorial status.
74	**gloria iusta** continues the vocatives of line 73; Maecenas's patronage lends Propertius distinction both while he is alive and after his death. Cf. Hor. *Carm.* 1.1.1, referring to Maecenas as *dulce decus meum*.
75	**uia proxima** takes the dat. and refers either to a literal road or more abstractly to Maecenas's journey that would bring him near to the poet's tomb.

76 **esseda ... Britanna** originally a British and more broadly a Gallic war-chariot that the Romans later adopted as a luxury pleasure vehicle (cf. **2.32.5**). The appropriation of a military mode of transport for use as a light-weight touring carriage symbolizes the way elegy as a genre incorporates epic imagery into its own refined and soft style.

caelatis ... iugis a yoke embossed with fancy metal-work

78 Spoken by Maecenas as he passes Propertius's tomb, these words suggest an epitaph, a concise statement in keeping with the poet's imagined *breue in exiguo marmore nomen* (72). Several conventions of the Roman epitaphic tradition are present here: an invitation to the passerby to read the inscription, mourning for the lost one, and circumstances of the death (Herrera 1999:195). Such commemoration also recalls Greek funereal elegy even as it ironically confirms the earlier assertion that it is "glorious to die in love" (47). Propertius often invokes such conventions: he explicitly composes his own inscription in 2.13.35–36, where he gives instructions for his funeral; the ghost of Cynthia, in 4.7.85–86, dictates her own epitaph after enjoining the poet to burn all his verses about her; and Cornelia, the speaker of 4.11, the daughter of P. Cornelius Scipio, narrates her past as though from the tomb itself (36).

dura puella the conventional epithet for the elegiac mistress (see Introduction, pp. xxii–xxiii)

∽ *Elegy 2.10*

A variation on the *recusatio*, this time addressed to Augustus himself, 2.10 has convinced scholars and editors in the past to consider it a sincere attempt to celebrate the emperor. However, at the time of the poem's publication, all the countries and regions mentioned in the poem were as yet unconquered territories or the sites of embarrassing military losses. The reference to "virgin Arabia" in line 16 suggests 26–25 BCE as a date of composition, before an ill-fated expedition to that country ended ruinously in 24 BCE. Although the poem begins in a laudatory vein, the speaker eventually defers his praise to the future, when Augustus will have made good on his own imperialistic ambitions. A closer analysis thus reveals the poem as a parody of a praise poem, one that transposes the language of elegiac love to the military sphere of potential conquests: the countries on which Augustus has imperial designs appear as "mistresses" to be conquered. By recasting Augustus's ambitions in the rhetorical terms of elegiac passion, the poem performs a humorous send-up of Augustan foreign policy.

The poem can be divided into three sections: lines 1–12 announce the poet's encomiastic intent with a mock-portentous drumbeat of expectation that becomes redundant; lines 13–18 celebrate Augustus's conquests; lines 19–26 back away from such praise and claim insufficient poetic prowess.

1–2 Two spatial metaphors, Mount Helicon and the plains of Thessaly, express the intended transition from private, erotic themes to public verse that celebrates the accomplishments of Augustus Caesar. Both vertical height and horizontal expanse suggest epic aspirations.

tempus Supply *est*.

lustrare "to range across" or "survey," but the meaning "to purify" is implicitly present for it looks ahead to the liquid imagery of the final couplet

aliis ... choreis an allusion to poetry in the grand manner and to the opening of Hesiod's *Theogony*, which features an image of the Muses dancing on Mt. Helicon. It is here that Hesiod first received instruction from the Muses as he begins his epic; cf. **3.3.1**; 3.5.19–20. Although the phrase implies a change in meter, Propertius launches his encomium in elegiacs.

2 **campum ... dare ... equo** i.e., to give the horse free rein over the field

COMMENTARY 2.10

Haemonio ... equo Haemon was the father of Thessalus and both were eponyms for the region of Thessaly that was famous for its horses. Luc. 6.397 points to their use in war. As the homeland of Achilles, Thessaly specifically evokes Homeric epic.

3 **fortis ... ad proelia turmas** "troops brave in battle"

4 **mei ... ducis** an ambiguous phrase that suggests both the poet as soldier and the authoritative role increasingly assumed by Augustus Caesar

5–6 Propertius here hedges his bets. If his celebratory intentions fall flat, the mere daring will bring him praise.

quod si deficiant ... erit mixed condition with future-less-vivid protasis and future-more-vivid apodosis: tentativeness about the positive outcome yields to confidence in the effort.

5 **quod si** "but if"

6 **uoluisse** subject of *est*

7 **canat** jussive subjunctive

8 **quando scripta ... est** a notorious crux whose ambiguity lies at the heart of the poem: if *quando* is translated as "since," then the statement becomes causal and explains the subject matter of the present poem as the *bella* to which the poet turns, now having closed the chapter on Cynthia, his *scripta puella*. However, by the end of the poem, the speaker has deferred his praise for Augustus to a future date. This deferral and the presence of Cynthia in later poems of this and the following book allow a retrospective reading of *quando* as "when," "at the time that."

9–12 Two more couplets announce the speaker's intentions with mock gravity and parodic redundancy, suggesting a greater focus on the poet and his craft than on the purported subject of the poem. The repetition of *nunc* (9) ... *nunc* (10) ... *nunc* (12) creates the poetic equivalent of the anticipatory drum roll.

9 **subducto ... uultu** abl. absolute; "with raised visage," referring to the attitude of a singer undertaking a more elevated style

11	**surge ... ex humili** The phrase underscores the hierarchy of genres: encomia of Augustus's military exploits rank higher than private love elegies.
13–18	These six lines constitute the heart of the panegyric and provide a glimpse of the various campaigns and foreign interests of the Augustan regime in the mid 20s BCE. However, a closer scrutiny of the actual historical backdrop of each reference reveals a certain indeterminacy and even misrepresentation in the speaker's claims about Augustan imperial conquest. Moreover, employing the trope of personification, Propertius casts Rome's relationship to the lands and territories that yield to Augustus's power in the elegiac rhetoric of erotic relations.
13–14	The gist of the couplet is clear: the Parthians pose a diminished threat to Rome. However, the syntax of line 13 is ambiguous: either *negat* takes *tueri* as a complementary infinitive (also known as an object infinitive; cf. Bennett sec. 328), with *equitem ... Parthorum* as the object of *tueri*, or *negat* introduces indirect statement with *equitem* as the subject-acc. of *tueri*. In the first reading, the Euphrates refuses to protect the Parthian horseman *post terga* ("behind its back"), suggesting that Augustus's power extends to territory beyond the river. In the second reading, the Euphrates claims that the Parthians no longer "look behind their backs"—that is, they do not engage in their celebrated battle tactics of shooting arrows from behind as they retreat.
14	**Crassos se tenuisse dolet** indirect discourse with *se*, referring to the Euphrates, as the subject-acc. of the infinitive. In 53 BCE the Romans suffered a major defeat by the Parthians at Carrhae and M. Licinius Crassus Dives, one of the "first triumvirate," and his son both died in the battle. The line may refer to graves of the Crassi or merely to their ashes. Regardless, the pose of suffering suggested by *dolet* falsely implies punishment or military action taken by Rome against Parthia at the time of the poem's composition. In fact, Augustus maintained a diplomatic neutrality, or even-handedness, towards Parthia

and the dynastic rivalry that bedeviled it throughout the decade of the 20s. Furthermore, the military standards captured by the Parthians in 53 BCE were not returned to Rome until 20 BCE, although Dio Cassius dates negotiations for their return as having begun in 23 BCE. The verbs *negat* (13) and *dolet* (14) and their cognates appear frequently in the context of Propertian erotic relations, the former to express the mistress's refusal of her favors and the latter to refer to the painful condition of elegiac love (cf. 1.16.21, 25, 35; 1.18.3, 13, 26; 2.14.20; 3.8.10; 3.21.7).

15 **India . . . tuo dat colla triumpho** Personified as a human captive, India presents her neck to bear chains in a triumphal procession (cf. **2.1.33**). Again, such reference to Augustan conquest of India greatly exaggerates the actual political backdrop: despite any ambitions to extend the empire to the far East, Rome had only received ambassadors from India in 26/25 BCE. In purely amatory contexts the neck bowed in military surrender serves as a trope for erotic submission (cf. **1.1.4**; 1.13.15; 2.5.14; 2.30A.8). The personification of India here allows the military imagery to take on such erotic resonance as well.

16 **domus intactae . . . Arabiae** *domus* means here "country" or "land" and the entire phrase suggests the region of Arabia as not yet subject to foreign conquest and therefore full of resources yet untapped by the Romans (cf. Hor. *Carm.* 3.24.1–2: *Intactis . . . thesauris Arabum et diuitis Indiae*). In 26 BCE Aelius Gallus, a newly appointed prefect of Egypt, launched an expedition into Arabia, apparently motivated by Augustus's interest in controlling trade routes for luxury goods—gems, spices, etc.—from the East. However, the campaign failed disastrously, with heavy Roman losses, in 24 BCE. Scholars speculate that Propertius's poem must have predated the military debacle and that the image of Arabia trembling before Augustus (*te tremit*) refers to the period when the expedition is getting under way. Dating issues

aside, the rhetoric again exaggerates Augustan conquest even as the specific diction eroticizes and feminizes Arabia as an "untouched" (*intactae*) virgin.

17 **qua ... tellus** indef. pronominal adj. agreeing with its noun in the nom.; "any land" withdrawing to the furthest edges of the world likely refers to Britain, where Augustus intended to campaign before uprisings in Spain deterred him in 26 BCE.

extremis ... oris both dat. of direction and dat. with the compound verb *subtrahit*

18 **sentiat** jussive subjunctive

tuas ... manus In the military context, this refers to Augustus's troops; however, the double-entendre of "your hands" provides the climax to the metaphor of erotic conquest. The f. demonstrative pron. *illa* plays into this rhetoric and the echo of this line in 2.15.18 (*scissa ueste meas experiere manus*) reinforces the trope of imperial expansion as violence against the elegiac mistress (see Introduction, p. xxiii).

19-20 After six lines of exaggerated claims about Augustus's military successes in the present (cf. the anticipatory *iam ... iam* and *nunc ... nunc* in lines 2-3 and 9-10), this couplet defers all praise to the future—suggesting that Propertius can only write *encomia* when Augustus gives him inspiration to do so! Note that the poet focuses on the fame that singing his leader's accomplishments will bring to his own self.

19 **haec ego castra sequar** Although this serves as a metaphor for Propertius's intent to celebrate Augustus's military exploits, it also alludes to the actual practice of poets accompanying generals on their campaigns for such a purpose.

canendo gerund; abl. of means

20 **seruent** jussive subjunctive

21-22 The speaker conceives of poetry as a garland to be placed on the head of a colossal statue of the gods—such as that of Jupiter Capitolinus, in whose lap a *triumphator* would place his golden crown at the end of his triumphal procession down the

COMMENTARY 2.10 63

Via Sacra through the Roman Forum. However, as is typical of a *recusatio*, the poet declares his prowess to be insufficient, and thus places his wreath at the statue's feet.

21 **ubi non est tangere** "when it is not possible to reach"

22 **his** dat. of possession, referring to *signis* ("statues") in line 21

23-26 Propertius continues to spin metaphors for his poetic offerings and his incapacity to write verse in the "high" style. Picking up on the previous image of statuary heads eluding the poet's grasp, the theme of height also looks back to Mount Helicon in line 1 and to the imperative to rise from humble song (*ex humili . . . carmine*) in line 10.

23 **inopes laudis conscendere carmen** "unable to scale the song of praise," a bold metaphor that has led some editors to print *culmen* or *currum*.

24 **pauperibus sacris** abl. of manner, denoting that in accordance with which something is done (Bennett sec. 220.3); cheap incense was the poor man's offering.

25-26 This final couplet alludes to the bathing of the Muses in the opening of Hesiod's *Theogony* (1–9) as well as to a passage in Vergil's sixth eclogue (64–73): here, one of the Muses leads the first Roman love elegist, Gallus, from the stream of Permessus, symbolizing elegy, up the slopes of Mt. Helicon, where the poet Linus then presents him with the pipes of Hesiod, thus initiating him into the select group of epic poets.

25 **nondum etiam** Translate as *nondum*.

Ascraeos . . . fontis Note the *-is* acc. ending; Hippocrene and Aganippe, high-mountain sources for the river Permessus, symbolize elevated poetry. They are located on Mount Helicon, home of the Muses, on the slopes of which was the town of Ascra, the birthplace of the epic poet Hesiod.

norunt syncopated pf. form instead of *no[ue]runt*

26 **Permessi . . . lauit Amor** Not attaining the sacred heights of Helicon, Propertius's poems take their elegiac inspiration from the lower streams of Permessus: *carmina*, although the

subject of *norunt* in line 25, is the object of *lauit* understood as a transitive verb. The image of *Amor* dipping Propertius's poems in these waters is both humorous and suggestive of the elegiac rhetoric of lines 13–18.

༄ *Elegy 2.16*

A poem that illustrates well the elegiac condition as one of frustrated desire, 2.16 also advertises and eroticizes empire by highlighting the luxury goods of Rome's growing imperial resources. The speaker anguishes over his separation from Cynthia, who, as a courtesan (*meretrix*) dependent on her clients for a living, has taken up with a wealthy praetor just returned from the provinces. The poem is interesting for the tension between a discourse of moral censure, adopted by the speaker, and the erotic appeal of Cynthia as an emblem of Roman imperialist expansion. A cameo inset of lines referencing Octavian's recent victory over Antony at Actium lends political implications to the rivalry between the speaker and the praetor.

The poem divides into four sections: the first twelve lines set the stage of the speaker's predicament—the return of the *praetor*—and advise Cynthia to fleece and send him packing; lines 13–36 indulge the *amator*'s erratic emotion, vacillating between jealous vindictiveness, moral outrage, wistful nostalgia, and self-recrimination; lines 37–42 compare the speaker's plight to Antony's fateful infatuation, with added praise for Octavian; and lines 43–56 combine wishes and threats, warning Cynthia to avoid material greed and beware the gods' wrath, incited by perjury.

1 **praetor** the term used as shorthand for *legatus pro praetore*, a Roman who has held the praetorship in Rome and who then advances to serving as governor of a province; this arrangement preceded the redistribution of provinces in 27 BCE, at which time Illyricum came under the authority of the Senate and was governed by a *proconsul*. The *praetor* here plays the role of the *diues amator* ("wealthy lover"), a stock figure who rivals Propertius for his mistress's affections.

COMMENTARY 2.16

Illyricis ... terris Illyria was the area of the Balkan peninsula along the eastern shore of the Adriatic sea and a region in which Octavian carried out successful campaigns against the Pannonians in 33 BCE, later celebrated in his triple triumph of 29 BCE.

2 **praeda ... cura** both in apposition to *praetor*; the term *praeda* connotes wealth acquired from military conquest, suggesting as a metaphor not only the rapacity of the *praetor*'s extortionate relationship to his province but also, the speaker implies, Cynthia's mercenary attitude toward him.

3 The speaker wishes the *praetor* had been shipwrecked. The statement here suggests an unfulfilled wish, an implied protasis of a past contrary-to-fact condition that is expressed in the apodosis of the next line.

saxo ... Cerauno locative abl. or abl. of cause; Acroceraunia, a treacherous promontory of what is now Albania. Cf. Hor. *Carm.* 1.3.2.

4 **darem** impf. subjunctive in the apodosis of a pres. contrary-to-fact condition—if the speaker's wish had come true and the *praetor* had died at sea, "what kinds of gifts would I give you, Neptune!"

5-6 The repetition of *sine me* emphasizes the speaker's condition as an *exclusus amator* or "locked-out lover," even though Cynthia's door remains open to the *praetor* and other guests at the *conuiuia*.

5 **plena ... mensa** abl. of attendant circumstance; the phrase refers either to the abundant and sumptuous food or possibly to the number of guests, making the table literally "full."

7-8 In two different metaphors the speaker now recommends that Cynthia should take advantage of the proffered harvest and fleece the *praetor* for all he is worth!

7 **ne desere** negative imperative; "don't let slip"—i.e., the opportunity

8   **pleno uellere** either abl. of separation or abl. of attendant circumstance, "when his fleece is full"

carpe the verb adds the idea of "good pickings" to the metaphor of shearing or "fleecing" the *praetor*; cf. Ovid *Am*. 1.8.91 in reference to profiting from a lover: *et soror et mater, nutrix quoque carpat amantem*.

stolidum ... pecus here, "the stupid beast," although usually *pecus* is a collective sing.

9   **consumpto ... munere** abl. absolute—when the man has nothing left to give

10   **dic ... nauiget** a substantive clause introduced by a verb of command (Bennett sec. 295.1); supply *ut*.

alias ... Illyrias acc. of direction without the prep. *ad*; i.e., other provinces as profitable as Illyria

11-12 Although clearly the *praetor* has both *fascis* and *honores*, the speaker here claims that Cynthia is immune to the attractions of political status and focuses rather on a suitor's wealth.

11   **fascis** acc. pl. with alternative ending; the Roman *fasces* were traditionally a collection of rods bundled together with a protruding axe-head and they symbolized political authority; they would be carried by the lictors in attendance on a provincial governor.

12   **una** "uniquely," in the sense of better than any other gold-digging mistress or courtesan—in a class of her own

sinus acc. pl.; "folds" of the Roman toga, where a pocket would hold money, and hence "purse" or "wallet." Other meanings of *sinus*—"lap" and "harbor"—have a connotative resonance here, given the erotic relationship with the *praetor* as one who provides a "safe harbor" in the form of financial stability.

13   **nostro ... dolori** dat. with compound verb

COMMENTARY 2.16

14 **rumpat ut ... membra** substantive result clause (Bennett sec. 297) dependent on the invocation to Venus for assistance; the line recalls Catullus 11 where the speaker describes Lesbia as holding 300 senators at once, bursting the loins (*ilia rumpens*) of each. The subject of *rumpat* is the *praetor*.

16 **perit** "is ruined" in the sense that Cynthia "goes bad" by allowing herself to be purchased; however, *perire* also has erotic implications—Cynthia "is dying from love" that is bought—as well as the connotation that she "perishes" in the speaker's affections.

indigna merce The adj. can be taken adverbially to stand for *indigne*, modifying the entire sentence, or as an abl. in strict agreement with the wares or merchandise that are not worthy of Cynthia; *merce* can also stand for *mercatura*, the abstract concept of trade; abl. of price or cause.

17–18 Not only the *praetor* but Propertius too experiences Cynthia's demands for goods.

17 **Oceanum ... gemmas** pearls from the Atlantic or, alternatively, from bodies of water to the East of the Mediterranean—the Red Sea, the Arabian Sea, or the Indian Ocean

mittit ... quaerere infinitive of purpose with a verb of motion

18 **ipsa ... Tyro** The ancient Phoenician city Tyre was famous for its purple dyes, excreted from sea snails. Fabrics dyed in this purple color became a symbol of wealth and status.

19 **Romae** locative case

19–20 **utinam ... esset ... posset** optative subjunctives in the impf. to express contrary-to-fact wishes

ipse ... dux Augustus Caesar

20 **straminea ... casa** the image of a straw hut may be an allusion to the house of Romulus, replicas of which stood on both the Palatine and Capitoline Hills during the Augustan period. The nostalgic sentiment here expressed by the elegiac

68 A PROPERTIUS READER

speaker ironically dovetails with Augustus's emphasis on the *mos maiorum*. Indeed, according to Suetonius (*Aug.* 72.1), Augustus himself did live in a modest dwelling and projected the image, at least, of temperate austerity.

21–23 **numquam ... essent ... fieret ... cubares** three verbs in the impf. subjunctive in a series of contrary-to-fact apodoses. The protasis of the condition must be inferred from the impossible wish in line 19, *utinam ... nemo esset diues*: "would that no one were rich ... if that were the case, then never ..."

21 **ad munus** "for a gift" or "with regard to a gift"

22 **una ... domo** idiomatic for "in one relationship"

fieret cana i.e., would turn grey with age

23 **seiuncta** separated from Propertius

24 **foedo ... uiro** abl. of place where or dat. with an implied compound verb, understanding *circumfusa* for *fusa*

bracchia acc. object of *fusa*, functioning as a Greek middle (Bennett sec. 175.2.d); also known as Greek acc. of respect

25 **non quia peccarim** a syncopated pf. subjunctive (the -*ue*- having dropped out) in a causal clause where the reason for her infidelity with the *praetor* is rejected

uulgo adv., "in general" or "commonly"

26 **formosis ... amica** "a companion to beautiful women"—i.e., "goes hand in hand with"

leuitas "fickleness" in the sense of "lack of loyalty" (cf. **2.1.49–50**)

27–28 By referring to the *praetor* as *barbarus*, the speaker indulges in slander that was common in political invective, suggesting that his competitor initially came to Rome as a foreign slave before rising to prominence as the governor of a province.

27 **exclusis ... lumbis** abl. absolute, literally "his loins shut out," a phrase that crudely echoes the *exclusus amator*

agitat uestigia moves his feet back and forth on the doorstep—i.e., "impatiently paces"

28 **felix** "happy" or "fortunate" but also "wealthy," a meaning that resonates with the idea that the *praetor* enriches himself from his province

mea regna poetic pl. referring to Cynthia; however, the political and territorial metaphor anticipates the reference to the battle of Actium and the rivalry between Mark Antony and Octavian in lines 37–42.

29-30 Two mythological examples of women murdered as a consequence of their material greed. Polyneices, at war with his brother Eteocles, successfully bribed Eriphyla to persuade her husband, Amphiaraus, to join the expedition of the "Seven Against Thebes." After the death of Amphiaraus, their son Alcmaeon murdered his mother, in keeping with the wishes of his father who, as a seer, had foreseen that he would not survive the battle (Diod. 4.65.56; Apollod. 3.81). Creusa, daughter of the king of Corinth, died from a poisonous dress and crown given to her by Medea, who was taking revenge for Jason of the Argonauts' betrayal of their relationship and decision to marry the Corinthian princess (Eur. *Med*.1136–1220).

quid ... inuenit ... arserit ... quantis ... malis indirect questions with a colloquial use of the indicative followed by the more usual subjunctive

29 **donis ... amaris** poetic pl. and abl. of cause; the gift was bitter not only because it specifically brought about Eriphyla's death (*Od*. 11.325ff) but also because it was the necklace of Harmonia, an object that doomed all who acquired it.

30 **quantis ... malis** abl. of attendant circumstance; "with how much suffering"

31-32 The speaker wonders whether he is so far gone in his erotic suffering that no offense committed by Cynthia would bring him to his senses and allow him to cease his lamentations.

33-34 **tot iam abiere dies, cum** "it's been so long since ..." The *cum* clause is temporal, taking the indicative; *abiere* is the alternative form for *abierunt*.

cura theatri ... Campi objective gen. dependent on *cura*; neither the theater nor the Campus Martius, typical venues for the leisure time of the young Roman male, hold their appeal any longer for Propertius. The speaker's lassitude and lack of interest in civic pastimes are the typical posture of the elegiac lover who rejects the norms of ancient Roman masculinity. Note that references to playing games and exercising on the Campus Martius appear frequently in Augustan poetry—cf. Hor. *Carm.* 1.8.4 and 3.7.26.

35–36 This couplet voices the anonymous censure of the *mos maiorum* that the speaker expects and mimics and to which he then responds with an aphoristic platitude that justifies his behavior. The lines also serve to introduce the following reference to Marc Antony, a public personage exemplifying the adage that shameful love has deaf ears.

35 **at pudeat** "but surely it should shame him . . ." a potential subjunctive that, repeated, becomes the apodosis of a mixed condition with indicative in the protasis

quod aiunt The rel. pron. refers to the entire *nisi* clause and the phrase indicates a popular saying.

36 **surdis auribus** abl. of quality

37 **ducem** refers here to Marc Antony but the word tellingly echoes *dux* in line 20, emphasizing that the battle of Actium conclusively decided the rivalry between Octavian and Antony for control of Rome. Although war was declared against Cleopatra alone, her Roman consort had a sizeable army, including approximately 500 warships, a fleet more numerous than Octavian's. In the period leading up to the decisive sea-battle, possibly in excess of 300 senators had departed Rome in support of Antony.

fremitu ... inani abl. of material or means; the groaning of soldiers is "empty" and "pointless" because Antony, in his single-minded devotion to and pursuit of Cleopatra, was deaf to the suffering of his men.

COMMENTARY 2.16

38 **damnatis ... militibus** abl. absolute implying the source and reason for the cries; note that the groaning comes from the men but that Antony, the subject of *compleuit* (37), is responsible. By fleeing the battle he abandons his men and dooms them to death at sea or to captivity and punishment as traitors. As it turned out, those soldiers of Antony who survived the battle—and many did—soon turned to Octavian, who treated them with clemency, as line 42 below implies.

39 **hunc ... dare terga** the finite verb *iussit* in line 40 governs the infinitive phrase, "to take flight," for which *hunc* (*ducem*) serves as the subject-acc.

uersis ... carinis abl. absolute

40 **extremo quaerere in orbe fugam** a second infinitive phrase dependent on *iussit*. The "end of the earth" exaggerates Antony's actual flight in his passion-driven retreat to Egypt. Note that the language here echoes line 17 and reinforces the comparison of the speaker to Antony.

41-42 Lines of egregious flattery, this couplet has struck many as gratuitous and out-of-place. However, the mention of Augustus does reinforce the element of public conflict between the triumvirs that structurally parallels the speaker's private rivalry with the *praetor*.

42 **illa ... manu** abl. of means and antecedent introducing the rel. clause *qua uicit*

condidit arma refers here to putting away arms, as in sheathing a sword, and thus underscores the virtue of *clementia* ("mercy") that Augustus claimed to embrace after his rise to power; ironically, the verb *condere* appears in the inverse context of vengeance at the end of the *Aeneid*, when Aeneas buries his sword in Turnus's chest: *hoc dicens ferrum aduerso sub pectore condit* (12.950). *condere* also means "to found" a city or "to compose" literature and such meanings resonate as underlying connotations here.

43 **quascumque ... uestis** indef. rel. adj. modifying a long *-is* acc. pl., "whatever clothing"

44 **quosue** Understand *uel quoscumque*.

dedit The subject is the *praetor*, but the elision of an explicit reference conflates him with the victorious Caesar of the previous couplet and underscores again the parallel between the triumvirs' political conflict on the public level and the speaker's erotic rivalry on the private level.

flauo lumine abl. of quality

chrysolithos literally, "golden stone" in Greek; peridots were gems of a transparent yellowish-green hue.

45 **uideam** optative subjunctive introducing the infinitive *ferre*, for which *procellas* serves as a subject-acc. and *haec* as the direct object in the acc.

in uanum "into the void"

46 **tibi ... tibi** ethical datives (Bennett sec.188.2.b)

uelim an interjected potential subjunctive that reinforces the optative subjunctive in the parallel rel. clauses *quae ... quae ... fiat*. Understand *fiat* for both clauses. The n. nom. pl. rel. pron. *quae* is subject (with antecedent *haec* referring to the rival's gifts), but *fiat* takes its number from the sing. predicate nom. *terra* in the first rel. clause and *aqua* in the second.

47–56 The speaker ends the poem with menacing words that insist on exceptions to the commonplace that Jupiter merely laughs at the false vows of lovers (cf. Tib. 1.4.21–4; Ovid *Ars Am.* 1.633–4). And yet, that Jupiter's storms derive from his empathy for the jilted, because he too has suffered deception in love (line 54), rings hollow given the lack of stories that bear witness to the god as the victim of erotic mistreatment.

47 **amantis** acc. pl.

48 **surda ... aure** abl. of manner. Contrary to Antony, whose oblivious passion makes him deaf to the cries of his men (line 36–38 above), Jupiter hears the prayers of injured lovers (or so the speaker claims).

49 **toto ... caelo** abl. of place where; "throughout the sky"

49–50	**percurrere ... desiluisse** infinitives in indirect discourse after *uidistis*, with *sonitus* and *fulmina* as subject-accusatives in close metonymic relation with each other
50	**aetheria ... domo** abl. of place from which, "from the vault of heaven." Note that *domo* is f.
51	**Pleiades ... Orion** constellations whose setting from the October/ November sky signaled the advent of stormy weather
52	**de nihilo** "for no reason"
55	**ne ... sit** jussive subjunctive
	tanti gen. of value
	Sidonia uestis refers to clothing dyed a deep crimson-purple from the same region as Tyre (see line 18 above), which was originally settled by inhabitants from Sidon. Situated in present-day Lebanon, the two cities were significant economic centers of the ancient world. On an intertextual level, the adj. *Sidonia* conjures up Dido, whom Vergil frequently describes with the epithet, although it is impossible to tell how much of the *Aeneid* Propertius would have heard or read at the time of writing this elegy.
56	**ut timeas** result clause; the speaker warns Cynthia that greed for gifts might elicit Jupiter's wrath in the form of the turbulent south wind. Whether this would directly threaten Cynthia or, more probably, the life of the rival gathering such luxuries from abroad, is left unclear.

༄ *Elegy 2.31*

The most complete description of the Palatine temple to Apollo that has come down to us, 2.31 holds a special interest for art historians and archaeologists. It also raises issues concerning the regime's use of sculpture, monument, and the urban environment as a means of propaganda. Although the poem makes no explicit mention of contemporary events, scholars have recognized in the temple's sculpture various allegorical permutations of the conflict between Octavian and Antony. The poem's focus on Apollo (with whom Augustus increasingly identified after Actium) and on the seductive appeal of visual media suggests that Propertius here subtly explores the political uses of art. Octavian vowed to build the temple after the defeat of Sextus Pompeius at the battle of Naulochus in 36 BCE but only completed it several years later. The dedication ceremony of 28 BCE provides the occasion for the poem in that the opening lines make the ritual festivities the excuse for the speaker being late to his date with Cynthia. Almost in the manner of a tour guide, the speaker unveils the brilliant features of the temple as a visitor might experience them successively, moving from the portico around the sacred precinct to the cult statue of the god within the building. The precision of his description may also reveal his wish to convince Cynthia that he was really there—i.e., that the temple is not just a pretext for his having been with another woman.

Fig. 3. Danaid hermsculpture from the portico of the Temple to Apollo on the Palatine. Palatine Antiquarian Museum. The raised arm suggests the Danaids' eternal punishment—carrying vessels of water to fill a leaking jar. Photo: P. Lowell Bowdich.

COMMENTARY 2.31 75

1   **ueniam** subjunctive in an indirect question

1–2 **aurea ... porticus** most likely refers to the gilding of the coffered ceiling of the portico; an architectural structure favored by the Romans, the portico as a covered walkway provided shade from the hot urban sun and a public venue in which to see and be seen.

2   **aperta fuit** The past pple. here functions as a predicate adj. after the pf. of *esse* (in place of the usual pf. pass. form *aperta est*).

3   **tantam erat in speciem ... digesta** The subject is *porticus* and the sense is "arranged to so great visual effect."

    Poenis ... columnis abl. of specification; the columns were carved from African marble, with "Punic" referring to the city Carthage, which was settled by Phoenicians. The geographic adj. underscores Rome's imperial reach and appropriation of foreign, material goods as a visual display of her military dominance in the Mediterranean.

4   **Danai femina turba senis** Supply *erat*. Between the columns were statues of the Danaids, the daughters of Danaus, all but one of whom murdered their cousin-bridegrooms on the eve of their wedding and, in the underworld, were condemned for eternity to carry water to fill a leaking vessel. Ironically, the Danaids committed their horrific act as an act of filial duty. When commanded by Danaus's brother, Aegyptus, to marry his fifty sons, they fled their homeland of Egypt with their father to settle in Argos. Danaus subsequently allowed his fifty daughters to leave with the cousins who had pursued them, but secretly ordered the prenuptial murder. Archaeological excavations have revealed a few of the statues of these women in postures suggesting their punishment, with vases carried on their heads. Originally from Egypt, the violent daughters of Danaus may well have symbolized Cleopatra, another transgressive woman from the East. Statuary representing their punition would thus evoke Augustus's righteous victory at Actium. However, according to Ovid (*Ars* 1.73–74, *Tr.* 3.1.60–62), a sculpture of the father with raised

sword, inciting the crime, was also present in the portico, and a scholiast to Perseus 2.55–56 indicates that there may have been statues of the cousins on horseback. This has encouraged the opposite interpretation: it is the Danaids' murder of their cousins—rather than the punishment for that act—that allegorizes the Romans' defeat of the Egyptians. From either perspective, the intergenerational and interfamilial conflict points to the Roman civil wars of the first century BCE.

femina an unusual use of the noun as an adj. (instead of *feminea*)

5–6 In the portico of the temple, *hic*, the first sculpture of Phoebus Apollo, playing his lyre, seems to the speaker more beautiful even than the god himself. Such a claim raises the issue of art's capacity to represent and evoke divinity but it also verges on the humorously sacrilegious. The exaggeration in the statement may be attributed to Propertius's flattery of Augustus: there is some evidence that in the grounds of the temple sanctuary the *princeps* placed a statue of himself in the dress and posture of Apollo and some scholars believe this to be Propertius's reference here (schol. *ad* Hor. *Epist.* 1.3.17; Serv. *ad* Verg. *Ecl.* 4.10).

uisus mihi pulchrior Supply *est* and understand the verb as expressing both literal perception, "was seen by me," and subjective impression, "seemed to me." In the first reading, *mihi* serves as a dat. of agent with the pf. pass., a not uncommon use in poetry. The compar. adj. *pulchrior* must be understood as a substantive: "one more beautiful than . . ."

marmoreus The adj. has a concessive force to it—"though made of marble."

uisus . . . carmen hiare Again, supply *est* to complete the meaning with complementary infinitive; although usually intransitive, *hiare* here functions as a transitive verb with *carmen* as a direct object.

COMMENTARY 2.31

tacita ... lyra concessive abl. absolute

7 **aram circum** The prep. is postpositive, coming after its noun.

steterant the plpf. instead of the impf. here

armenta The collective sing., *armentum*, usually refers to a herd of cattle, but the pl. can also signify a group of individual cattle or horses.

7–8 **Myronis ... artificis** As both Pliny (*Nat. Hist.* 34.57) and Petronius (*Sat.* 88) attest, the fifth-century Greek sculptor Myron was much admired for his naturalistic representation of animals.

8 **quattuor ... boues** in apposition to *armenta*, as is *signa*

9 **medium** within the surrounding portico

claro ... marmore abl. of material

10 **et** for *etiam*, "even"

carius compar. n. adj. in the nom. agreeing with *templum*

patria ... Ortygia abl. of comparison; Ortygia was a mythological island identified with Delos, the birthplace of Apollo.

11 **in quo** The antecedent is *templum*, line 9.

Solis ... currus The chariot of the sun, on the roof of the temple, may refer to the work of Lysias, a marble *quadriga* with Apollo and Diana riding within.

12 **ualuae** Supply *erant*; these were the two leaves of the temple door.

Libyci ... dentis i.e. ivory

13–14 The scenes fashioned on each of the doors underscore Apollo as an avenging deity, in distinction from the statues in the portico and within the temple that feature him as the god of poetry and the lyre. One scene alludes to the unsuccessful attempt by the Gauls in the third century BCE to sack Apollo's temple at Delphi, at the base of Mt. Parnassus. The other depicts the deaths of the sons and daughters of Niobe, a mythological figure who boasted that, on account of her fourteen children, she was superior to Leto, the mother of Apollo and

Diana. In an act of horrifying punition, the divine brother and sister killed all of Niobe's offspring.

altera . . . altera maerebat Either the verb here functions as a kind of *zeugma* (see **1.3.16** and note), or, in keeping with the second door's "mourning" the deaths of Niobe's children, an appropriate verb must be supplied for the first of the two doors.

13 **deiectos . . . Gallos** The trope of *hyperbaton* (the departure from conventional word order and thus, for inflected languages, the separation of modifier and noun) here reinforces the sense of the Gauls hurled off the mountain.

uertice abl. of separation; although the Gauls did not in fact climb Mt. Parnassus, the image evokes the theme of divinely vanquished arrogance and may well draw from the various myths of the Titans and the Giants attempting to scale Mt. Olympus and assail the Olympians.

Fig. 4. "Apollo Barberini." Glyptothek, Munich. The god holds the *kithara* or lyre in his left arm. First to second century CE probable copy of the cult statue in the Temple of Apollo on the Palatine. Wikimedia Commons.

14 **Tantalidos** Greek patronymic in the subjective gen. (Bennett sec. 199), "of the daughter of Tantalus," i.e., Niobe. The *funera* refer to the deaths of her children as the loss that she suffered

15-16 **deus ipse** Inside the temple, flanked by sculptures of Latona and Diana, was a cult statue of Apollo in flowing drapery. Note that the word order here reflects the statement about the statuary positions.

16 **Pythius** a cult title for Apollo that derives from *Pytho*, an earlier name for Delphi

∾ *Elegy 2.32*

The speaker's jealous suspicions raised by Cynthia's travel to various shrines outside of Rome provides the premise for 2.32, which is neatly divided between condemnation, and then acceptance, of her potential infidelities. Printed as one continuous piece in the manuscript tradition, 2.32 should be read in close conjunction with the preceding 2.31. Both poems explore the role of vision, but in contrast to the implicit gaze of the aesthete selecting details of the temple, 2.32 openly features the erotic gaze of desire and the proprietary surveillance that it engenders. Such desire and scrutiny take place against the backdrop of Rome and the outlying environment. The temple to Palatine Apollo, with its portico of Danaids, anticipates the description in 2.32 of the newly renovated Portico of Pompey: both precincts exemplify the urban amenities of Rome, where the speaker would prefer that Cynthia take her promenades. However, she flees the city, he believes, to avoid his watchful gaze. After fearing for Cynthia's reputation and the gossip that surrounds it (1–24), the speaker then excuses any sexual betrayal as a minor transgression (25–30): both goddesses and mythological heroines acted similarly with no consequences (31–40) and the climate of contemporary Rome is rife with lax morals (41–52); after the flood survived by Deucalion and Pyrrha, female chastity declined—a fact both Pasiphae and Danae attest (53– 60); given Greek and Roman precedents, Cynthia should be "free" (61–62). The anti-/pro-Cynthia structure suggests a courtroom debate and the pervasive legal language may indicate the historical background of a first failed attempt at legislation that criminalized adultery and that

Augustus later successfully passed in 18 BCE. 2.32 is also important in its references to Catullus 68, a poem considered the prototype for, or even the first, Roman love elegy.

1–2 With this opening couplet (which some editors transpose to follow line 10 so that the *qui* refers to the observing *turba* of line 8), the speaker expresses his anxiety at Cynthia's excursions beyond Rome—she could be the victim of the male gaze and all to which it may lead. A more subtle reading interprets the lines as the speaker's mocking summary of Cynthia's own excuses for leaving the city (in order to avoid unwanted male attention). In either case, the couplet displays the ancient idea that erotic desire is stirred by the vision of beauty, and specifically by images "penetrating" or entering the eyes of the viewer (cf. **1.1.1** where it is Cynthia's own eyes that wound the speaker). This is referred to as "intromission," a theory propounded by the atomists Leucippus and Democritus, and supported by Epicurus (Diog. Laert. *Lives* 10.48–49) and Lucretius, who championed the philosopher's vision in *De Rerum Natura*.

qui ... is Translate as an indef. pron. in a simple conditional clause, followed by a pron.: "if anyone ... he ..." or "whoever ... he ..."

peccat The verb refers here to sexual wrongdoing, with implications of adultery. Although Cynthia's identity often suggests a courtesan (making adultery irrelevant), it is variable and depends on context. In many poems, the speaker projects a nostalgic wish for the values of the *mos maiorum* onto his beloved, desiring in her the fidelity and chastity of a wife. Cf. **2.1.48**; 2.6.37–42; 2.7.19–20; 2.34.9–12.

qui te non uiderit ergo/ non cupiet Again, the rel. clause functions similarly to the protasis in a future-more-vivid condition, with the fut. pf. for greater emphasis (translate it as a pres.). Translate *qui* as "whoever," as the equivalent to an indef. pron. that would ordinarily follow *si*—"if anyone ..."

2 **facti lumina crimen habent** lit. "eyes hold the charge of the deed"—i.e., eyes are the guilty ones because they initiate the crime; *facti* is gen. dependent on *crimen*, "charge" or "indictment," and the entire phrase, in addition to *peccat*, initiates the juridical tone of the poem.

3–4 **quid** acc. sing. n. interr. pron. used as adv., best translated as "why," "to what end"

Praenesti locative sing. (found only here). Praeneste (n. sing.), modern Palestrina, was the site of a famous oracle and shrine to Fortuna Primigeneia ("the First-born," cf. Plut. *Quaest. Rom.* 106). Cf. Cic., *Div.* 2.85–86 for a description of the origins of interpreting lots at this oracle, a practice still current in Cicero's and Propertius's time. In the early and mid-republican period Hercules, rather than Fortuna, was the primary deity for the town, as he was at Tibur (see line 5). The sanctuary-complexes at Praeneste and Tibur were models for the great portico-garden complex adjoining Pompey's temple to Venus Victrix and mentioned in lines 11–16.

dubias . . . sortis acc. pl.; supply the verb *petis* from line 4, where *moenia* is the direct object in parallel syntax that also introduces a question with *quid*, "why?" Note that *dubias* literally suggests the ambiguity of the oracle's pronouncements, but may also imply the speaker's skepticism about Cynthia's claims that she leaves Rome to make religious pilgrimages.

4 **Aeaei . . . Telegoni** refers to Tusculum, founded by *Telegonus*, son of Ulysses and Circe. His epithet *Aeaei* derives from the island Aeaea, his mother's home. Cf. *Od.* 10.135; Hor. *Epodes* 1.29–30, *Carm.* 3.29.8; Ovid *Fast.* 3.92, 4.71. Although the other sites mentioned by Propertius featured cults that drew worshippers, Tusculum was known mostly as an area favored by affluent Romans, such as Cicero, for their villas outside of Rome.

5 **Herculeum . . . Tibur** Tibur, modern Tivoli, was home to a prominent temple to Hercules Victor that attracted many visitors in antiquity. *Tibur* is acc. n. sing. expressing direction to, without prep.

esseda nom. n. pl. Originally a war-carriage used by the Gauls, it was later adopted as a light traveling vehicle. Cf. **2.1.75–76**.

6 **Lanuuium** [an emendation for the MSS *ducit anum*]: acc. expressing direction to, without prep. Supply the verb *deportat* from line 5, which has parallel syntax. Famous for its temple of Juno Sospita, Lanuvium was a town reached by the Via Appia, the principal road stretching south from Rome to Brindisium, in Apulia. In **4.8**, Cynthia visits the temple there with her lover.

7 **utinam** introduces an optative subjunctive.

spatiere 2nd person sing. alternate ending; *spatiari* refers to a leisurely promenade or stroll in public venues. Ovid devotes much of Book 1 of the *Ars Amatoria* to public places in which the lover might stroll and encounter possible love-interests.

Fig. 5. Apollo fighting with Hercules over the Delphic tripod. Palatine Antiquarian Museum. The struggle allegorically suggests the conflict between Octavian and Antony that culminated at the battle of Actium. Painted terracotta relief from the Temple of Apollo on the Palatine. Photo: P. Lowell Bowdich.

hoc ... loco abl. of place where, prep. omitted; refers to the city of Rome, in distinction to the sanctuaries of rural Latium that Cynthia visits, and looks ahead to the portico-garden complex of Pompey evoked in lines 11–16. Editors who transpose lines 7–10 to the beginning of 2.32 understand *hoc ... loco* in reference to the temple to Apollo on the Palatine described in 2.31. Cynthia's flight to rural sanctuaries suggests her rejection of Augustan Rome and its opulent new buildings.

quodcumque indef. pron. acting as an internal acc. for the verb *uacabis*—"whatever free time you will have"

8   **tibi** dat. with *credere*

9   **deuotam** refers to Cynthia as a worshipper or "devotee" and serves as subject-acc. of *currere*. It suggests Cynthia's state of being "bound" by her vow to the goddess.

accensis ... taedis abl. absolute expressing circumstance

uidet the gaze of the crowd here is ambiguous, either suggesting the gaze of desire to which lines 1–2 refer, or the observation of an eyewitness to Cynthia's potential infidelities.

9–10   **currere, ferre** infinitives in indirect discourse introduced by *uidet*

10   **lumina** object of *ferre*; lit. "lights" or "torches" but suggestive of "eyes" and the theme of the gaze that runs throughout the poem.

Triuiae ... deae refers to Diana Nemorensis and her cult in a sacred grove (*nemus*) near the town of Aricia, close to Lanuvium. *Triuiae* serves as an adj. here but more often is a title, orginally of Hecate, as goddess of the crossroads, who was identified with Artemis and hence Diana. Ovid *Fast.* 3.263–70 describes a rite in which women carry torches and visit the grove of this goddess as thanksgiving for the fulfillment of prayers.

11–16   These lines refer to Pompey the Great's portico-garden, part of a temple-theater complex established with war booty in honor of Venus Victrix after the general's victory over Mithridates of Pontos. With its lavish artwork including statues of the Muses, of Greek poetesses, and of famous courtesans, the portico-garden seemed to celebrate female creativity and sexuality and became a favorite haunt of poets and those of either sex seeking erotic adventure. In the *Res Gestae* (20), Augustus claims to have renovated the theater of Pompey, adjacent to the garden complex. The sentence here describing certain features of the architectural structure is clear until lines 15–16. The simplest reading takes the sing. verb *sordet* as followed by a series of subjects, *porticus* (12) . . . *ordo* (13) . . . *flumina* (14), each of which, with their modifying phrases, adds detail. The rel. clause *quaeque . . . cadunt*, dependent on *flumina*, then governs the abl. of separation in line 15 (making *nymphis* parallel to *Marone* in 14) and leads into the *cum* clause of line 16. Alternatively, the *cum* clause of line 16 can function as a substantive and fourth additional subject of *sordet*, with line 15 as an abl. absolute contained within the clause.

11 **scilicet ... sordet** The speaker's tone here is ironic—the opulence of Pompey's portico-garden should not elicit Cynthia's disdain.

umbrosis . . . columnis abl. of material; see the note on **2.31.1–2**.

12 **aulaeis ... Attalicis** tapestries richly embroidered with gold, a type of weaving that Pliny (*Nat. Hist.* 8.196) attributes to Attalus, king of Pergamum; abl. of specification with *nobilis*

13 **platanis ... ordo** a sequence of plane trees, planted close together (*creber*) and trimmed to grow at an equal height; *platanis* is an abl. of specification with *creber . . . ordo*.

14 **flumina ... quaeque** The *-que* is enclitic with the rel. pron., so read *et flumina quae*.

sopito ... Marone abl. of separation; in Homer, Maron is Apollo's priest, among the Cicones, who gives Odysseus the wine with which he later inebriates the Cyclops before putting out his eye (*Od.* 9.197; cf. Eur. *Cycl.* 141). The reference here is to the statue of a sleeping figure from whose mouth water streams down.

15 **nymphis ... crepitantibus** abl. of separation, parallel to *sopito ... Marone*—i.e., the *flumina* stream both from the Maron figure and from the nymphs. This assumes actual sculptures surrounding the Triton figure. The verb *crepitare* suggests here a light splashing but also means "to chatter."

tota ... urbe abl. of place where; i.e., the noise is heard throughout the city. The improbability of a lightly (*leuiter*) splashing sound being heard all about the city has led to the emendation of *urbe* to *orbe*, which is adopted by many editors. However, given that bad gossip about Cynthia has struck the speaker's ears in line 23 and spread *in tota ... urbe* in line 24, it is possible that the splashing, chattering nymphs anticipate this idea of the rumor mill.

16 **cum ... Triton ... recondit aquam** Triton, son of Neptune, suddenly swallows water that has been sent into the air.

17–20 From the speaker's perspective, Cynthia deceives herself if she thinks she conceals her cheating trysts from him: her departure from the city indicates her wish to escape his proprietary gaze. The ploys of her treachery, however, are ineffective (*inanis*, 19) with one so experienced (*docto ... mihi*, 20).

17 **tui** either possessive (and redundant) gen. with *ista ... uia*, "that path of yours," or agreeing with *amoris*

furtum ... amoris objective gen., "a covert affair"; *furta* often indicates such in the pl.

19 **nil agis** "you accomplish nothing"

20 **tendis ... retia** The image is one of laying traps for animals.

iners "clumsily," "without skill"

21 **sed de me minus est** "but it concerns me less"

famae ... pudicae objective gen.

86 A Propertius Reader

22 **tanta ... erit** "will cost you, poor girl, as much as you deserve"; lit. "will be as great for wretched you as is deserved"

tibi miserae dat. of disadvantage

23–24 **me laedit ad auris rumor** Supply a pple.—i.e., "a rumor, having arrived at my ears, injures me."

25 **tu non ... credere linguae** This line has occasioned confusion and hence emendation by some editors. Why should the speaker be telling Cynthia not to believe malicious gossip? She knows whether or not the rumors are true. As a consequence, in order to retain the manuscript text, some have attributed this line to the speaker in a moment of self-apostrophe, and others interpret lines 25–26 as spoken by Cynthia. But the speaker may simply be telling Cynthia not to pay attention to those who would malign her.

26 **semper ... fuit** "rumor has always been the price of beauty"; lit. "the penalty for those who are beautiful..." Cf. **2.16.26** for similar phrasing.

fabula in the immediate context, "rumor" or "gossip," but also "story" or "tale," a meaning that anticipates the mythological examples of legendary ladies that the speaker soon adduces to condone any erotic misdemeanors on Cynthia's part

27 **deprenso ... ueneno** "by poison apprehended"—i.e., in Cynthia's possession; abl. of cause. The idea is that Cynthia's transgressions, if any, have been minor. Poison was a conventional means of murder and often associated with women in ancient Rome.

28 As the sun-god, Phoebus Apollo observes all and can serve as a witness, in any judicial case brought against Cynthia, that her hands are clean—i.e., free of pollution from the crime of murder. Ironically, despite this implicit juxtaposition of major crimes (murder) and misdemeanors (sexual infidelity), it is in fact Apollo who *does* serve as the snitching witness to the famous case of divine adultery, the affair of Mars and Venus, to which the speaker refers five lines later.

Commentary 2.32

testis eris ... uidere The idea of being a witness and giving testimony serves to introduce an indirect statement construction, with Apollo as the implied subject of the infinitive.

29 **una aut altera** "one or two"

longo ... lusu abl. of manner; "in drawn-out lovemaking"

31–40 These lines provide mythological *exempla* of divine and mortal women who indulged in erotic dalliance and, in the first two cases, adultery, without judicial consequence. Here the speaker abandons his earlier attitude of censure and condones Cynthia's possible transgressions by appealing to precedent.

31 **Tyndaris** Helen, the daughter of Tyndareus. Of course, Helen's infidelity had catastrophic social consequences, but she did not suffer any legal penalty for her actions. Cf. **2.1.49–50**, where Cynthia ironically censures the *Iliad* on account of Helen.

externo ... amore abl. of cause; refers to Paris, son of Priam, king of Troy

32 **sine decreto** i.e., without judicial sentence or verdict

domum acc. of direction, without a prep.

33–34 The story of Venus and Mars, discovered by Apollo and caught in a finely-woven net by Vulcan, first appears in the *Odyssey* 8.266–366 and figures also in Ovid *Ars Am.* 2.561–93.

34 **honesta** means not just "honorable" but also connotes high social rank.

35–40 These lines do not logically follow in a list of *exempla* referring strictly to adulterous liaisons. The reference to a crowd of Hamadryad sisters—woodland nymphs—and Sileni gazing at the spectacle of a *deam* having sex with a shepherd on Mt. Ida points to the story of Paris's relations with the nymph Oenone. See Parthenius, *Amat. Narr.* 4 and Ovid *Her.* 5 for lengthier versions of the affair. The *exemplum* makes sense as an instance not of illicit sex but rather of conspicuous lovemaking between a mortal and a divine being that elicits a benign gaze and acceptance by the pastoral community. Here the gaze emanates neither from a potential aggressor nor from an informing witness, engaged in surveillance. Subtle allusion to the *Homeric Hymn to Aphrodite*, lines 257–63, underscores that nymphs such as Oenone and her sisters have multiple sexual partners and the community does not censure them.

35 **quamuis Ida ... dicat amasse** indirect discourse with a syncopated pf. infinitive (instead of *amauisse*); Mt. Ida, where Paris grazed his sheep, is personified as the speaker. The force of *quamuis* (with subjunctive) is that despite Oenone's affair with a mortal she did not earn the censure of her community.

36 **accubuisse deam** The nymph (*deam*) is the subject-acc. of the infinitive.

37 **hoc** refers to the sexual congress of Paris and Oenone.

Hamadryadum ... sororum partitive gen.; Hamadryads refer specifically to tree nymphs, whereas Oenone was a river-nymph or Naiad, the generic name that appears in the vocative in line 40. The two terms, however, are also used interchangeably to refer simply to nymphs. Note that the crowd, *turba*, of sister nymphs echoes the female crowd of old Danaus, *Danai femina turba senis*, the Danaids, who were also sisters, at the temple to Apollo (**2.31.3–4**). However, the benign, pastoral spectatorship of the woodland nymphs differs from gazes of the city, statuary included, that Cynthia flees.

38 **Silenique senes** aged satyr-figures; note again the echo of **2.31.4** in *senes*.

pater ipse chori Silenus himself, father and leader of the chorus of satyrs in a satyr-play; see note on **3.3.29–30** below.

39 **cum quibus** all those mentioned in the previous couplet

Idaeo legisti poma sub antro At first glance, the activity of gathering apples seems impossible in the milieu of a cave. However, the erotic suggestiveness of *sub antro* (cf. Hor. *Carm.* 1.5.1–3, *Quis ... te puer ... urget ... sub antro*) and the allusion to the passage in the *Homeric Hymn to Aphrodite* reveal apple-picking (or, here, gathering) as a metaphor for having

COMMENTARY 2.32

sex (cf. Sappho 105 L-P, a fragment to which Longus alludes in *Daphnis and Chloe* 3.33–34). The prep. *sub* here suggests "within" or "beneath the cover of."

40 **supposita ... manu** "with cupped hand"; cf. **1.3.24**.

41 **in tanto stuprorum examine** a partitive gen. construction. The focus now shifts back to Rome and its moral climate of sexual vice, but given the mythological *exempla* of the preceding lines as well as the references to Lesbia, Pasiphae, and Danae in 45, 57, and 59, the "swarm of sex crimes" resonates in both urban and mythic contexts. The term *stuprum* can refer to adultery, but technically, after the Augustan *lex Julia de adulteriis*, it applied to any illicit sexual act with a free unmarried woman of honorable status. Propertius's poem was published around 25 BCE, seven years before the Augustan marriage and adultery laws were implemented. However, the poem's frequently legal language and tone explore the very issues that the legislation was intended to address.

42 These questions suggest the prosecution or defense in a courtroom and echo the language of Cicero's speeches (cf. *Rosc. Am.* 74). Here, the questions point to a woman accused of being excessively rich and receiving money, presumably for prostitution.

cur haec tam diues Supply *est*; *haec* is the nom. f. sing. subject and *diues* the predicate adj.

43–44 So vice-ridden is the current moral climate that Rome is very lucky even if just one girl acts contrary to the present depraved standards. The adv. *nimium* suggests that this is perverse. The sentiment and diction of the couplet recall Cic. *Catil.* 1.2, *o tempora! o mores!*

43 **nostro ... tempore** abl. of time when or within which

felicem ... Romam acc. of exclamation

45–46 Here the speaker appeals to literary precedent and specifically Lesbia, the mistress who figures prominently in Catullus's lyric and elegiac poems. Most scholars agree that Lesbia is a metrically equivalent pseudonym for Clodia Metelli, a woman vilified by Cicero in the *pro Caelio*, his defense of Clodia's former lover, Caelius Rufus, whom she accused of trying to poison her. Cicero's slanderous representation of Clodia, railing against her sexual profligacy, served as a diversionary tactic in the courtroom.

46 **quae sequitur, certe est inuidiosa minus** "the woman who follows suit, is surely less blameworthy." The rel. pron. and clause precede the grammatical antecedent. Note the etymological root of *inuidiosa* in *uidere*, in keeping with the poem's emphasis on the communal gaze in relation to shame (see line 9).

47–48 **qui . . . hic** The rel. pron. precedes its antecedent.

47 **Tatios ueteres durosque Sabinos** The generic pl. is used here for Titus Tatius (i.e., "old Tatii"—or "old Tatius types"), the Sabine king, who reconciled with Romulus after the rape of the Sabine women and then jointly ruled Rome with him for five years. Here, people of ancient Italian stock represent the *mos maiorum*, the austere morality of the past. The reference to one seeking such values as recently having set foot in the city may subtly allude to Augustus's swift and recent ascent to power.

49 **tu** Propertian elegy often shifts addressees within the poem and speaks to a general audience or readership.

49–51 **prius . . . poteris siccare . . . deligere . . . quam facere, ut . . .** The auxiliary verb *poteris* goes with the infinitives modified by both *prius* and *quam*, "sooner . . . than . . ." The infinitive *facere* then introduces a substantive result clause. Note the rhetorical figure of the *adunaton* or "impossibility" here.

52 **Saturno regna tenente** abl. absolute with acc. object of the pple.; the speaker here views the period of Saturn's rule as a golden age of sexual morality.

53–54 After the golden age Jupiter became angered at human crimes and flooded the earth, allowing only Deucalion and Pyrrha to survive.

53 **fluxere** 3rd pl. pf. act. indicative; alternative form for *fluxerunt*

55 **dic mihi** Note that this phrase introduces a direct rather than an indirect question. The questions here and in line 56 are the independent clauses following the subordinate *cum* and *post* clauses of lines 53–54. The speaker continues to address a general audience and the legal language of the poem suggests the defense before a jury.

56 Even gods and goddesses are unable to maintain monogamous relations, so why should humans be expected to (as the speaker implicitly reasons)?

quae an interr. adj. modifying *dea*, a nom. subject parallel to the interr. pron. *quis* in line 55

uiuere Supply *potuit* as an auxiliary verb from line 55.

57 **uxorem ... magni Minois** Pasiphae, the wife of Minos, king of Crete, fell in love with a bull. The famous craftsman-artist Daedalos built a wooden cow by which Pasiphae had sex with the bull and conceived the Minotaur (cf. Verg. *Ecl.* 6.45–60; Ovid *Ars Am.* 1.289–326; Ovid *Met.* 8.136–68; Hyg. *Fab.* 40).

59 King Acrisius enclosed his daughter, Danae, in a bronze tower because of a prophecy that he would die at the hands of a son born to her. Despite the king's efforts Danae was impregnated by Jupiter and gave birth to Perseus. In most versions of the myth Jupiter seduces her as a shower of gold (cf. Pind. *Pyth.* 12.917; Soph. *Ant.* 944–53; Isocr. 10.59; Ovid *Met.* 4.610), an image interpreted by later artists such as Rembrandt as a ray of sunlight penetrating her chamber. Danae serves in Propertius's poem as a symbol of chastity corrupted, but the emphasis in the *exemplum* lies more in the inefficacy of external restraints (the bronze wall) rather than on the willful agency of the woman.

nec minus "similarly"

aerato ... muro abl. of means

60 **magno ... Ioui** dat. with *negare*

61-62   Propertius cleverly exploits the double-entendres permitted by Cynthia both as his mistress and as a figure for elegiac poetry. To imitate "*Graias . . . Latinas*," then, suggests on a literal level that Cynthia conforms to Greek and Latin precedents of human and divine behavior, as in the previous *exempla* of Helen, Venus, Oenone, and Lesbia. On a metaphorical level, however, the imitation is an aesthetic one, wherein love elegy draws on previous literature for models. Indeed, Catullus 68 provides one such model—written in elegiac couplets, the poem treats Lesbia's infidelity in a manner similar to Propertius's elegy. Note, too, that the *exempla* suggest a range of genres—not only elegy, but epic (the *Iliad* and *Odyssey*), pastoral, and lyric.

62   **uiue meo libera iudicio** the idea of Cynthia's "freedom" here is rich in connotations. To live freely could mean to live loosely, with no fear of the speaker's negative judgment, or, from the perspective of the poem as a form of legal defense, responding to a prosecution, Cynthia is now "free" since acquitted in the court of the speaker's opinion. In the first reading, *meo . . . iudicio* would be abl. of separation; in the second, abl. of manner.

ᴄᴡ *Elegy 3.3*

One of the five programmatic poems of Propertius's third book, 3.3 confirms his Callimachean poetics with an allusion to the Alexandrian poet's prologue to the *Aetia*, when Apollo gives him guidance, and to his vision of the Muses on the slopes of Mount Helicon, where Hesiod had first encountered them. Propertius's poem describes the speaker's own dream set on Helicon, sacred abode of the Muses, as he sets out to write Roman historical epic in the tradition of Ennius. Recalling the paradoxical form of the *recusatio*, the speaker makes several references to significant events in Roman history before Apollo intervenes to redirect his talents to love poetry. Other versions of this Callimachean scene and the dream motif appear in Vergil's sixth eclogue and Ennius's *Annales*, lending the Propertian application of the motif a rich intertextual backdrop. The speaker then visits the grotto of the Muses, where Calliope gives him further instruction.

COMMENTARY 3.3

The poem illustrates well how elegy defines itself through its invocation of an Alexandrian aesthetic and through oppositions (hard/soft; epic/elegy; public/private) that it also calls into question. Although more developed than 2.10, as a form of *recusatio* 3.3 shares a similar movement of epic intentions diverted, thwarted, or jettisoned.

The poem's structure is neatly symmetrical, consisting of four sections of twelve lines each, with a couplet capping the development of each twenty-four–line half. Lines 1–12 feature the dream of writing in the Ennian tradition, followed by the admonitory vision of Apollo (13–24) and his actual redirection of the speaker (25–26) to visit the Muses' grotto (27–38), where Calliope further advises him (39–50) and anoints him with the water of Philitas (51–52).

1-4   **uisus eram** The pass. plpf. form is completed by the infinitive *posse* (4) on which *hiscere* (4) then depends: "I had seemed to be able to open wide my mouth and tell about . . ." —i.e., "I dreamt that I was able . . ." *hiscere* is usually intransitive but here takes *reges . . . et . . . facta* as direct objects (cf. **2.31.6**).

1   **molli recubans . . . in umbra** The language recalls the opening of Vergil's first eclogue, but *molli* lends an elegiac coloring to the pastoral setting of this dream vision (see Introduction, p. xxiii and the note on **2.1.1–2**). Cf. also Hor. *Carm*. 3.4.6–7: *audire et uideor pios/ errare per lucos, amoenae/ quos et aquae subeunt et aurae.*

2   **Bellerophontei . . . umor equi** refers to Hippocrene, the spring created by the horse of Bellerophon, Pegasus, when his hoof dashed open the ground upon landing on Mt. Helicon (Ant. Lib. *Met*. 9). The two pursued the Chimaera, a fire-breathing monster with three heads—of a lioness, a goat, and a dragon (Pind. *Ol*. 13.84–90; Hes. *Theog*. 319–325).

3   **Alba** refers to Alba Longa, the settlement founded by Ascanius, the son of Aeneas, who came to Italy from Troy in order to initiate the Roman race. Alba Longa was the residence of the rulers who came after Ascanius until Romulus established the city of Rome. By apostrophizing *Alba* in the

vocative, Propertius personifies the town, referring thus to "your kings." The repetition of words, although in different cases (*polyptoton*), lends a prosaic quality to the line, suggestive of the annalistic epic that the speaker initially attempts in his dream.

4 **tantum operis** "so great a work"; the adj. *tantum* functions here as a substantive on which a partitive gen. depends. The phrase is technically in apposition to *reges . . . et . . . facta*, but really describes the entire undertaking of an epic on the kings of Alba Longa.

neruis . . . meis The basic meaning of "sinew" or "string" could suggest either the abstract sense of "with my strength" or the more literal sense of "accompanied by (the strings of) my lyre."

5 **magnis . . . fontibus** dat. of direction with a compound verb. The idea and language of lines 4–5 recall **2.10**, where the speaker sets out to write *magni . . . oris opus* (12), "a work of great inspiration" (lit., "work of a great mouth"), asks his poems to summon strength, *iam, carmina, sumite uires* (11), but then accepts that they have not yet come to know *Ascraeos . . . fontis* (25), i.e., Aganippe and Hippocrene.

admoram syncopated plpf. form, i.e., *admoueram*

6 **pater . . . Ennius** the "father" of Roman historical epic; at the beginning of his *Annales* he relates a dream in which Homer visits him on Mt. Helicon and claims that he, Ennius, is the reincarnation of the Greek epic poet.

7–12 These lines list episodes from Ennius's *Annales*, but not in chronological order. Nonetheless, they are a good example of how the *recusatio* incorporates elements of the repudiated epic genre into the lyric or elegiac form and compass.

7 **Curios fratres et Horatia pila** The three brothers *Curiatii* (the normal spelling) fought the three *Horatii* in the battle between the cities of Alba Longa and Rome during the reign of Tullus Hostilius (673–642 BCE). Livy 1.24–26 recounts the

story in which all the brothers were killed except for one of the *Horatii*. After this conflict, Alba Longa merged with Rome.

pila n. pl.; refers to weapons of the conquerors or the conquered dedicated as a commemorative trophy.

8 **Aemilia ... rate** abl. of means; the royal trophies borne "on Aemilius's boat" refer to the triumphal passage of booty up the Tiber in 167 BCE, after Aemilius Paullus's victory over Perseus, the king of Macedon. Since Ennius died in 169 BCE (according to Cicero, *Brut.* 78, *Sen.* 14) Propertius is likely attributing this episode to Ennius's *Annales* by conflating it with the conquest of a different Aemilius who, in 190 BCE, vanquished King Antiochus of Syria at sea, but brought back no significant war spoils.

9 **uictricesque moras Fabii** refers to *Fabius Maximus Cunctator*, the "Delayer," famous for his tactic of postponing battle with Hannibal and the Carthaginians during the second Punic War.

9–10 **pugnamque sinistram Cannensem** the battle of Cannae, in 216 BCE, which was "ill-fated" because the Romans lost 70,000 men to the forces of Hannibal

10 **uersos ad pia uota deos** After the battle, the gods paid attention to the offerings of the Romans (Livy 23.11).

11 **Hannibalemque Lares ... fugantis** The Lares, or household gods, put to flight Hannibal, who approached the city of Rome but never entered it.

Romana sede abl. of separation; refers to "their Roman home" in the sense that the city of Rome was the home writ large for the Lares, although each household had its own gods.

12 **tutum ... fuisse Iouem** indirect discourse with *Iouem* as subject-acc. and *tutum* as predicate adj., dependent on *cecinit* in line 7

anseris ... uoce abl. of means; in 387 BCE noisy geese woke those protecting the temple of Jupiter on the Capitol and saved it from destruction by the Gauls (Livy 5.47).

13-26 Apollo's intervention to redirect the speaker from epic back to elegy draws from a similar scene in the prologue to Callimachus's *Aetia*, where the god advises the poet to "feed the sacrificial victim to be fat" but to "keep the Muse slender" (1.23–24) and to ride his chariot on "unworn paths" and not along a "broad course" (1.27–28). In Callimachus's *Hymn to Apollo*, the god declares that the Assyrian river, though powerful, carries mud along with it, in contrast to the pure and slender stream that springs from a holy source (105–12). Propertius works all of these metaphors into his poem as tropes for the contrasting genres of epic and elegy (see Introduction, pp. xxiv–xxv).

13 **Castalia . . . arbore** a tree next to the Castalian spring, actually on Mount Parnassus, but which Propertius here locates on Mount Helicon

14 **nixus** a deponent verb that takes the abl.: "leaning" on his lyre

15 **quid tibi cum tali . . . est flumine** an idiomatic construction in which *quid* acts as a predicate nom. and the prepositional phrase *cum tali . . . flumine* as the subject in question—lit. "what is to you with . . . ," i.e., "what are you doing with such a river?"

15-16 **te . . . tangere iussit** The verb of command introduces an infinitive with subject-acc. construction.

carminis heroi gen. of quality

17 **hic** adv. referring to *carminis heroi . . . opus* as its antecedent

tibi dat. of agent with pass. periphrastic

18 **mollia . . . prata** The metaphor of poetry as a chariot race goes back to the epinician lyric of Pindar, but the diction here, with the programmatically charged adj. *mollis*, refers to elegy, and this dovetails with the great/small opposition implicit in *paruis . . . rotis*, recalling the opening line of the poem.

19 **ut . . . iactetur** purpose clause

20 **quem legat** rel. clause of purpose—a book to read while waiting for a date; the image of reading in solitude here demonstrates the gradual transition, in ancient Rome, from hearing literature read aloud to consuming it in private.

COMMENTARY 3.3

21 **praescriptos euecta est … gyros** The pass. verb here takes an acc. object of the prepositional prefix *e-*, "your page is borne outside of its prescribed rounds." The line continues the metaphor of chariot racing from line 18.

pagina stands metonymically for Propertius's poetry.

22 **non est … cumba grauanda** The light boat or "skiff" of Propertius's genius should not be overburdened—another permutation of the Callimachean contrast between the high style of epic and the refined smaller poem.

ingenii … tui gen. of quality

23 **radat** jussive subjunctive with *alter remus … alter* as its subject—"let one oar … let the other …" The two different oars and their respective domains suggest the elegiac couplet, with its epic hexameter followed by elegiac pentameter.

tibi possessive dat.

24 **medio … mari** abl. of place; the sea is a metaphor for epic poetry, the genre that attracts the *maxima turba* and therefore constitutes the "broad course," travelled by many but avoided by Callimachus (see note on 13–26 above).

25 **plectro … eburno** abl. of means

26 **noua … semita facta … est** The idea of the "new" or "fresh path" evokes the Callimachean metaphor of "untrod paths" for poetry. Cf. **1.1.18** and Introduction, pp. xxiv–xxvi.

muscoso … solo abl. of place

27–36 The cave of the Muses, to which Apollo directs the speaker, has musical instruments and figurines attached to the walls as decoration, and a spring in which the doves of Venus dip their beaks. This "source" provides inspiration for elegy but confusingly appears, in the dream, to be identified as well with the spring created by Pegasus, from which the speaker had started to drink at the poem's outset and from whose powerful stream or river Apollo deflects him in line 15.

27 **affixis … lapillis** abl. of quality; the cave or grotto has small stones fixed to its roof in the style of a mosaic.

28   **cauis ... pumicibus** abl. of place where; "from its hollowed rocks." The phrase suggests an artificial grotto constructed from rocks and bits of concrete and designed to imitate a natural setting. This was a common feature of Roman construction in such spaces as *nymphaea* (sanctuaries dedicated to water nymphs) or gardens or outside dining areas.

tympana drums or tambourines used to accompany ritual dances

29   **orgia Musarum** the ritual paraphernalia that accompanied the worship of the Muses

29-30   **Sileni patris imago fictilis** the earthenware figurine of father Silenus, the rustic deity who leads the chorus of satyrs in a satyr-play. Brought up by Dionysus, the elderly Silenus is often depicted as drunk, fat, and snub-nosed, but also as a wise character who, when compelled, reveals his wisdom. Cf. Verg. *Ecl.* 6.

30   **Pan Tegeaee** vocative; the god of bucolic poetry, Pan plays the syrinx or "panpipes" (*calami*) and inhabits the pastoral landscape of Arcadia in which Tegea was located.

31   **Veneris ... uolucres ... columbae** Venus flies in a chariot pulled either by swans or by a flock of doves, birds sacred to her as a goddess (cf. Sappho 1; Hor. *Carm.* 4.1.10; Ovid *Meta.* 14.597); these are called *mea turba*, in apposition, because the speaker identifies with them—he too, as an elegiac poet, is in the service of the goddess of love.

32   **Gorgoneo ... lacu** abl. of place; refers again to Hippocrene (see line 2 above), the spring created by Pegasus, since the winged horse sprang from the Gorgon Medusa's blood after Perseus had slain the monster. However, rather than produce a powerful river (*tali ... flumine*, 15) the source gives rise to a calm pool.

punica rostra the scarlet-red "beaks" of the dove; the color resonates with the implicit image of the Gorgon's blood in the background myth. The words could also, however, mean "the beaks of Carthaginian ships" (a weapon projecting from the bow that was used for ramming other ships), since *punicus* derives from *Poeni*, the Phoenicians, who settled Carthage. This martial image underlying the primary meaning only underscores how the themes of historical epic are in fact intertwined with the motifs of love and passion in elegy and particularly in the *recusatio* form.

33 **diuersae** agrees with *puellae* but also has an adverbial force that modifes *sortitae iura*: the nine Muses "diversely allotted domains" of activity, i.e., jurisdictions; *iura* is an acc. of respect. Despite this idea of different tasks, the association of specific genres with different Muses had not yet become established.

34 **in sua dona** the prep. here has a purposive force: "for their own respective gifts"

35 **hederas ... in thyrsos** The *thyrsus* wand, carried by Maenads as followers of Bacchus, was used in ritual celebrations of the god. Arguably a symbol of fertility, it consisted of a fennel rod wrapped in ivy with a pine cone at the tip.

35–36 **carmina neruis aptat** "fits songs to her strings," implying the writing of music for the lyre

36 **texit ... rosam** refers to the making of wreathes, with the sing. *rosam* serving as a collective sing.

37 **e quarum numero ... una dearum** lit. "from the number of these goddesses, one ..." The rel. pron. is sometimes used in a new sentence with the force of a demonstrative pron. referring to the previous sentence.

38 **Calliopea** the Muse most associated by Propertius with his patroness (cf. **2.1.3**; 3.2.16; **3.3.51**; 4.6.12); Calliope only later becomes identified with epic poetry.

39 **niueis ... cycnis** Venus rides in a chariot drawn either by doves (31, above), or, as here, by swans (cf. Hor. *Carm.* 3.28.13–15).

uectabere Note the alternative 2nd person sing. fut. pass. ending (necessitated by the meter).

40-46 These lines all evoke concerns of the martial, military world that Calliope tells Propertius to dismiss. It is typical of the *recusatio* form to include such a series of allusions to public, historical events in a poem that makes a programmatic statement declining to celebrate them. In this poem, it is Apollo first and then Calliope who instructs the poet to eschew historical epic in favor of personal love elegy. The irony and paradoxical quality of elegy lie in its seeming repudiation but simultaneous embrace of the public events of history.

40 **fortis equi ... sonus** As in **2.1.18**, the idea of the Propertian speaker engaging in warfare—here, drawn by the sounds of spirited war-horses—serves as a metaphor for writing epic in contrast to elegy. Cf. **2.10.2**: *et campum Haemonio iam dare tempus equo.*

41-42 **nil tibi sit ... flare ... tingere** The infinitives are the subject and *nil* the predicate nom.—"let it be nothing to you to blow ... or to stain ..."

41 **praeconia classica** "martial summons"; *classica* derives from *classis*, "fleet," and can refer to naval warfare as well as to trumpet calls.

rauco ... cornu abl. of means

42 **Aonium ... nemus** the grove of the Muses on Mt. Helicon, which is located in Aonia, a region of Boeotia

tingere Marte The idea of staining the grove with warfare or blood recalls the image of doves dipping their scarlet beaks in the spring of Hippocrene (32, above), and although the surface logic of the poem intends a contrast between writing historical epic and writing elegy, the rhetorical resemblance between the two images belies and undercuts the opposition.

43-46 **quibus in campis ... stent ... refringat ... uectet** The indirect question governs all three verbs in the subjunctive and the clause also serves as a further subject of the *nil tibi sit* construction in line 41: "let it be nothing to you on what plains . . ." Alternatively, another infinitive such as *dicere*, parallel to *flare* and *tingere*, may be supplied as the subject: " . . . to tell on what plains . . ."

43–44 **Mariano . . . signo** abl. of attendant circumstance, "under Marius's standard"; the Roman standard, carried by legions and other divisions of the army, was a tall pole with a symbol at the top, frequently in the shape of an animal. Gaius Marius instituted the eagle as the legionary standard and it is his victories over German forces (*Teutonicas . . . opes*), the Teutoni and Ambrones at Aquae Sextiae (Aix-en-Provence) in 102 BCE and the Cimbri in the Po valley in 101 BCE, that Calliope alludes to here.

proelia . . . stent both abstractly in the sense of "where the battles took place" but also with a more literal sense of battle formation

45–46 **barbarus . . . Rhenus . . . uectet** This clause technically depends on *quibus in campis* (43), but it reads more smoothly if an *ut* ("how") or something equivalent is substituted. Note that the river is personified, made to grieve, and cast as "barbarian" in keeping with the Roman perception of those inhabiting the Rhinelands. The Rhine river carrying wounded bodies recalls the Scamander glutted with the war-dead in Book 21 of the *Iliad*, as well as Vergil's Tiber (*Aen.* 8.540), reinforcing the epic status of such imagery.

Sueuo . . . sanguine abl. of means or specification; refers to the defeat of the Suebi, another German tribe, who after crossing the Rhine in 29 BCE were vanquished by C. Carrinas, a victory celebrated as part of Augustus's triple triumph of the same year, along with the conquest of Illyria, the annexation of Egypt, and the success at Actium.

46 **maerenti . . . aqua** abl. of place where

47–50 Calliope now turns to the elegiac topics that *will* be the Propertian speaker's poetic domain. She specifies that his poems will benefit lovers, while Apollo earlier instructed him to write for the *puella* awaiting her man (20). Love elegy proves useful for both populations, since they constitute the same demographic.

47 **coronatos alienum ad limen amantis** The *exclusus amator* or "locked-out lover" typically comes from an evening of revelry and continues to wear his garland from the symposium, or *conuiuium*, when he arrives at the doorstep of another man (*alienum*) with whom his girl resides.

48 **nocturnae . . . fugae** objective gen.; refers to the stealthy nighttime flight from her house that the mistress will take; cf. 4.7.16, where the ghost of Cynthia reminisces about her covert trysts with Propertius: *et mea nocturnis trita fenestra dolis* ("my window worn down by nighttime wiles").

ebria signa the evidence left of fugitive trysts after a party—burned-out torches, garlands, etc. Others interpret the phrase to mean a drunken sign communicated by the lover to the mistress—perhaps the waving of torches outside her window. The military definition of *signa* as "standards," however, suggests other connotations in a *militia amoris* context.

49 **ut . . . sciat** purpose clause

clausas . . . puellas Just as the lover or *exclusus amator* is locked-out, so his mistress is locked-in by her husband or guardian.

excantare The verb evokes those serenades or elegiac poems, sung or recited by the lover, that charm the girl to come out as though responding to a magic spell or incantation. The Greek term for the "poem at the closed door" of one's beloved is the *paraklausithyron*. In 1.16 Propertius writes a parody of such a poem by putting it in the mouth of the door itself.

50 **qui uolet** The subject of the rel. clause is the subject of *sciat* in line 49.

austeros . . . uiros either husbands or guardians; the adj. suggests the morality of the *mos maiorum*.

51 **talia Calliope** Supply *dixit*.

lymphis . . . petitis abl. absolute

52 **Philitea ... aqua** i.e., the water that Philitas drank. Both a scholar and a poet, Philitas of Cos wrote poems in the elegiac meter during the second half of the fourth century BCE. He was a great influence on Callimachus, in the following generation, during the heyday of the Alexandrian period (see Introduction, pp. xxv–xxvi). Note, however, that as the spring from which Philitas drank still seems to be Hippocrene (the *magnis ... fontibus* that inspire Ennius in lines 5–6), Propertius may be suggesting that elegy and epic paradoxically do draw from the same source (see line 32 above and accompanying note).

ᴄᴠ *Elegy 3.11*

A contradictory poem, **3.11** sets up a parallel between the private domain of elegiac enslavement to a mistress and the public sphere where mythology and recent history offer examples of domineering women exercising their power. The initial rhetorical gambit invokes these examples as a way of justifying the speaker's situation, but the poem then evolves into an exaggerated caricature of Cleopatra and the public shame that Rome would have endured had Augustus not ultimately triumphed at Actium. Thus, when the poem turns from myth to recent history, the *exemplum* emphasizes the oppressiveness of subjugation by a woman in terms of potential monarchy. Private gender politics become dangerous as actual political systems. As often in Propertius, propaganda comes close to parody. Cleopatra as the public analogue for the tyrannical elegiac mistress also looks back to the comparison that the speaker makes in **2.16** between his and Marc Antony's situations. Here, in **3.11**, the vision of the fallen Egyptian queen may well serve as a veiled threat and warning to Cynthia, anticipating her decline in the lover-poet's affections by the end of the book. On the level of propaganda and the distorted polarization between Rome and the Orientalized East, the depiction of Cleopatra is profitably compared to Horace's lyric treatment of the same material in *Carm.* 1.37, to Vergil's epic account in *Aen.* 8.675–713, and to Propertius 4.6, the aetiological elegy on the Palatine temple to Apollo.

The structure of 3.11 consists of four sections: the lover-poet's defensive query about his own condition (1–8); the catalogue of famous powerful women from myth and then history (9–28); the vituperative sketch of Cleopatra (29–58); and significant events of Roman history followed by gratitude to Augustus for safeguarding Rome's identity (59–72).

1–2 The opening couplet addresses an unidentified reader, but one that suggests the homosocial audience of **1.1**, the male friends whom the speaker warns about erotic love in his programmatic elegy of Book 1. Cf. the similar address to the city of Rome itself in 1.12.1–2: *Quid mihi desidiae non cessas fingere crimen ... conscia Roma.*

1 **quid mirare** The interr. n. pron. acts here as an adv., "why are you amazed if..." Note the alternative form for the 2nd person sing. pres. pass. indicative.

uersat "controls" or "influences" but there is likely also a pun on the idea of the woman controlling the speaker's elegiac verses (*uersus*); cf. Catul. 50.12 for the same double-entendre, but in reference to homoerotic passion: *ut ... toto indomitus furore lecto uersarer* ("so that ... I was tossed on all my bed, wildly, by my passion"), a line that suggests Catullus stayed up all night writing erotic verse.

2 **trahit addictum ... uirum** The metaphor here draws from creditors and debtors, where a man indebted to another (*addictus*) becomes his "property" and thus enters the condition of debt-bondage or slavery; the usual phrase for leading off such a man from court is *addictum ducere* so that *trahere* may look forward to the conventional metaphor of the yoke, drawn from agriculture, in line 4 below.

sub sua iura "beneath her jurisdiction"

3 **ignaui capitis** gen. of charge; "slothful creature," with *caput*, lit. "head," used colloquially here

mihi dat. of reference

4	**fingis** implies that the charges are contrived, unfair, and imaginary.
	quod nequeam subjunctive in a clause that gives the supposed grounds for the charge
	fracto ... iugo abl. absolute; translate as though a separate infinitive phrase (*frangere iugum*) with *nequeam*, parallel to *rumpere uincla*.
5–8	Each profession or way of life allows a person to speak from experience and the lover-poet is no exception.
5	**uenturam ... mortem** Supply *esse* for the active periphrastic in indirect discourse introduced by *praesagit*.
6	**uulneribus** abl. of cause
	didicit ... habere object infinitive with *discere* (Bennett sec. 328)
7	**praeterita ... iuuenta** abl. of time when; in the naiveté of his bygone youth the speaker spoke the same deluded words as his addressee.
8	**exemplo ... meo** abl. of means
	disce timere object infinitve with an imperative
9–28	With the exception of the last couplet implying Jupiter's shameful subordination to the female sex (a problematic statement; cf. **2.16.47–54** and note), the list of powerful women in these lines moves from the realm of myth to the historical, if legendary, Semiramis in line 21, to the recent history of Cleopatra that begins the next section. The list of dominant females is striking for their "Oriental" otherness—their Eastern origins compounded by their gender make their aspirations to power doubly threatening to the patriarchal worldview of the Roman male. And yet, despite the power they covet or in some cases hold, most of these women experience a tragic downfall of one kind or another, a narrative pattern underlying the myths associated with each figure. The bleak back stories of these powerful women reinforce the message conveyed by the ultimate *exemplum* of Cleopatra—the female gender should be wary of attempting to exercise too much authority.

9–12 In her hometown of Colchis, near the Black Sea, Medea helped Jason of the Argonauts to perform the trials set by her father as conditions to acquiring the Golden Fleece. Jason successfully yoked flame-breathing bulls that sowed the earth with dragon's teeth from which fully armed soldiers sprang forth—only to destroy each other in battle. When Medea realized that her father, Aetes, intended to cheat Jason of his reward, she used her potions to lull to sleep the serpent (or dragon) guarding the Golden Fleece, thus enabling Jason to bring it back to his uncle and claim (unsuccessfully) his right to the throne of Iolcus. On account of Medea's subsequent murder of Jason's uncle, Pelias (see note to **2.1.51–56**), the two fled to Corinth where Jason abandoned her, whereupon Medea killed their two children, his new wife, and his new father-in-law, the king, in revenge. Propertius focuses on the events in Colchis, the earlier part of the myth, recounted in detail in books three and four of the *Argonautica*, an arguably Callimachean epic by the Hellenistic poet Apollonius of Rhodes (see Introduction, p. xxv).

9 **Colchis** an adj. functioning as a substantive here, "the Colchian woman"—i.e., Medea

flagrantis an acc. pl. ending as the scanned hexameter reveals

adamantina . . . iuga Adamant was considered the hardest substance and later became associated with diamond; note that the image of the hard yoke controlled by a woman looks back to line 4.

10 **proelia** By helping to sow dragon's teeth that became warriors in the *armigera . . . humo*, Medea effectively sowed "battles."

11 **feros . . . hiatus** the gaping jaws of the dragon, lit. "the fierce gapings"

12 **iret ut** purpose clause with the verb preceding the conj.

Aesonias . . . domos poetic pl. in the acc. with verb of motion without a prep.; the home of Aeson, Jason's father, who was deposed by his brother from the throne

13-16   Penthesilea, queen of the Amazons, fought at Troy against the Greeks. According to the *Posthomerica* of Quintus Smyrnaeus, a late fourth-century CE epic poet, Penthesilea came to Troy to die in battle, as propitiation to the gods because she killed her sister, Hippolyta, in a hunting accident. The lost epic, *Aethiopis*, tentatively dated to the eighth to the seventh century BCE, recounted the story of her death at the hands of Achilles, who fell in love with her when she removed her helmet.

13   **ausa** Supply *est*.

14   **Maeotis** "Maeotic," describing Penthesilea as coming from the region of Lake Maeotis (now the Lake of Azov, north of the Black Sea), an area reputed to have been inhabited by the Amazons

15   **aurea cui postquam nudauit cassida frontem** The rel. *cui* serves as a possessive dat.; translate "after whose golden helmet laid bare her visage..."

17-20   Hercules served as a slave in the palace of Omphale, the queen of Lydia and daughter of King Iardanus, who achieved her monarchic authority by chance: Omphale came to rule after her husband Tmolus, the legitimate king of Lydia, was killed by a bull. Some versions of Hercules's one-year bondage to the queen have him sold to her in fulfillment of the oracle at Delphi, as compensation for his murder of Iphitus, the son of Eurytus whom Hercules defeated in an archery contest (Soph. *Trach.* 69–71). However, following line 16 that describes the conquering Achilles as conquered by Penthesilea's lovely face, the Propertian narrative here ascribes Hercules's enslavement to Omphale's distinctive beauty. As her slave Hercules dressed as a woman and performed women's tasks (cf. Prop. **4.9.47–50**; Ovid *Her.* 9.53–118; *Fast.* 2.303–58), while Omphale wore the Nemean lion's skin, the hero's garb, and carried his club (as vase paintings reveal). Such gender inversion dovetails with the conventions of love elegy, where the mistress dominates a feminized lover or *servus amoris* such as Hercules (see Introduction, pp. xx–xxiii).

17 **Omphale** In keeping with the feature of *correption* in Greek prosody, the name scans as a dactyl with the final *-e* shortened and not elided with the following *in*.

in tantum . . . processit honorem "advanced to such great esteem . . ." The phrase implies a public recognition of her beauty.

18 **Lydia Gygaeo tincta puella lacu** The phrase is in apposition to *Omphale*, in line 17. Propertius conceives of the lake of Gyges, mentioned by Homer (*Il.* 2.865, 20.390), as the source of the river Pactolus, famous for its gold. The logic of the image then implies that such gold-bearing waters also enhance beauty.

19 **qui . . . statuisset** subjunctive verb in a rel. clause within a result clause

pacato . . . in orbe The phrase suggests the *pax Augusta*, although Hercules's enslavement by a woman parallels Cleopatra's domination of Antony, the implicit figure in the following lines. As a mythological figure, Hercules had contradictory political uses. From the perspective of "positive propaganda," Vergil's Cacus episode in Book 8 of the *Aeneid* (the major intertext for Prop. **4.9**) connects Augustus (i.e. not Antony) with Hercules and Aeneas as the forces of piety overcoming chaos.

columnas "the pillars of Hercules," the rocks of Gibraltar and Ceuta, between which flow the straits of Gibralter. The term *columnas* metaphorically suggests a victory monument established by Hercules after he had rid the Mediterranean of all monsters.

19-20 **ut . . . traheret pensa** result clause; refers to the drawing from an allotment or "weight" of wool off a distaff before spinning it into skeins

20 **dura . . . manu** abl. of means. Note the opposition between Hercules's hard hand and the soft wool: this contrast between *durus* and *mollis* resonates with connotations of genre,

aligning with epic and elegy. Moreover, the activity of spinning—as well as weaving—frequently serves as a metaphor for writing poetry, thus transforming the epic Hercules into an elegiac poet, "spinning" his soft threads into poems.

21-26 Diodorus Siculus (2.4.2–20.5) appears to be the source for these details about Semiramis, the Assyrian queen of Nineveh, who restored and enlarged Babylon in the ninth century BCE. See also Strabo 2.1.31 for her foundation of Babylon. Although Propertius does not here focus on her potent sexuality and instead emphasizes her urban renovations, Diodorus chronicles her power over her husbands as well as over other men. Similar to Omphale, the Babylonian queen came to power after the death of her (second) husband, Ninus. She later meets her own end at the hands of her son, Zoroaster. As a legendary female ruler with a basis in historical fact, Semiramis marks a transition from the mythical Medea, Penthesilea, and Omphale, to the contemporary Cleopatra, another powerful and ambitious queen who, as presented in 3.11, aspired to govern Rome.

21 **Persarum ... urbem** in apposition to *Babylona*, the "capital" of the Persian empire

22 **ut ... tolleret** a result clause, although best translated with a pple., "raising a sturdy structure ..." Note that Semiramis's actions (*statuit*, 21; *tolleret*, 22) parallel those of Hercules who established (*statuisset*, 18) memorial pillars. However, in contrast to the epic hero's spinning the soft threads of elegy, as it were, Semiramis's urban *solidum ... opus* metaphorically suggests the genre of epic.

cocto ... aggere abl. of material; "on a brick fortification," referring to the walls of baked brick for which Babylon was famous

23 **duo ... mitti ... currus** Supply *possent* from line 24.

in aduersum ... per moenia "in opposite directions along the walls"

24	**nec possent ... stringere ... latus** "and were able not to graze the side [of the other] with touching wheel-axles..." The conj. *nec* negates the infinitive rather than *possent*. The idea is that the walls are so massive that two chariots could drive in opposite directions without scraping each other.
25-26	**duxit et ... iussit et** The conjunctions are postpositive.
25	**medium, quam condidit, arcis** "through the middle of the city that she built..." The partitive gen. *arcis* depends on *medium*, which modifes *Euphraten*.
26	**subdere Bactra** object infinitive with subject-acc. following *iussit*; the phrase *imperio subdere caput*, "bow its head to her power," suggests a captive enslaved in war, an image that becomes a conventional metaphor for the lover's relationship to his mistress or to *Amor* itself. Cf. **1.1.4**: *caput impositis pressit Amor pedibus* ("His feet placed above, Love pushed my head down").
27	**nam quid ... raptem** deliberative subjunctive: "for why should I..." After a list of powerful women who, either implicitly or explicitly, dominated heroic men, the speaker breaks off with a rhetorical query asking why he should (continue to) "drag heroes or gods into court," subjecting them to the criminal charges leveled at him in line 3 (*crimina ... mihi ... fingis*). Line 27 can be confusing, since no gods have been mentioned, and thus may be taken as signaling an omission of further development—a kind of *praeteritio* (cf. **4.8.23** and accompanying note). Line 28 then makes a nod to the category of "gods" about which the speaker does not elaborate save brief mention of Jupiter, who brings shame on both himself and his house (and, as the line implies, thus incriminates himself without the speaker's assistance).
29	**quid, modo quae** "what about the one who recently..." The full phrase, without colloquial abbreviation, would read *quid de ea dicam modo quae ... uexerit*, which explains the subjunctive as dependent on the deliberative subjunctive of *dicam*.

COMMENTARY 3.11   111

30   **et ... femina trita** "a woman even worn away," in apposition to *quae* in line 29. The scandal and disgrace that Cleopatra brought to Roman arms is compounded, the speaker implies, by her sexual profligacy with slaves, a charge for which there is no actual evidence. Cf. Hor. *Carm.* 1.37.7–10: *regina ... contaminato cum grege turpium morbo uirorum.*

31   **coniugii obsceni** The "obscene marriage" refers to Antony's relationship with Cleopatra, a liaison flaunted with great spectacle and contracted as a marital union in 37 BCE, before he had divorced Octavia, the sister of Octavian-Augustus, much to the shock of Roman citizens.

31-32   **Romana ... moenia et addictos in sua regna Patres** As the "price" of marriage, Cleopatra demands the city of Rome as well as its system of government, its "senators enslaved as bondsmen to her rule." Cf. the speaker's situation in line 2: *addictum sub sua iura uirum*. The poem has begun to make an about-face and the *exempla* adduced to justify the speaker's private relations with a woman become unacceptable at the public level of contemporary politics.

33-35   These lines apostrophize the cities of Alexandria and Memphis, making them stand metonymically for Egypt, the "land most adapted to deceit," where the desert sands, the site of Pompey the Great's burial, stripped him of the three triumphs he had celebrated for foreign conquests. The imagery also evokes two generations of Roman civil wars fought against an Egyptian backdrop, both Julius Caesar's conflict with Pompey and Octavian's showdown with Antony at Actium. There is no main verb but rather two vocative phrases, followed by a relative adverbial clause introduced by *ubi* in line 35.

33   **dolis aptissima tellus** in apposition to the vocative, *Alexandria*. Although Egyptian treachery and deceit were a staple of propaganda, this phrase also suggests Pompey's fate: after suffering defeat at the battle of Pharsalus, he fled to Egypt, pursued by Julius Caesar, and was murdered with the

Pharaoh's involvement, before reaching the shore. According to Plutarch (*Pomp.* 80.1–4), the body was beheaded and thrown into the water but soon thereafter cremated on the beach (cf. *harena*, 35).

34 **totiens . . . Memphi cruenta** vocative phrase, with *Memphis* as the Greek nom. Situated in lower Egypt, Memphis did not in fact experience warfare. However, metonymically evoking the country as a whole, the city's "so often bloodied" status refers to Pompey's gruesome demise; to Julius Caesar's involvement in the Alexandrian civil wars in Egypt after the death of Pompey; and to Octavian's defeat of Antony and Cleopatra.

nostro . . . malo dat. of disadvantage with *cruenta*

35 **tris . . . triumphos** Pompey celebrated three triumphs for victories in Africa over Sulla's enemies (79 BCE); in Spain over Sertorius (71 BCE); and over Mithridates in Asia (62 BCE). It was to commemorate this last conquest that Pompey established the theater and temple-garden complex in honor of Venus Victrix, a public Roman space renovated by Augustus and which figures prominently in **2.32** as disdained by Cynthia.

Pompeio dat. of disadvantage and dat. with a compound verb, *detraxit*

36 **hanc . . . notam** the mark of disgrace left by Pompey's ignominious murder

tibi dat. of disadvantage

37–38 This couplet wistfully states that Pompey's death either on the battlefield or from illness would have been preferable for him than his murder in Egypt. The syntax implies a contrary-to-fact past condition: a plpf. subjunctive of *ire* in a protasis with suppressed *si* in line 37 and an impf. active periphrastic in the indicative, *daturus eras*, in place of *dedisses* in a second protasis in line 38. The apodosis is simply supplied by *melius* with an implied *fuisset* or *esset*.

37 **issent . . . funera** suggests the procession of a funeral and grave-bier.

Phlegraeo ... campo abl. of place where; in myth the battle between the Olympian gods and the giants took place in the "Phlegraean plain" and tradition locates the site either in the volcanic area near Naples or in Thessaly, close to Pharsalus, where in 48 BCE Julius Caesar defeated Pompey in battle. Earlier, in 50 BCE, Pompey became gravely ill in Naples, a condition that Cicero discusses in a passage of *Tusculan Disputations* (186). Either location is therefore possible as a reference to a place where Pompey might have died more nobly than being murdered off the shores of Egypt.

38 **tua ... socero colla daturus eras** As a means of reinforcing the alliance known as the first triumvirate, which included also Marcus Licinius Crassus, Pompey married Julius Caesar's daughter in 59 BCE. Her death in 54 BCE contributed to the disintegration of the relations between the men. The image here of Pompey giving his neck to his father-in-law suggests surrender (also preferable to treacherous murder) as well as the grisly detail of what did in fact happen: after the Pharaoh's men cut off Pompey's head they offered it up as a prize to Julius Caesar. Finally, the image of a neck-in-surrender, drawn from the rhetoric of warfare, perversely echoes in the context of elegiac love where it suggests the submission of the lover (cf. **1.1.4**; 2.30A.8: ... *Amor ... /grauis ipse super libera colla sedet*).

39 **incesti ... Canopi** The town of Canopus, located in the Nile-delta, had a reputation for debauchery and dissolute living, features that Juvenal assails in his sixth satire. However, here too the city functions in part as metonymy, in this case suggesting the actual incest of the Egyptian royal family.

meretrix regina The phrase evokes Cleopatra's reputation as a loose *femme fatale*, her relations with both Julius Caesar and Mark Antony, and her attempt to seduce Octavian; but the words also constitute an oxymoron in terms of status. It is precisely this inversion of status, wherein the non-citizen courtesan has the upper hand over the citizen lover, that love elegy explores in its experimental imagining of alternate social relations. The phrase thus also alludes to Cynthia through the figure of Cleopatra.

40 **una Philippeo sanguine adusta nota** a difficult and ambiguous line. Keeping the abl. *sanguine* the line admits two readings in which *una . . . adusta nota* refers to Cleopatra and is in apposition to *regina* in line 39: (a) "the single disgrace branded on Philip's blood," understanding an abl. of place where; or (b) "a singular disgrace branded [on us, Rome] by Philip's blood," understanding an abl. of means. The Ptolemaic genealogical line, which included Cleopatra, claimed descent from Philip of Macedon, the father of Alexander the great.

41–46 **ausa** Supply *est* in order to introduce the series of infinitive phrases as the actions that Cleopatra actually dared, or dreamed of daring: *opponere . . .* (41), *cogere . . .* (42), *pellere . . .* (43), *sequi . . .* (44), *tendere . . .* (45), *dare . . .* (46). With propagandistic near-hysteria these lines present Cleopatra as the forces of the East threatening to undermine Western culture.

41 **Ioui nostro** dat. with compound verb, *opponere*

latrantem . . . Anubim Anubis was the Egyptian god with a jackal's head who was associated with the dead.

42 **Tiberim . . . ferre minas** The infinitive phrase is the object of *cogere*, with *Tiberim* as the subject-acc. and *minas* as the object of *ferre*.

43 **crepitanti . . . sistro:** abl. of means; the *sistrum* was a rattle used in the worship of Isis.

44 **baridos . . . contis** The Egyptian barge (*baris, baridos*, f.) was a flat-bottomed boat propelled by poles, *conti*.

rostra Liburna "The Liburnian beaks" refer metonymically to the light and easily maneuvered ships of the Liburni, an Illyrian tribe of pirates. Octavian's victory at Actium was attributed in part to these lightweight galleys, although outnumbered by the forces of Antony and Cleopatra.

COMMENTARY 3.11

45 **conopia** "mosquito nets," which were considered effeminate by the Romans

Tarpeio . . . saxo The Tarpeian rock, situated on the Capitoline Hill, derived its name from Tarpeia, the Vestal Virgin who betrayed Rome out of her passionate love for the Sabine chief, Tatius, only to be killed by him for her treachery. Subsequently, murderers and traitors were thrown from the rock in punishment. Cf. 4.4 for Tarpeia's story as an aetiological love elegy.

46 **iura dare et** The *et* is postpositive.

statuas inter et arma Mari The *inter* is postpositive; the image refers to memorials of and trophies won by Marius for his defeat of Jugurtha, the Cimbri, and the Teutones. These were set up on the Capitoline Hill. Alternatively, *statuas* could refer to statues of the kings of Rome.

47 **quid nunc . . . iuuat** "in what way now does it help . . ." The subject of *iuuat* is the infinitive clause, *fractas esse . . . securis*, with subject-acc. and past pple., "that the axes of Tarquin were broken . . ."

Tarquinii Tarquinius Superbus was the last king of Rome, ruling from 534–510 BCE, according to tradition. After his son raped Lucretia, the Roman nobility avenged the act by driving out the Tarquins, overthrowing monarchic rule, and establishing the Roman republic (cf. the note to **1.3.41–42**).

securis the axes, "rods" or "*fasces*," were a symbol of authority carried by the lictors in attendance on the Etruscan kings and later by those who accompanied magistrates of the Roman republic (see **2.16.11** and note).

48 **nomine . . . simili** abl. of manner; i.e., the name of *Superbus*

49 **si mulier patienda fuit** pass. periphrastic in the pf. indicative (rather than the subjunctive in a contrary-to-fact protasis); this completes the question posed in line 47—i.e., the liberation from the tyranny of the Tarquins becomes meaningless if Rome had had to endure the rule of Cleopatra, a woman.

Note how political systems here become associated with gender and sexuality: the phrase *pati muliebria*, "to endure womanly acts," refers to a man's experience of anal penetration, a metaphor for the emasculation Roman citizens would have suffered under Cleopatra's monarchic domination.

cane, Roma, triumphum The poet now invites the city to sing "*io triumphe*" in celebration of Octavian's defeat of Cleopatra. This was in fact celebrated in the triple triumph of 29 BCE, several years prior to the publication of this poem, but the following six lines, in particular 52–56, comprise a kind of flashback memory of the event on the part of the speaker.

50 **longum Augusto salua precare diem** Now that Rome is "safe," she should make a prayer for the long life of her savior, Augustus. The *princeps* did not receive this name until 27 BCE, two years following the triple triumph of 29 BCE, but the speaker uses the later nomenclature even in his recollection of the earlier event.

precare imperative of the deponent *precor*, with *Roma* as the subject

51 **fugisti tamen** The subject is Cleopatra and the concessive adv. is in relation to her daring and aspirations as described in lines 41–46.

timidi uaga flumina Nili Ancient rivers were commonly personified not only as a literary trope, where they metonymically represent a region or country, but also on floats during an actual triumph through the center of Rome. The personification here, coupled with the emphasis on the different branches of the Nile's delta, recalls the description of Octavian's triple triumph at **2.1.31–32**, where the river, "with its seven captive streams, went weakened, dragged through the city."

52 Of course Cleopatra's hands did *not* in fact receive the chains of Romulus (i.e., Rome), since she committed suicide and thus famously eluded being taken to Rome for Octavian's triumph. However, these lines function figuratively to express her

defeat and they may also refer to the effigy of Cleopatra that Dio Cassius (51.21.8) claims was carried during the triumphal procession and which lines 53–56 appear to evoke.

Romula uincla The use of the adj. *Romulus* to mean "Roman," may also suggest Augustus specifically, since he almost adopted the name of Romulus, the first king of Rome.

53 **bracchia spectaui sacris admorsa colubris** The speaker emphasizes his role as spectator observing the effigy of Cleopatra borne along during the triumphal spectacle. Cleopatra killed herself, as most sources claim, by allowing poisonous asps to infect her arms with toxins. Cf. Hor. *Carm.* 1.37.25–28: *ausa et iacentem uisere regiam/ uultu sereno, fortis et asperas/ tractare serpentis, ut atrum/ corpore combiberet uenenum.*

colubris dat. of agent or abl. of means

54 **trahere ... membra** subject-acc. and object infinitive after *spectaui* (53).

occultum ... soporis iter "the hidden journey of sleep," in reference to death. It is hidden because the poison is unseen; appositional gen.

55–56 The speaker here imagines the effigy of Cleopatra speaking and, in keeping with the portraits of her in Hor. *Carm.* 1.37 and Plut., *Ant.* 28.1–4, as a debauched inebriate given to excessive drink.

55 **hoc ... tanto ... ciue** abl. absolute—"with such a citizen as this ..." The reference is to Augustus and the idea is that Rome, protected by such a citizen, should not have feared Cleopatra.

tibi dat. of agent with pass. periphrastic, *fui ... uerenda*

56 **et** = *etiam*; that is, even though she is drunk and presumably slurs her speech

lingua the subject of *dixit*

57 **septem ... iugis** abl. of specification; the seven hills of Rome comprise the Capitoline, Palatine, Aventine, Caelian, Esquiline, Viminal, and Quirinal.

toto ... orbi dat. with a compound verb

58   **femineo . . . Marte** abl. of cause; almost an oxymoron that underscores the perversity, to the patriarchal Roman sensibility, of political domination by a woman. Line 58, however, is uncertain and missing from the oldest manuscript N.

67-68   Most editions transpose these lines from their place in the manuscripts since they clearly belong to the list of Rome's past glories that, in the speaker's logic, become undercut if the city stands in thrall to a woman and her threat of monarchy.

67   **nunc ubi** Two related interpretations are possible: supply *sunt* and the speaker elevates the victory at Actium by implying that past Roman glories pale in comparison; supply *essent* and Augustus has saved not only the city but the entire history on which her cultural renown and identity are based—"where now would be . . ." The underlying question here asks "what would be the significance of these Roman victories if Rome had fallen to Egyptian Cleopatra?" In this case, supply verbs that would follow a contrary-to-fact construction.

Scipiadae classes "the fleets of Scipio," with a possessive gen. (sing.). Scipio Africanus sailed with his army to Africa and defeated Hannibal in 205 BCE, bringing about the end of the Second Punic War.

signa Camilli It was M. Furius Camillus who defeated the Gauls in 387 BCE at the time of their invasion. The *signa* either serve as a metonym for Camillus's battle prowess or they refer specifically to standards recovered after their capture by the Gauls at the battle of Allia. Cf. Verg. *Aen.* 6.825 *referentem signa Camillum*.

68   **Pompeia . . . capta manu** Supply *signa* from the previous line; refers to the enemy standards captured by Pompey the Great's hand (or band, another meaning for *manus*) in his defeat of Mithridates, king of Pontus (on the southern coast of the Black Sea), in 65 BCE.

59-60   This couplet continues the list evoking prominent Roman victories. The series of phrases with nom. nouns and their

COMMENTARY 3.11 119

modifiers requires *nunc ubi sunt* or *nunc ubi essent* to be supplied from line 67 (transposed above).

59 **uicti ... Syphacis** objective gen.; an ally of Hannibal in the Second Punic War, Syphax was king of Numidia. Scipio Africanus defeated him in 203 BCE.

60 **Pyrrhi ... gloria fracta** refers to Pyrrhus, king of Epirus, whose military successes in southern Italy subsequently foundered at Malventum in 275 BCE, after his defeat by the Romans.

61 **Curtius expletis statuit monumenta lacunis** "Curtius established a memorial by the chasm he filled"; this refers to the heroic action of Marcus Curtius, who rode in full military garb into a chasm that opened in the Roman forum. His act was a response to a soothsayer's claim that Rome would thrive if it sacrificed "that in which the Roman people were most powerful" (Livy 7.6), a statement interpreted as referring to the city's youth. Propertius follows the aetiological story given by Livy and Varro (*LL* 5.148) for the irregular monument, the Lacus Curtius, in the Forum Romanum.

expletis ... lacunis abl. of means or abl. absolute; poetic pl.

62 **Decius ... proelia rupit** "Decius broke through the battle-lines"; P. Decius against the Latins in 340 BCE (Livy 8.9) and his son in 295 BCE (Livy 10.28–29) both practiced *deuotio*, a ritual military action in which the general rides full-tilt into the forces of the opposing side, after "devoting" himself and the enemy forces in sacrifice to the gods of the underworld, as a means of securing victory for his own side.

misso ... equo abl. absolute; on a horse at full speed

63 **Coclitis abscissos testatur semita pontis** Horatius Cocles kept the approaching Etruscans at bay until the bridge over the Tiber was torn down, thus preventing their access to Rome (Livy 2.10). He later swam back across the river to the city. His *semita* or "path," however, can hardly be this crossing and remains obscure.

64   **est cui** "there is one to whom . . ."

        habere an infinitive of purpose following *cognomen coruus . . . dedit*. In 348 BCE, Marcus Valerius Corvinus fought in single combat against a Gaul with a crow perched on his helmet; thus he received his *cognomen*, Corvinus, the adjectival form of *coruus*, "crow."

65   **haec di . . . haec di . . .** *moenia* should be read in both clauses; in the second clause, the gods include Augustus himself, as the following sacrilegious pentameter suggests.

66   **uix timeat saluo Caesare Roma Iouem** potential subjunctive; the panegyric here becomes distinctly hyperbolic and almost profane by placing Augustus on equal footing with Jupiter. The *princeps* had forbidden his *numen* to be worshipped as a god within the boundaries of the city. Augustus here is safe not only because he has defeated Cleopatra but also because, unlike Jupiter in line 28, he has proved himself immune to erotic domination by a woman.

        saluo Caesare abl. absolute

69   **Leucadius . . . Apollo** refers to the temple of Apollo on the island of Leucas near Actium, from which vantage the turned ships (or battle lines—*uersas acies*) and flight of Antony and Cleopatra could be observed.

        memorabit "will memorialize"

70   **tantum operis** gen. of the whole; "so much labor" or perhaps "such a force." Note the identical phrase in **3.3.4**, where it refers to epic poetry. With Octavian-Augustus's victory at Actium, epic battles and their celebration in the epic genre are a thing of the past.

71-72   The final couplet asserts the geographical supremacy of Augustus Caesar, controlling all the Ionian Sea and its ports, but also the mindful thoughts of the sailor. With the mention of *nauita* the reader recalls line 5 and the anticipation of death, an unsettling echo for the poem's ending.

ᴄᴏ *Elegy 4.8*

One of only two poems about Cynthia included in Book 4, a collection that overall addresses Roman patriotic themes, 4.8 describes an event, possibly a "flashback," in which the speaker attempts to assuage his jealousy over Cynthia's trip to Lanuvium with a rakish rival. Despite the speaker's efforts to distract himself, his dinner party with two loose women proves disastrous. A truly comic poem, with many touches of realistic detail, 4.8 makes only a cursory nod at the aetiological premise of the fourth book as a work indebted to Callimachus's *Aetia*, a collection of elegiac poems connected by the theme of "origins." Although refraining from a full explanation of the snake cult at Lanuvium, Propertius's poem provocatively juxtaposes a description of the fertility ritual with the sexual politics of the speaker's affair with Cynthia. Scholars have read this elegy as a mock-epic episode that casts Cynthia in the role of the vengeful Odysseus, returning from adventures "abroad" to a house full of rivals.

After two introductory couplets, the poem's structure consists of three internal sections of 22 lines each: an abbreviated description of the ritual at Lanuvium and Cynthia's supposed journey there (3–26, with 19–20 moved after 1–2); the calamitous gathering at the speaker's house (27–48); and Cynthia's surprise arrival and the mock-epic battle that erupts (49–70). A concluding eighteen lines set the terms for peace and bring about the lovers' reconciliation (71–88).

1   **disce** The verb evokes Lucretian epic even as it purports to introduce an aetiology: in this case, the "origins" of the event on the Esquiline are elided—or juxtaposed—with the cult of Lanuvium with its ritual as the actual topic of antiquarian interest.

   quid . . . fugarit indirect question with syncopated pf. subjunctive

   Esquilias . . . aquosas Under Augustus, the Esquiline was the fifth region of Rome and an upscale residential district. It was also the site of various gardens, including those of Maecenas, as well as fountains and a complex system of imperial aqueducts, hence the epithet *aquosas*. The adj. also looks ahead to the cry for water in line 58.

hac nocte "last night"

2   **nouis ... agris** abl. of place where; new land that Augustus included in the Esquiline, extending it beyond the borders of the region during the period of the republic.

19-20   These lines clearly do not belong in their current place in the manuscript tradition. Many editors transpose them here, since they develop the action introduced in the first couplet and make the transition to the description of the ritual at Lanuvium less abrupt.

arcana ... taberna "hidden tavern," suggesting a dark alley or otherwise less visible place. The description looks ahead to *obscurae prima taberna uiae*, the place into which lines 61–62 imply that Cynthia chases her rivals before returning, victorious, to Propertius.

famae ... meae objective gen. dependent on *labe*

3   **Lanuuium** subject of the sentence, with *tutela* in the predicate nom. A city approximately 30 km southeast of Rome, Lanuvium was most famous for its cult of Juno Sospita and the temple dedicated to her worship. Set deep within the shrine was a cave in which a snake resided. As Propertius narrates the details of the ritual associated with the cult, young girls would descend with food for the snake. If it took the food, this signified that the girl was a virgin and boded well for the year. If it rejected the food, the girl was considered impure and this was not a good omen.

annosi ... draconis either objective or subjective gen., depending on whether *tutela* is understood as "guardian" or "object of protection"

uetus The adj. here reinforces the longstanding status of the protective relationship between the town and the snake and thus anticipates the antiquarian interest that line 4 confirms.

COMMENTARY 4.8

4   **tam rarae non perit hora morae** "the hour spent on such an unusual place of interest is not wasted..." The word *mora* can refer to the actual time spent in Lanuvium or to the object of attention—the town itself or the temple and its associated ritual. Cf. Hor. *Epist.* 1.13.17–18: *carmina quae possint oculos aurisque morari Caesaris* ("poems which may interest the eyes and ears of Caesar"). Understand *tam rarae ... morae* as a gen. of quality.

5   **hic sacer abripitur caeco descensus hiatu** "here, the sacred descent breaks off steeply in a dark, gaping chasm..." Understand *abripitur* as intransitive and *caeco ... hiatu* as an abl. of specification.

6–7 **qua penetrat (uirgo, tale iter omne caue) ... honos** Although *honos* is the subject of *penetrat*, the parenthetical statement *uirgo ... caue* initially suggests *uirgo* as the subject with *honos* in apposition, and, as a result, evokes a macabre but symbolic inversion of gender relations where the maiden, as offering, penetrates the snake's dark cave.

7   **ieiuni serpentis** objective gen. dependent on *honos*, the offering that honors the snake

8   **ex ima sibila torquet humo** "hurls hissings from the deepest earth"

9   **talia ... ad sacra** "at such sacred rites"

10 **anguino ... ore** an unusual abl. of place rather than a dat. with *credere*

11 **sibi** dat. with the pple., *admotas*, of a compound verb

12 **ipsa canistra** So great is the fear of the virgin that her trembling hands cause "even the basket" itself to shake; *canistra* is a poetic pl. Sacred offerings of food were provided in this way. On the use of baskets in the sacred rites of Osiris cf. Tib. 1.7.48: *Et leuis occultis conscia cista sacris*.

13 **si fuerint castae** Propertius teasingly omits the contrary case. Note the use of the pf. subjunctive as a gnomic pf. in a protasis of repeated action (Bennett 262.*B*.1 and 302.3a).

in colla "to the embrace"

15 **detonsis ... mannis** abl. of means; ponies with close-clipped manes were a sign of luxury; cf. Hor. *Epodes* 4.14. Note that the trimmed hair of the ponies anticipates the similarly close-shaved appearance of the dandy, in lines 23 and 26, with whom Cynthia cavorts.

16 **sed mage causa Venus** supply *fuit* from the first half of the pentameter. The speaker suggests that Cynthia's excursion to Lanuvium to visit the temple of Juno Sospita is merely a pretext for an affair. Such alleged erotic dalliance contrasts with the chaste virgin who elicits the farmers' jubilant forecast of fertility in lines 13–14.

17 **Appia** vocative address to the Appian Way, the main road leading out of Rome to the southeast

17–18 **dic quaeso, quantum te teste triumphum egerit** The imperative *dic* introduces an indirect question with pf. subjunctive; *quaeso* is a polite interjected request that may be viewed as introducing *dic*. Note the appeal to the Appian Way as a witness to provide the details of Cynthia's wild triumphal ride. This rhetorically seeks to establish the "reality" of what can only be the speaker's imagination of the scene. In addition, the legal language of *te teste* recalls the similar address to Apollo as a witness in **2.32.28**, where the god asserts Cynthia's innocence in regard to crimes more serious than suspected infidelities that use religious excursions as a pretext. Note that Augustus had finally passed the *Lex Iulia de ordinibus maritandis* and the *Lex Iulia de adulteriis* in 18 BCE (see Introduction, p. xvii), just two years before Propertius publishes his fourth book of verse in 16 BCE.

17 **te teste** abl. of attendant circumstance

triumphum The idea of Cynthia's triumphal procession demonstrates well the use of military rhetoric as a metaphor for erotic conquest in elegy. She has conquered both the lover with whom she leaves Rome and the speaker whose imagination and feelings she dominates. Note, too, that while the Roman *triumphator* as a successful general celebrating his victory would wear the dress of Jupiter Optimus Maximus, it is the goddess Juno who, at least as a pretext, is here connected to Cynthia's triumphal ride.

18 **effusis ... rotis** abl. absolute; "at full speed." The ususal expression is *effusis habenis* with reference to horses' reins being let out to give them full scope at a gallop.

21 **spectaclum** in apposition to *ipsa sedens*; the idea of Cynthia as a spectacle for others continues the rhetoric of the military triumph with an onlooking audience. Cf. 3.13.11–12: *matrona incedit census induta nepotum et spolia opprobrii nostra per ora trahit*, where the censorious speaker inveighs against matrons who parade their wealth through the streets like triumphing generals dragging their spoils of conquest. In her own spectacle, driving the carriage down the Appian Way, Cynthia similarly takes on a masculine role.

primo temone pependit "she hung over the very end of the yoke-pole," with *primo* referring to the edge of the pole; abl. of place where

22 **impuros ... locos** literally, here, "dirty places" or "obstructed places," understanding *purus* as "free from impediments" (*OLD* sv 7). The idea is that Cynthia boldly drives the chariot through mud and other obstacles; however, the moral connotation of *impuros* resonates with the earlier context of the ritual at Lanuvium as well as in relation to Cynthia's and Propertius's infidelities to each other.

ausa ... frena mouere in reference to steering the carriage

23 **serica ... carpenta** a poetic pl.; it is unclear which part of the *carpentum*, a two-wheeled luxury carriage, would be "silken" here—perhaps the cushions or perhaps a covered roof. The substantive point is the effeminacy of the vehicle belonging to Cynthia's companion.

nam taceo a clear example of Ciceronian *praeteritio*, where a rhetorical gesture of seeming to "pass by" and not to mention a certain subject in fact serves to emphasize it all the more pointedly

uulsi . . . nepotis "of her smooth-skinned playboy"; the removal of all facial and body hair by plucking it out (*uellere*) was considered a sign of elegance that verged on effete decadence. Cf. Ovid *Ars Am.* 1.505–8 for condemnation of the practice as unmasculine. The first meaning of *nepos* as "descendant" (*OLD* sv 1) evolved into the meaning of "prodigal spendthrift, playboy" (*OLD* sv 4) from the idea of dissipating one's inheritance in a debauched lifestyle.

24 **armillatos colla Molossa canis** "dogs adorned with elaborate collars about their Molossian necks"; *armillatos* derives from *armilla, -ae,* "bracelet, armband," and takes *colla* as a Greek acc. of respect. *Molossa*, in agreement with *colla*, is a transferred epithet and refers to Molossian dogs, a famous working breed (and thus not generally ornamented in this way).

25 **qui dabit immundae uenalia fata saginae** lit. "who will give over his life for sale to squalid gladiatorial fare"; in this reading, *immundae . . . saginae* stands metonymically for the gladiator's school and is thus in the dat. case. The term *sagina* for gladiatorial food refers to the fattening or "stuffing" of animals for slaughter; *fata* here has the sense of "allotted span of life," which is precisely what the gladiator sells.

26 **uincet ubi erasas barba pudenda genas** "when a shameful beard will conquer his shaved cheeks"; as soon as the *nepos* has dissipated all his money and is no longer able to maintain his elegant lifestyle (symbolized here by his smooth-skinned appearance), then he will be forced to sell himself to a gladiatorial school for his food (*saginae*) and upkeep.

27 **cum fieret** a causal *cum* clause with subjunctive in secondary sequence

nostro . . . lecto dat. of disadvantage

COMMENTARY 4.8

28 **mutato ... toro** abl. absolute expressing more literally the meaning of *castra mouere*, a military metaphor as is common in love elegy; *castra* is a poetic pl.

29 **Auentinae ... uicina Dianae** "who lives near the temple of Diana on the Aventine"; from a less literal perspective, Phyllis by no means resides "in the neighborhood of" the goddess of chastity.

30 **sobria grata parum** the two adjectives are technically in apposition to *Phyllis*; however, translate by making two clauses that parallel the second half of the pentameter: i.e., *cum sobria est, grata parum est* ("when she is sober, she is not particularly appealing").

omne decet "everything about her seems right"

31 **Tarpeios ... inter ... lucos** refers to a place called *inter duos lucos*, a depression or "saddle" between two sacred groves originally situated on the Capitoline Hill, one on the northern end, sometimes referred to as the *Arx*, and another on the southern height, where Tarpeia was buried. Here, according to tradition, Romulus established an *asylum* for newcomers to the city and granted them citizenship (Livy 1.8.5–6; Dion. Hal. 2.15.3–4).

32 **candida** "fair" but with ironic hints of "morally pure, innocent" (*OLD* sv 8b)

potae i.e., *Teia*; dat. with *satis*

non satis unus erit refers to Teia's sexual appetite when drunk.

33 **his ... uocatis** abl. absolute; refers to Phyllis and Teia

33–34 **lenire ... nouare** object infinitives following *constitui*

34 **et Venere ignota furta nouare mea** an ambiguous statement that can be understood a few different ways, depending on whether *mea furta* (as a poetic pl.) refers to the relationship with Cynthia or to extramarital erotic liaisons more generally, including the stolen—if unsuccessful—pleasures with Phyllis and Teia: (a) "and to rekindle my love for Cynthia

with unfamiliar passion," or (b) "and to engage once more in illicit love with unsampled women . . ." *Venere ignota* has also suggested "unfamiliar kinds of sex" in the sense of two women at once.

35 **secreta . . . herba** a garden or, more precisely, lawn, at the innermost part of the house; the hidden location echoes the snake's lair at Lanuvium.

lectulus a diminutive of *lectus*, the couch specifically for dining; three persons per couch would be a standard arrangement for ancient Rome.

36 **concubitus** usually refers to sexual intercourse but here signifies the order of seating, which was codified and specific in ancient Roman dining practice; all the same, the sexual connotations are relevant to the context here.

37 **ad cyathos** "servicing the wine-ladle"; *cyathus* was the ladle used for drawing wine from the mixing-bowl and transferring it into individual wine cups.

uitrique aestiua suppellex "summer dinner service of glass"; gen. of material—note the emphasis on glass here as a sign of luxury.

38 **Methymnaei . . . meri** Methymna was a city on Lesbos, which island was famous for its quality wines; *saliua* refers specifically to "flavor."

39 **Nile, tuus tibicen erat** Egypt was particularly renowned for its flute or "aulos"-players; the Nile river often serves as a metonym for Egypt. Cf. Tib. 1.7.21–26.

crotalistria †Phyllis† "castanet-dancing Phyllis," although the manuscript tradition is suspect and certainly corrupted: it is problematic that the dancer be the same Phyllis as the guest.

40 **et facilis spargi munda sine arte rosa** "and the rose, elegant without art, ready for strewing . . ." *spargi* is an infinitive with adj. (Bennett sec. 333), also known as an epexegetical infinitive, here with *facilis* as "ready at hand" (*OLD* sv 6).

41 **nanus et ipse suos breuiter concretus in artus** "and even a dwarf shrunken [condensed] compactly into his own frame ..." The intensive pron. *ipse* should be taken to emphasize the possessive pron. *suos* (*OLD* sv *ipse* 2b) or to emphasize the presence of the dwarf himself (*OLD* sv *ipse* 9); *artus* in the pl. refers to the body's frame as a whole. Pliny *NH* 7.75 attests to dwarves as entertainment. Dwarves were also popular as figures in Nilotic scenes after the Augustan annexation of Egypt. Such mural scenes would decorate the homes of wealthy Romans. The coupling of a flute-player from the Nile with a dancing pygmie or dwarf in Propertius's poem may well draw on such cultural conceptions of the "Egyptian Other" in the Roman cultural imagination.

42 **truncas ... manus** "his stumpy arms," lit. "truncated hands"

caua buxa The "hollow boxwood" likely refers to the *tibia*, the hollow flute often described as made of boxwood: cf. Ovid *Fast.* 6.667 *caua tibia* and 6.697 *terebrato buxo*. The pl. suggests the double *aulos* (Greek term) or *tibia* (Latin term). That the dwarf dances to the accompaniment of the Egyptian flute-player rounds out this Nilotic scene at the speaker's house.

43-44 The inconstant and flickering flame, despite the recently filled oil lamps, and the collapsing table bode ill for the speaker's plans with Phyllis and Teia. Moreover, each of these events, in addition to the dwarf with his "truncated limbs," has erotic and sexual connotations. The flame of the speaker's desire burns in fits and starts, threatening to go out; and the table falling back or "contracting" against its feet (the flat top folding into a vertical position and the entire structure collapsing supine on the ground?) metaphorically suggests the speaker's impotence.

43 **suppletis ... lucernis** concessive abl. absolute

44 **reccidit inque suos ... pedes** Note the similar syntax to line 41: *ipse suos ... concretus in artus*. Both lines feature a verbal action followed by *in* with the acc. of a body part which, in each case, has impaired functioning—hence the sexual connotations.

130 A PROPERTIUS READER

45-46 The couplet refers to the Roman game of throwing dice. These dice (*tali*), made of animal bones, had four exposed faces and the lucky "Venus throw" consisted of each of four *tali* coming up with a different number. Had the speaker achieved this, it would have been a favorable omen for his erotic adventures. However, *damnosi . . . canes* keep jumping up instead. Four faces with all the same number "1" comprised the losing "dog throw."

45 **me . . . quaerente** concessive abl. absolute

quoque i.e., in addition to the other bad omens of 43-44

47-48 The speaker is blind and deaf to the charms of his guests (in keeping with the earlier imagery that symbolically suggests his impotence). Rather, all his imagination is focused on the town of Lanuvium, a point that underscores his role in creating the vision of Cynthia and her latest paramour in lines 15-26.

49 **cardine** "on their hinges," with the sing. here standing for the pl.; technically an abl. of cause or means

50 **leuia . . . murmura** probably not in reference to hushed tones but rather voices indistinctly heard from within; take as a second subject with *sonuerunt* or supply *sunt* with *facta*.

ad primos . . . Laris "at the entrance to the house," with *Laris* (note the long *-īs* acc. pl. ending) as the tutelary, protective gods of the household (*Lares Domestici*) serving as a metonym here. There may be, however, a more precise reference to a shrine, *lararium*, at the front of the house.

51 **nec mora** Supply *erat*.

resupinat a use of the historical pres. for lively narration of a past action (Bennett sec. 259.3); Cynthia's forceful entrance flings open and slaps back the two halves of the double doors so they figuratively lay flat "on their backs" against the wall.

totas best taken adverbially: "completely"—i.e., "wide open"

52 **comis** abl. of specification

furibunda decens "attractive in her rage"

53-54 This couplet alludes to *Odyssey* 22 when Odysseus and Telemachus have begun to take their vengeance. The Propertian speaker's loss of grip echoes 22.17, where the "cup fell from the hand" of the first suitor killed. Note that the speaker, rather than Teia and Phyllis, here occupies the position of the rival suitors.

53 **remissos** "slackened" or "limp"

54 **ipso ... mero** abl. of means; though in agreement with *mero*, the *ipso* gives emphasis to *labra*: "even my lips, loosened by the wine, became pale."

55-56 This couplet underscores the epic intertext, but introduces Iliadic imagery to the Odyssean theme of revenge on the suitors. The thunderous lighning-bolts shot from Cynthia's eyes liken her to Jupiter even as her rage recalls Achilles. Cf. Hom. *Il.* 19.16-17, where Achilles's eyes flash angrily when he beholds and receives his divine armor, a sign of his own demi-god status.

55 **quantum femina saeuit** = *tantum saeuit quantum femina potest*

56 **spectaclum** echoes line 21 but here it is not just Cynthia as a spectacle but the mayhem of the entire scene that her sudden entrance has provoked. Moreover, it is the sight of panicked women—in this case, Teia and Phyllis—that often characterizes a "sacked city" and that likely motivates the comparison here.

capta ... urbe abl. of comparison; evokes Troy in the Greek epic intertext, but other cities as well

57 **iratos in uultum ... unguis** a conventionally "feminine" weapon (cf. Hor. *Carm.* 1.6.17-18); note that (self-imposed) nail-scratches on the face also characterize female mourning for the dead in a wartime context.

conicit suggests the "hurling" of a spear in battle.

58 **uicinas ... aquas** As though there were a fire, Teia cries out for water from the neighbors; it is also possible to take *uicinas* in reference to the Esquiline as the "neighborhood of aqueducts" (see line 1 above and accompanying note). In either case, Teia pretends that there is a fire in an attempt to create a disturbance that will facilitate her escape from Cynthia.

59 **lumina ... elata** torches that have been raised high, possibly by neighbors, in order to see what is happening; the light then disturbs, *turbant*, and wakes up other sleeping citizens, *Quiritis* (note the long -īs acc. pl. ending).

60 **omnis ... semita** "the entire street," but possibly "every street," i.e., in the neighborhood

insana ... nocte abl. of time, "in the crazy night"; alternatively, an abl. of manner in a kind of *hypallage*, wherein the syntactic relation of the two words is inverted in relation to the actual meaning so that *insana* should be the noun and *nocte* the adj.: "with late-night lunacy."

61 **direptisque comis tunicisque solutis** abl. of attendant circumstance; note that torn hair, like a (self-inflicted) scratched face, often signifies mourning and thus looks back to the figure of the sacked city in line 56. The loosened tunics suggest not only the haste of their flight but also the erotic dalliance that Cynthia interrupts.

62 **obscurae ... uiae** gen. of the whole dependent on *prima taberna*, where Cynthia chases her rivals

63-66 Propertius omits any details about the encounter with Phyllis and Teia in the tavern, but Cynthia clearly comes out the victor and the rhetoric of warfare continues as she confronts the Propertian speaker. Note the series of active verbs in the "historical present," with Cynthia in charge and the speaker her victim. In these lines and in the following description of her reconciliation with him, the rhetoric vacillates between figurative and literal, particularly as she initially wounds and strikes him.

63 **gaudet in exuuiis** As though a warrior from the battlefield, Cynthia rejoices in her "spoils," probably pieces of the other women's clothing.

64 **peruersa ... manu** a back-handed slap that cuts the speaker's face with her nails

mea ... sauciat ora Love's wound becomes actual.

65 **imponitque notam collo** Cynthia makes a mark of possession on his neck (*collo* is a dat. with a compound verb), almost like branding an animal; the diction recalls **1.1.4**: *et caput impositis pressit Amor pedibus*.

66 **oculos, qui meruere** as though to suggest that, ultimately, his crime consisted in his "wandering eyes." Note that in line 47 he is *caecus* to the women's bared breasts. Cf. **2.32.1–2**: *Qui uidet, is peccat: qui te non uiderit ergo, non cupiet: facti lumina crimen habent*.

67 **nostris ... plagis** abl. of cause and poetic pl.; "my beating" in the sense of "beating me"

68 **ad plutei fulcra sinistra** "by the raised end of the couch at the left"; the *pluteus* refers usually to the back or headboard, but here may stand metonymically for the couch as a whole.

69 **geniumque meum ... adorat** Lygdamus appeals to the speaker's *genius*, his divine spirit. A person's *genius* had a protective function and might receive such prayers from servants desiring their master to intercede on their behalf.

70 **nil potui** "I could do nothing"

tecum ego captus eram The military rhetoric continues here and echoes the *capta ... urbe* of line 56; it also recalls the erotic use of the metaphor in **1.1.1**: *Cynthia prima suis miserum me cepit ocellis*.

71 **supplicibus palmis** abl. of manner; with upturned palms the speaker supplicates his mistress for peace.

71–72 **tum demum ad foedera ueni, cum ... pedes** A treaty is struck only when Cynthia allows him to touch her feet.

71 **foedera** a poetic pl.; with *ad ... uenire*, "to come to" or "have recourse to" a policy, etc. (*OLD* sv *uenio* 9)

73 **admissae ... culpae** "the wrong you perpetrated"; dat. with *ignoscere*, which is an object infinitive with subject-acc. (*me*) introduced by *uis*

74 **accipe ... quae ... formula ... erit** Supply *eam* as the antecedent for the rel. pron. *quae* as the subject of *erit*.

nostrae formula legis predicate nom. phrase; Cynthia uses legal language here: "the terms of our agreement" or even "the letter of my law," with *formula* referring quite literally to the precise language (*OLD* sv 5 and 6). Given that Cynthia is in fact imposing her conditions, *nostrae* may well refer to her alone (Bennett sec. 242.3).

75–76 In contrast to the speaker's anxiety about Cynthia's excursions as narrated both here in 4.8 and earlier in 2.32, she simply lays down the law about where he is not permitted to stroll, elegantly turned out, in the city.

75 **Pompeia ... in umbra** the shade provided by Pompey's portico, part of the temple-theater complex (see note on **2.32.11–16** above)

spatiabere connotes a leisurely pace; cf. Ovid *Ars Am.* 1.67, *Pompeia lentus spatiare sub umbra*, where the narrator instructs his readers and pupils in the best urban spots to trawl for women.

76 **cum lasciuum sternet harena Forum** in reference to gladiatorial shows occasionally staged in the Forum, hence the need for sand; *lasciuum* indicates the decidedly non-business purpose for which the Forum would serve in this case.

77–78 **caue inflectas ... det** The imperative here governs prohibitive subjunctives and is identical to *caue ne* (Bennett sec. 276b)

77 **colla ... obliqua** "your neck at an angle"

ad summum ... theatrum towards the top rows of the theater where women were seated (Suet. *Aug.* 44.2–3), as required by the *lex Iulia theatralis* passed sometime between 26 and 17 BCE (although earlier laws made similar stipulations)

78 **tuae se det ... morae** lit. "present itself for your delay"; i.e., "catch your attention and cause you to tarry"

lectica ... aperta Opened curtains invite the onlooker's gaze; the covered litter was not just for elite women but also for members of the imperial family and other Roman officials.

79-80 It is unclear precisely why Cynthia holds Lygdamus chiefly responsible as the source of her problem and complaint—possibly because he had served as a go-between and had facilitated the speaker's liaisons with other women or perhaps because the night with Phyllis and Teia had been his idea. In 4.7.35-36, Cynthia's ghost accuses Lygdamus of having poisoned her and, in a dream, demands that he be tortured with hot irons.

79 **in primis** "most of all" in the sense of "foremost to be dealt with"

mihi dat. of reference

80 **ueneat** jussive subjunctive, as is *trahat*; Lygdamus is to be put up for sale and, in the meantime, wear shackles on both legs.

81 **legibus utar** abl. with *utor*; a formal declaration that the speaker accepts Cynthia's terms

82 **riserat** the plpf. used instead of the pf. here

imperio ... superba dato gives the reason for her triumphant laughter; note the language of military and political *imperium*, particularly with *dare*, suggesting proconsular power. Here, despite the drama that has unfolded with Cynthia taking the role of victor and the speaker as defeated victim turned subject, the phrase *imperio ... dato* hints at the actual balance of power in gender relations beyond the fanciful inversions of elegy: that is, the very political status that the narrator would in fact possess as a citizen male, this power he "grants" to Cynthia in an elegiac drama of military conquest.

83-86 Cynthia now turns to cleansing the house and ridding it of all pollution introduced by the intruding women. In keeping with the Homeric intertext, the scene recalls the purification of the palace in Book 22 of the *Odyssey* after the suitors have been killed.

83 **quemcumque locum** indef. rel. adj. and noun in the acc. as the object of *tetigere* in the rel. clause but also of the main verb *suffiit* in line 84 (supply *hunc locum* for further clarity)

85 **totas ... mutare lucernas** infinitive phrase as object of *imperat*—"to change the lamps completely," understanding *totas* as adverbial. Cynthia orders that the lamps be filled with new oil because they have been witness to the narrator's scandalous tryst and are thus polluted.

86 **sulpuris** gen. of material

87 **mutato ... lecto** abl. absolute

per singula pallia "down to the last coverlet"

88 **respondi** the repetition from line 81 makes this verb suspect in the manuscript tradition; if it is kept, it suggests that the narrator experiences anew his sexual virility.

toto soluimus arma toro The elegiac rhetoric of *militia amoris* is here inverted: instead of the more typical "waging war" as a metaphor for sex, the phrase *soluere arma* in the sense of "make peace" refers both to lovemaking and its aftermath. For *soluo, -ere*, as "to make less tense or firm," see *OLD* sv 8a and cf. Hor. *Epodes* 12.8, *pene ... soluto*, and Lucr. 6.798.

ᕼ *Elegy 4.9*

This poem purports to describe the origins of the *Ara Maxima* and the rule that forbids women to worship there. Vowed in thanksgiving by Hercules, the altar commemorates his victory over the monster Cacus who, living near the Palatine, had stolen the hero's cattle. The poem combines an aetiological narrative with parody of Vergilian epic (*Aen*. 8.184–279), the primary source for the story about Cacus, even as Hercules's reference to his own cross-dressing past casts him in the ambiguously gendered role of an elegiac male. The first twenty lines summarize the conflict with Cacus and the subsequent fifty recount the hero's encounter at the shrine of the Bona Dea. Here, the priestess denies his request for water from the stream within the sacred precinct—it is a space reserved for women alone. Hercules responds by forcing entry to slake his thirst and then, in vengeance, forbidding female worship at his own altar.

There is, then, a kind of ring structure in which the story explaining the origins of the *Ara Maxima* and its exclusion of women (1–20; 67–70) encloses a narrative about women's rites celebrating the Bona Dea (21–66). As such, the poem explores the intersection of gender, ritual, and civic identity by mapping them onto the physical space of the city. Two final couplets engage hymnic language and stand apart from the main narrative (71–74).

1-6 These lines begin their aetiological narrative with a precise moment in mythic time, but contemporary Rome underlies the narrator's perspective and creates a kind of "double vision" of past and present that looks back to the opening poem of the fourth book, which is similarly indebted to Book 8 of the *Aeneid*. The unusually long sentence also expresses the geographic expanse traversed by Hercules from the straits of Gibralter to the city of Rome.

1 **Amphitryoniades** "the son of Amphitryon," i.e., Hercules. As a patronymic form, defining a person in reference to the father, the name is here misleading: Hercules was in fact the son of Alcmene and Jupiter, who only assumed the appearance of Amphitryon, her absent husband, in his sexual encounter with her. With this seven-syllable Greek word the poem begins on an elevated tone, but diction and images in the following lines soon deflate the epic sonority.

qua tempestate "at the time when"; a formal phrase in keeping with the tone of the patronymic

iuuencos the oxen of Geryon, the three bodied giant. As one of his twelve labors, Hercules was sent to bring back these cattle to Eurystheus, the king of Tiryns.

2 **Erythea** the island where Geryon lived, in the western Mediterranean

3 **pecorosa Palatia** a poetic pl. in apposition to *inuictos montis*; the Palatine as "grazed by sheep" is perhaps a pun, given the possible etymology of the hill's name from *balare*, to "bleat."

The juxtaposition of *inuictos* with *pecorosa* reinforces the poem's temporal "double-vision": early Rome as a place of agriculture in contrast to contemporary Rome with its explosion of urban buildings, including the temple to Apollo on the Palatine, which came to be associated with Augustus's victory at Actium and thus his "unconquered" status.

4 **fessos fessus** a jingoistic example of *polyptoton*, the repetition of a single word in different cases; here, it undermines the elevated tone of the poem's beginning

fessus et ipse "weary himself as well"

5 **Velabra** a poetic pl.; the *Velabrum* was a low-lying area bounded by the Forum, the Palatine Hill, the Tiber (and the adjacent Forum Boarium), and the Capitoline Hill. Before the construction of the *Cloaca Maxima* that ran through it, the area was covered with water and, as Propertius and others claim, allowed for the sailing of small boats. Even after it was drained the area would sporadically flood from the Tiber.

suo ... flumine abl. of means

quaque "and where"—i.e., *qua* with enclitic *-que*.

6 **urbanas ... aquas** here the poet imagines past and present superimposed

uelificabat with this verb Propertius points to a possible etymology for the *Velabrum*

7 **infido ... hospite Caco** abl. absolute expressing the attendant circumstances that resulted in the cattle not remaining safe

8 **furto polluit ille Iouem** By robbing Hercules's cattle, Cacus violated the sanctity of the guest-host relationship and the god who protected it. It is unclear whether Cacus actually welcomed Hercules into his home (not likely to be the "terrifying cave" of lines 9 or 12) or whether the monster, as a resident of the area, owed the hero hospitality as he passed through the region.

9 **incola** Both Vergil (*Aen.* 8.230) and Ovid (*Fast.* 1.551) represent Cacus as inhabiting the Aventine; however, it is clear from the preceding description that Hercules came to the Palatine.

| 11 | **ne ... forent** negative purpose clause; *forent* is an alternative form for *essent*.

manifestae ... rapinae an objective gen. dependent on *signa*; the adj. here is proleptic, showing what would be the consequences of the "sure evidence"—i.e., that the theft would have come to light.

| 12 | **auersos** "facing backwards," so that the marks left by the hooves would appear to be leaving the cave; cf. Verg. *Aen.* 8.209–11 for this strategy.

| 13 | **nec sine teste deo** "but not without the god's observation"— lit. "the god as witness," referring here to Jupiter as the deity who protects the sanctity of the guest-host relationship and the hospitality shown to strangers

furem sonuere iuuenci The lowing of the cattle revealed the thief—in the sense that their sounds "signified" the theft that had taken place.

| 13–14 | **furem ... furis ... fores** The *polyptoton* of the first two words, coupled with the assonance and consonance of all three, creates the same comically deflating effect as *fessos fessus* earlier (4).

| 14 | **furis et** = *et furis*

implacidas ... fores The doors are personified here with Cacus's attribute of cruelty.

ira of Hercules; the compression of narrative action leads to the omission of the hero's name, but the following lines identify him.

| 15 | **Maenalio ... ramo** abl. of means; Propertius here locates the origin of Hercules's club in Arcadia, where Mount Maenalus was situated. In its imagery, diction, and, indirectly, its sound the line echoes **1.1.13–14**: *ille etiam Hylaei percussus uulnere rami / saucius Arcadiis rupibus ingemuit*. Not only does *Maenalio* evoke the Arcadian landscape of the *exemplum* in the earlier poem, but it also echoes as a near anagram of Milanion, the mythological figure struck by Hylaeus's club. The epic action of Hercules, however, contrasts with the elegiac suffering of Milanion.

tria tempora Greek acc. of respect and body part affected (Bennett sec. 180), object of *pulsus*, "struck on his three heads"

16 **Alcides** a Greek patronymic, in this case referring to Hercules as the supposed grandson of Alceus, the father of Amphitryon. See line 1 and note above.

16–18 **ite boues . . . quaesitae . . . boues** Hercules here addresses his cattle as female in contrast to the bulls of line 13, *iuuenci*, and the masculine gender of line 12, *auersos . . . boues*. This may be due to scribal error, but the gender indeterminacy also resonates with the overall theme of the elegy, wherein ritual practice serves to demarcate male and female through exclusions and Hercules himself exhibits gender ambiguity (cf. 45–50).

16–20 **ite boues . . . ite . . . erit Romae pascua uestra Forum** Note the echo of Vergilian pastoral (*Ecl.* 1.74 *ite meae . . .* , *ite capellae*; 10.77 *ite domum . . . ite capellae*) and, from Hercules's perspective, the double vision of agricultural present and urban future, again recalling Book 8 of the *Aeneid*.

17 **nostrae . . . clauae** possessive gen. dependent on *labor ultime*, which apostrophizes the cattle seized from Geryon as the last of Hercules's famous ten labors, although elsewhere in the tradition there were more to follow

19 **sancite** "hallow," "confirm the status of" (*OLD* sv 1b)

arua . . . Bouaria The Forum Boarium lay between the Tiber and the Velabrum; Propertius has apparently already drained this area of the water covering it at the poem's outset (5–6). The aetiological explanation offered here differs from that in Varro (*Ling. Lat.* 5.146) where the place served as a cattle market.

20 **erit Romae . . . Forum** The sing. predicate determines the number of the verb here. This is not the *Forum Romanum* specifically but a future marketplace imagined by Hercules as a speaker in the past. However, the term resonates with contemporary associations for Propertius's urban audience.

21 **sicco . . . palato** abl. of cause

22   **terraque non ullas feta ministrat aquas** Propertius again seems to ignore the statement of lines 5–6; *feta* suggests that the earth has not yet "given birth" to water contained within it.

23   **inclusas ... ridere puellas** subject-acc. and infinitive in indirect discourse following *audit*; the image recalls Nausikaa and her playmates awakening Odysseus on the beach of Phaiakia (Hom. *Od.* 6.115–26) as well as the girl's laughter at the end of Horace's Soracte Ode: *nunc et latentis proditor intumo/ gratus puellae risus ab angulo* (*Carm.* 1.9.19–20). In the following context of the grove, *inclusas* suggests "hidden" or "shut in by the trees," but the idea of the "enclosed girl" points up the corollary elegiac condition of the "shut-out lover" (*exclusus amator*) who attempts to draw out his mistress with song: *ut per te clausas sciat excantare puellas* (**3.3.49**).

24   Both *lucus* and *nemus* mean "sacred grove," although the latter possesses a more generic sense of woodland. Here, the abl. of manner *umbroso ... orbe* suggests the circular arrangement of the trees in the *nemus*.

25   **femineae ... deae** with reference to the Bona Dea, an Italian goddess associated with fertility and chastity in women, with a temple on the Aventine. The celebration of her rites, which excluded men, involved the drinking of wine and blood-sacrifice, activities traditionally forbidden to women in ancient Roman culture.

loca clausa the second in a series of objects of *fecerat* (24); the "closed places" allude to the ritual exclusion of men even as the phrase connotes, in an elegiac context, the *exclusus amator*, an identity that Hercules subtextually acquires.

fontisque piandos the third object of *fecerat* (24); the gerundive *piandos*, "to be kept pure," also suggests sacrificial expiation.

26   **impune et** = *et impune*

nullis ... uiris dat. of indirect object; Propertius here alludes to Clodius Pulcher who, in 62 BCE, intruded on the rites of the Bona Dea and was later tried for his violation (Plut. *Caes.* 9–10).

27 **deuia** emphasizes the remoteness of the shrine.

limina literally "threshold" but metonymically standing for "doorway" or entrance here

28 **odorato . . . igne** abl. of means; the fire lets off a smell of incense and illuminates the hut (or, as the context implies, the temple).

luxerat plpf. for impf.

29 **populus et** = *et populus*

longis . . . frondibus here referring to long branches with foliage rather than to the shape of the leaves themselves

ornabat The verb aestheticizes the static scene.

30 **multa . . . umbra** The shade, foliage, and bird song all suggest features of the *locus amoenus*.

cantantis . . . auis acc. pl.

31 **in siccam congesta puluere barbam** "his dry beard matted with dust"—lit. "with dust heaped onto his dry beard." The prepositional phrase follows from the verbal action of the abl. absolute, which expresses attendant circumstances.

puluere f. here

32 **iacit** "utters" or "exclaims"

uerba minora deo words not suitable to—unworthy of—his future divine status: gods should not make the prayers of suppliants.

33 **sacro . . . antro** abl. of place where; not literally a cave, but rather the vaulted space created by the grove

34 **defessis . . . uiris** dat. of indirect object; pl. for the sing. but the generic class of weary men may also be implied

hospita The adj. is proleptic—i.e., it anticipates what would be the result of *pandite*.

35 **circaque sonantia lymphis** Understand *circa* as an adv. and *sonantia* as n. pl. nom. pple. acting as a substantive with a suppressed *sunt*: "and all about are places ringing with the sounds of water . . ."

36 **caua succepto flumine palma** *caua* instead of *plena* with the abl.: lit. "a hollow hand with the water scooped up"—i.e., a cupped handful of water. Cf. **1.3.24**: *nunc furtiua cauis poma dabam manibus*.

37 **tergo qui sustulit orbem** When Atlas went to gather the apples of the Hesperides for Hercules, the hero took on the job of carrying the globe on his back.

38 **ille ego sum** Hercules's boasting tone here is not likely to win him the sympathy of the women.

terra recepta i.e., which Hercules received from Atlas; *terra* functions as a metonym for *orbis* here. Some interpret *recepta* as referring to the earth "taken back" from monsters, in which case *terra* is literal.

39 **Herculeae ... clauae** possessive gen.

40 **numquam** modifies *irrita*.

ad uastas ... feras "against huge beasts"; the prep. here expresses an adversative relation. Note the epic connotations of *uastas* (and *orbem*) in contrast with *caua ... palma*: grand masculine conquest of beasts rather than humble supplication of women.

41 **uni ... homini** dat. of reference; "for one man alone," although other mortals made the journey later in mythological time—Theseus, Ulysses (Odysseus), and Aeneas—Hercules made the trip before becoming a god. Note that Hercules talks about himself in the third person.

Stygias ... luxisse tenebras infinitive and subject-acc. in indirect statement introduced by *quis ... non audit* in line 39. Sent by Eurystheus to fetch Cerberus, the guard-dog at the entrance to the underworld, Hercules successfully performed the task and returned to the world above. His journey to Hades as a living mortal caused the "Stygian darkness" (in reference to the river Styx) to become light.

42 In the manuscript tradition this line is later repeated as line 66. Following Camps's emendation, we mark a *lacuna* here and transpose lines 65–66 to follow line 41.

65-66 **angulus hic mundi . . . accipit . . . uix . . . patet** Although Hercules finds himself in this region of the world it scarcely welcomes him.

65 **mea fata trahentem** "dragging out my destined life," in reference to the labors that Hercules must accomplish

66 **fesso** The adj. has concessive force: "though tired."

43-44 **quodsi Iunoni . . . faceretis . . . non clausisset . . . ipsa nouerca** a mixed contrary-to-fact condition with pres. protasis and past apodosis. Hercules claims that if the women were worshipping Juno (rather than another deity not yet revealed to him) even she, despite her known cruelty to him, would not have denied him water.

nouerca Juno is called the stepmother of Hercules because he is the son of Jupiter, her husband, and Alcmene.

45-50 Hercules contrasts his present travel-worn appearance and symbols of heroic masculinity with his time spent dressed in women's clothing, performing the tasks of a female slave for Omphale, queen of Lydia (cf. **3.11.17-20** and accompanying note). The transvestism and earnest self-promotion of the hero cast him in a ludicrous light.

45 **saetaeque leonis** After Hercules killed the Nemean lion he wore its skin and shaggy mane draped about his shoulders.

46 **Libyco sole perusta coma** Hercules's labors—e.g., his pursuit of the apples of the Hesperides—took him through the sands of Libya. The image of his "sun-scorched hair" underscores the demanding and heroic nature of his epic quest.

47 **Sidonia . . . palla** abl. of attendant circumstance; Hercules wears the garment of Roman matrons, here dyed a deep crimson-purple from the shellfish of Sidon (cf. **2.16.55**). Such luxurious finery contrasts with the servile job of spinning wool and suggests the "dress-up" nature of Hercules's attire.

48 **Lydo . . . colo** abl. of means

pensa diurna See **3.11.19-20** and accompanying note.

COMMENTARY 4.9   145

49 **mollis et** = *et mollis*

fascia the band supporting a woman's breasts, here described as *mollis* to convey its feminine value, as appropriate to women, rather than its actual softness, although that meaning is present too

mihi dat. of reference, indicating possession

50 **apta** The adj. has concessive force: Hercules was a *puella* (a charged word in elegy, generally referring to a mistress), although one "equipped with" a man's hands.

manibus duris abl. with *apta*; the contrast of *durus* with *mollis* resonates with the generic values pertaining to epic and elegy; as often, Propertius plays with and dissolves the opposition by embedding epic imagery in elegiac form—or "dressing Hercules in women's clothing," as it were.

51 **talibus ... at talibus** Supply *dictis* and *ait*; then *dictis* and *responsit*.

52 **canas ... comas** Greek acc. of respect and body part affected, with pf. pass. pple. *uincta*

puniceo ... stamine abl. of means

53 **parce oculis** The verb takes the dat.; Hercules should "spare his eyes" in two senses: "refrain from looking" and to avoid the punishment of blindness that, the priestess goes on to imply, would ensue from the violation of his gaze.

luco ... uerendo abl. of separation

54 **tuta ... fuga** abl. of manner

55–56 **interdicta ... casa** "Forbidden to men, the altar, which protects itself in the secluded hut, is kept inviolate by a fearful law." The subject of *piatur* is *ara*, contained within the rel. clause (56), for which it also provides the antecedent. The verbs *piatur* and *uindicat* suggest that any transgression of the law forbidding men access to the altar requires religious expiation.

55 **uiris** dat. with *interdicta*

	metuenda lege abl. of means
56	**summota ... casa** abl. of place where
57-58	The priestess offers the cautionary *exemplum* of the prophet Tiresias who, in this variant of the myth about the cause of his blindness, observes the goddess Athena bathing naked and consequently loses his sight as punishment. However, Ovid (*Met.* 3.314–36) recounts a different version with which Propertius was surely familiar: after striking sacred snakes mating in the forest, Tiresias is changed into a woman and then later, under the same circumstances, back into a man. Since he has experienced the life of both genders Juno goes to Tiresias to settle a dispute that she has with Jupiter about whether men or women have more pleasure in sex. When Tiresias sides with Jupiter in his contention that women have greater enjoyment, Juno punishes Tiresias with blindness but Jupiter compensates him with prophetic vision. This myth hovers in the background of the figure of Tiresias here and shares many of the same themes as 4.9: transvestites and/or transgendered characters; the cruelty of Juno; patriarchal pronouncements and power; and gender difference in relation to the delineation of sacred space. Moreover, in the story to which Propertius directly alludes the goddess Athena also comes across as ambiguously gendered: she removes her badges of masculine identity and becomes feminine in her naked vulnerability to the gaze.
57	**magno** abl. of price
	posita Gorgone abl. absolute; the head of the Gorgon Medusa embellished Athena's aegis and serves here as a metonym for her armor.
59	**dent** jussive subjunctive
60	**auia ... unda** in apposition to *lympha* (59)
	secreti limitis gen. of quality; "out-of-the-way" or "hidden channel"
61	**sic anus** Supply *dixit*.

COMMENTARY 4.9

postis ... opacos The doorposts are covered by a tree's foliage and thus dark with shade.

62 **iratam ... sitim** Hercules's thirst becomes personified and stands for the hero himself.

63 **exhausto ... flumine** abl. absolute

64 **uix siccis ... labris** abl. absolute, with a pple. of *esse* understood

67–70 Hercules now states not only the origin of the *Ara Maxima*, but, more to the point, also the reason for the exclusion of women from his temple, a ritual "law" to which the entire dramatic episode leads and that constitutes the hero's vengeance for the women's refusal to allow him into their space to quench his thirst. The *Ara Maxima* was located in the *Forum Boarium*, adjacent to the temple of Hercules.

67 **gregibus ... repertis** abl. absolute expressing time when as well as cause

69 **haec** with reference to *Maxima quae ... Ara* in line 67

nullis ... puellis refers to women rather than "girls," but the elegiac *puella* resonates in the excluded gender, complementing Hercules earlier as the implicit *exclusus amator*.

pateat jussive subjunctive with *ueneranda*, a fut. pass. pple. that functions as a predicate adj. modifiying *haec*: "let this altar never be open to any women as a place of worship."

70 **ne sit** negative purpose clause, with *inulta* as predicate adj.

73–74 **hunc ... quoniam ... sanxerat ... Sanctum** transposed before the invocation of Hercules, in lines 71–72, this couplet explains the epithet for the hero as deriving from the past pple. of the verb *sancio*. However, this is a difficult etymology since *sanxerat* here appears, unusually, to mean "had purified" or "had made holy," as though the world is made *sanctum* by Hercules (who then receives the epithet, although he is the agent of the action). Some emend the epithet to *Sancum*, a Sabine name for Hercules, named thus because he "sanctified" the world.

73 **purgatum ... orbem** i.e., "cleansed" of monsters; the phrase recalls *pacato ... in orbe*, in 3.11.19.

74	**Tatiae ... Cures** The chief Sabine city, *Cures*, is here personified in terms of its inhabitants, with the name of their king, *Tatius*, serving as a modifying adj.
71-72	Invoking Hercules as hero-turned-god, the speaker seeks that the divinity be a propitious presence in his book.
71	**cui iam fauet aspera Iuno** The persecuting goddess, the source of all his labors, now favors Hercules.
72	**uelis** optative subjunctive

Appendix: Maps

∞ *Map of the ancient Mediterranean*
sites of major battles of the Roman civil wars, with an inset showing Rome and neighboring towns visited by Cynthia in Elegy 2.32

∞ *Map of Rome*

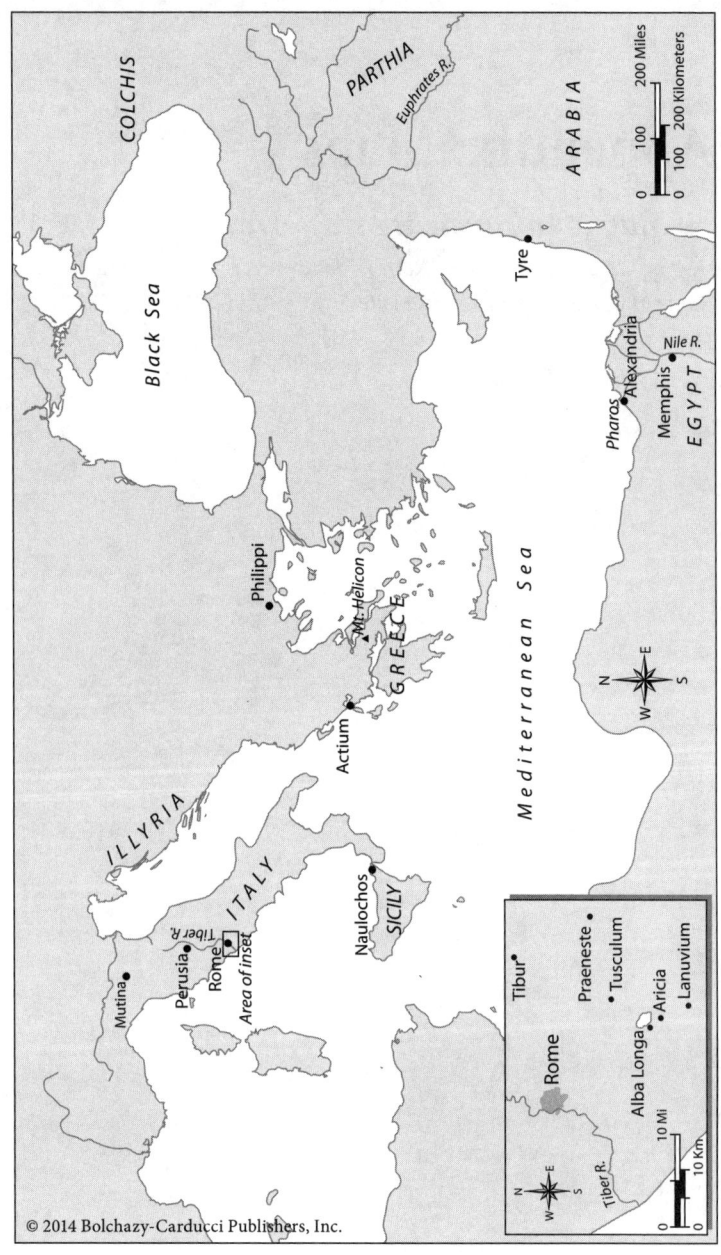

Appendix A: Maps

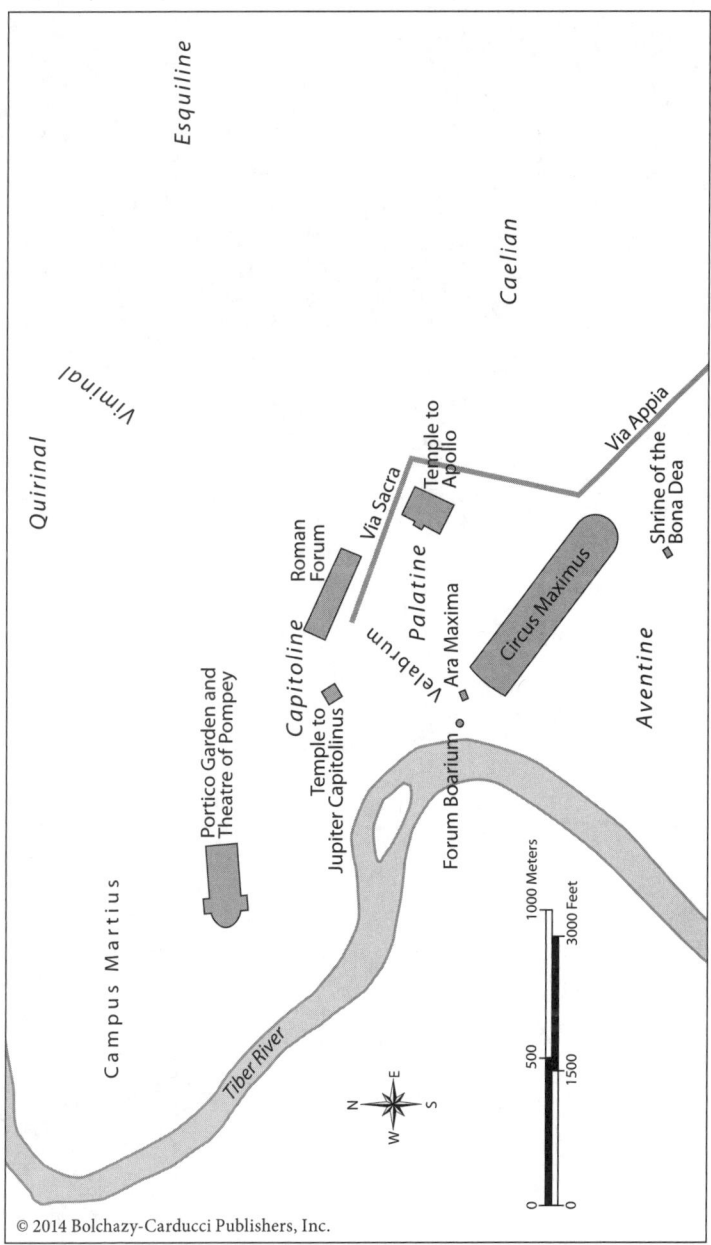

Complete Vocabulary

Latin orthography follows that of the *Oxford Latin Dictionary*, ed. P. G. W. Glare, Oxford, 1985 (= *OLD*).

ā. *See* **ab**
ab, *prep. + abl.,* from, by
abeō, -īre, -iī (-īuī), -itum, to go away, depart
abripiō, -ere, -ripuī, -reptum, to drag or snatch away; (pass., of a path) to be interrupted, come to an end
abscēdō, -ere, -ssī, -ssum, to go away, withdraw
abscindō, -ere, -scidī, -scissum, to break off, cut away
absum, abesse, āfuī, —, to be absent
accendō, -ere, -dī, -sum, to burn
accipiō, -ere, -cēpī, -ceptum, to receive
accumbō, -ere, -buī, -bitum, to lie down, recline, go to bed (with a person)
Achillēs, -is *or* **-ī (-eī),** *m.,* Achilles
aciēs, -ēī, *f.,* ranks, line
Actius, -a, -um, *adj.,* of, or connected with Actium

ad, *prep. + acc.,* to, towards, for, against, in front of
adamantinus, -a -um, *adj.,* of adamant or steel
addīcō, -ere, -dixī, -dictum, to make a slave, enslave; to assign a debtor to his creditor as property
adeō, -īre, -(i)ī, -itum, to come near, approach
admittō, -ere, -mīsī, -missum, to incur, to commit, to be guilty of, to allow
admordeō, -ēre, -(me)mordī, -morsum, to bite at, gnaw
admoueō, -ēre, -mōuī, -mōtum, to move near, bring into proximity
adnuō, -ere, -nuī, -nūtum, to nod assent or agreement, grant
adōrō (1), to appeal to, entreat
aduersus, -a, -um, *adj.,* facing, unfavorable, hostile
aduertō, -ere, -uertī, -uersum, to turn towards, give ear to, pay attention to

adūrō, -ere, -ussī, -ustum, to burn, scorch
Aeaeus, -a, -um, *adj.,* of Aeaea
aedēs *and* **aedis, -is,** *f.,* house, temple
Aegyptus (-os), -ī, *f.,* Egypt
Aemilius, -a, -um, *adj.,* of Aemilius or the Aemilii
aenum, -ī, *n.,* pot, cauldron
aequor, -oris, *n.,* expanse, sea
aerātus, -a, -um, *adj.,* made of bronze or brass
Aesonius, -a, -um, *adj.,* of Aeson
aestīuus, -a, -um, *adj.,* of, belonging, or occurring in summer
aestus, -ūs, *m.,* heat, rage
aetās, -ātis, *f.,* period or time of life
aeternum, *adv.,* for ever, eternally
aetherius, -ia, -ium, *adj.,* heavenly, ethereal
affīgō, -ere, -fixī, -fixum, to fix, attach
agedum, *interj.,* come!
ager, agrī, *m.,* field
agger, -eris, *m.,* earthwork, fortification, rampart
agitō (1), to move, stir, drive, provoke
agō, -ere, ēgī, actum, to drive, lead; to make, act
agricola, -ae, *m.,* farmer
ah, *interj.*
āiō, —, —, —, to say
āla, -ae, *f.,* wing
Alba, -ae, *f.,* Alba (a town in Latium)
Alcīdēs, -ae, *m.,* descendant of Alceus, Hercules
Alexandrīa, -īae, *f.,* Alexandria (a city in Egypt)
aliēnus, -a, -um, *adj.,* belonging to another; foreign, unfamiliar
aliquī, -qua, -quod, *adj.,* some, certain
alius, -a, -um, *pron.,* another, other
almus, -a, -um, *adj.,* kindly, gracious
alter, -ra, -rum, *adj.,* another, other
altus, -a, -um, *adj.,* lofty, tall, high
amans, -ntis, *m./f.,* lover
amārus, -a, -um, *adj.,* bitter, harsh
amātor, -ōris, *m.,* lover
āmens, *gen.* **–ntis,** *adj.,* demented, insane, frantic
amīca, -ae, *f.,* friend, mistress
amictus, -ūs, *m.,* garment, clothing; wrap, cloak
amīcus, -a, -um, *adj.,* friendly
amīcus, -ī, *m.,* friend
amnis, -is, *m./f.,* river, stream
amō (1), to love, like
amor, -ōris, *m.,* love, the god of love
Amphitryōniadēs, -ae, *m.,* male descendant of Amphitryon, Hercules
an, *particle,* can it be that ... ?; or, or whether; whether, if
Androgeōn, -ōnos, *m.,* Androgeon

Andromedē, -ēs, *f.,* Andromeda
anguīnus, -a, -um, *adj.,* of a snake
angulus, -ī, *m.,* corner
angustus, -a, -um, *adj.,* narrow, confined
animus, -ī, *m.,* mind, spirit
annōsus, -a, -um, *adj.,* aged, old
annuō. *See* **adnuō**
annus, -ī, *m.,* year
annuus, -a, -um, *adj.,* annual
anser, -eris, *m.,* a goose
ante, *adv.,* before, previously; *prep.* + *acc.,* before, in front of
antīquus, -a, -um, *adj.,* ancient, old
antrum, -ī, *n.,* cave, hollow place with overarching foliage
Anūbis, -is *or* **-idis,** *m.,* Anubis (an Egyptian god)
anus, -ūs, *f.,* old woman
Āonius, -a, -um, *adj.,* of Aonia, Boeotian
aperiō, -īre, -peruī, -pertum, to open
Āpidanus, -ī, *f.,* Apidanus (a river in Thessaly)
Apollō, -inis, *m.,* Apollo
Appius, -a, -um, *adj.,* Appian; **Via Appia,** Appian Way
aptō (1), to accommodate, fit
aptus, -a, -um, *adj.,* fitted for, good at, suited to
aqua, -ae, *f.,* water
aquōsus, -a, -um, *adj.,* rainy, watery

Āra Māxima, Ārae Māximae, *f.,* Ara Maxima (the altar of Hercules)
āra, -ae, *f.,* altar
Arabia, -ae, *f.,* Arabia
arātor, -ōris, *m.,* ploughman, plower
arbor, -oris, *f.,* tree
Arcadius, -a, -um, *adj.,* Arcadian
arcānus, -a, -um, *adj.,* secret
ardeō, -ēre, arsī, —, to burn
ardor, -ōris, *m.,* a burning, passion, desire
Argus, -ī, *m.,* Argus
arma, -ōrum, *n. pl.,* arms, weapons
armentum, -ī, *n.,* herd
armiger, -era, -erum, *adj.,* producing armed men
armillātus, -a, -um, *adj.,* wearing collars
ars, -tis, *f.,* skill, craftsmanship, art
artifex, -ficis, *m.,* craftsman, artisan
artus, -ūs, *m.,* limb; (pl.) frame
aruum, -ī, *n.,* field, land
arx, -cis, *f.,* citadel; city; hilltop
Ascraeus, -a, -um, *adj.,* of or connected with Ascra
asper, -era, -erum, *adj.,* rough, harsh
aspiciō, -ere, aspexī, aspectum, to look at, behold
assiduus, -a, -um, *adj.,* persistent, unrelenting

assuētus, -a, -um, *adj.,* accustomed, customary, usual
astrum, -ī, *n.,* star
at, *conj.,* but, however
atque, *conj.,* and in fact, and indeed
Attalicus, -a, -um, *adj.,* of King Attalus, rich, splendid
attrahō, -ere, -trāxī, -tractum, to draw with force, drag towards
audācia, -ae, *f.,* daring, boldness
audeō, -ēre, ausus, to dare, have the courage
audiō, -īre, -īuī *or* **-iī, -ītum,** to hear
āuehō, -ere, -uexī, -uectum, to carry off
Auentīnus, -a, -um, *adj.,* of the Aventine Hill, Aventine
āuersus, -a, -um, *adj.,* facing in the opposite direction, turned away
Augustus, -ī, *m.,* Augustus
auis, -is, *f.,* bird
āuius, -a, -um, *adj.,* out-of-the-way, remote
aulaeum, -ī, *n.,* curtain
aurātus, -a, -um, *adj.,* gilded
aureus, -a, -um, *adj.,* gold, golden
auris, -is, *f.,* ear
auspicium, -(i)ī, *n.,* auspices, omen from birds
auster, -trī, *m.,* the south wind
austērus, -a, -um, *adj.,* strict, stern

aut, *conj.,* or
autem, *particle,* on the other hand, while, moreover
auus, -ī, *m.,* ancestor, forefather
auxilium, -(i)ī, *n.,* assistance, help, aid, relief
axis, -is, *m.,* axle

Babylōn, -ōnis *or* **-ōnos,** *f.,* Babylon (a city on the Euphrates)
Bacchus, -ī, *m.,* Bacchus, Dionysus
Bactra, -ōrum, *n. pl.,* Bactra
barba, -ae, *f.,* beard
barbarus, -a, -um, *adj.,* uncivilized, uncouth, savage
barbarus, -ī, *m.,* foreigner (other than a Greek or Roman)
bāris, -idos, *f.,* flat-bottomed boat used on the Nile
Bellerophontēus, -a, -um, *adj.,* of Bellerophon
bellum, -ī, *n.,* war
bene, *adv.,* well, fittingly, suitably
bibō, -ere, -ī, —, to drink
bīnī, -ae, -a, *adj.,* two
bis, *adv.,* twice
bonus, -a, -um, *adj.,* good
bōs, bouis, *m./f.,* bull, cow, *pl.,* cattle
Bosporus (*or* **-os**), **-ī,** *m.,* Bosphorus
bouārius, -a, -um, *adj.,* of cattle
brāc(c)hium, -(i)ī, *n.,* arm
breuis, -e, *adj.,* brief, short

breuiter, *adv.,* for a short distance; narrowly
Britannus, -a, -um, *adj.,* British
bustum, -ī, *n.,* grave-mound, tomb
buxum, -ī, *n.,* flute, pipe made of boxwood

Cācus, -ī, *m.,* Cacus (a giant)
cadō, -ere, cecidī, cāsum, to fall
cadūcus, -a, -um, *adj.,* falling; ready to fall
caecus, -a, -um, *adj.,* blind
caelō (1), to adorn, emboss
caelum, -ī, *n.,* sky, heaven
Caesar, -aris, *m.,* Caesar (cognomen inherited by Augustus)
calamus, -ī, *m.,* reed
Callimachus, -ī, *m.,* Callimachus (third-century Greek poet)
Calliopē, -ēs, *f.,* Calliope (a Muse)
Camillus, -ī, *m.,* Camillus
campus, -ī, *m.,* plain, field
candidus, -a, -um, *adj.,* bright, white, fair; morally pure, innocent
canis (-ēs), -is, *m./f.,* dog
canistrum, -ī, *n.,* basket
Cannensis, -e, *adj.,* of Cannae
canō, -ere, cecinī, (cantum), to sing (of)
Canōpus (-os), -ī, *m.,* Canopus (a town on the Nile)
cantō (1), to sing, celebrate in song
cānus, -a, -um, *adj.,* white, grey

capillus, -ī, *m.,* hair
capiō, -ere, cēpī, captum, to take hold of, seize, catch, capture
captīuus, -a, -um, *adj.,* captured, taken prisoner
caput, -itis, *n.,* head
cardō, -inis, *m.,* pivot, hinge
carīna, -ae, *f.,* keel, hull, ship
carmen, -inis, *n.,* song, poem
carpentum, -ī, *n.,* two-wheeled carriage
carpō, -ere, -sī, -tum, to pluck, seize
Carthāgō, -inis, *f.,* Carthage
cārus, -a, -um, *adj.,* dear
casa, -ae, *f.,* cottage, hut
cassis, -idis, *f.,* helmet
Castalius, -a, -um, *adj.,* of Castalia, Apollo, or the Muses
castra, -ōrum, *n. pl.,* military camp
castus, -a, -um, *adj.,* untouched, upright, chaste
catēna, -ae, *f.,* chain; (pl.) fetters
Caucasius, -a, -um, *adj.,* of or belonging to the Caucasus, Caucasian
cauda, -ae, *f.,* tail
caueō, -ēre, cāuī, cautum, to beware, take care
causa, -ae, *f.,* motive, reason, cause
cauus, -a, -um, *adj.,* hollow, concave, porous
cēdō, -ere, cessī, cessum, to go, withdraw, depart

Cephēius, -a, -um, *adj.,* descended from Cepheus
Ceraunus, -a, -um, *adj.,* of Acroceraunia
cernō, -ere, crēuī, crētum, to see, look at; consider; judge
certē, *adv.,* certainly
certus, -a, -um, *adj.,* fixed, certain
Chīrō(n), -ōnis, *m.,* Chiron (a centaur famous for his medical skill)
chorēa, -ae, *f.,* dance
chorus, -ī, *m.,* band of revelers
chrȳsolithos, -ī, *m.,* topaz
Cimber, -brī, *m. and adj.,* one of the Cimbri (a German tribe)
circā, *adv.,* in the neighborhood, round about
Circaeus, -a, -um, *adj.,* of Circe, Circean
circum, *prep. + acc.,* around
circumdō, -are, -dedī, -datum, to put round, surround, enclose
cithara, -ae, *f.,* cithara, lyre
cīuīlis, -e, *adj.,* of, connected with citizens; of, connected with civil war
cīuis, -is, *m./f.,* citizen
clāmō (1), to shout
clārus, -a, -um, *adj.,* bright
classicus, -a, -um, *adj.,* of or connected with fleets or naval warfare; martial
classis, -is, *f.,* fleet
clāua, -ae, *f.,* club
claudō, -ere, clausī, clausum, to close, shut

clausus, -a, -um, *adj.,* inaccessible, enclosed
Cnōsius, -a, -um, *adj.,* of or pertaining to Cnossos, the ancient capital of Crete
Cocles, -itis, *m.,* Cocles
coctus, -a, -um, *adj.,* baked
coeō, -īre, -iī, -itum, to come together, meet
cōgitō (1), to think, ponder, consider
cognōmen, -inis, *n.,* cognomen
cōgō, -ere, coēgī, coactum, to compel, force, constrain
Colchis, -idis *or* **-idos,** *adj.,* of Colchis, Colchian
collum, -ī, *n.,* neck
colubra, -ae, *f.,* snake, serpent
columba, -ae, *f.,* dove
columna, -ae, *f.,* column, pillar
colus, -ī, *m.,* distaff
coma, -ae, *f.,* hair of the head
compleō, -ēre, -plēuī, -plētum, to fill, complete
compōnō, -ere, -posuī, -positum, to place; to settle (in repose); to establish, appoint
concidō, -ere, -dī, to fall down; to collapse
concrētus, -a, -um, *adj.,* composed, formed; condensed
concubitus, -ūs, *m.,* action of lying together (for sleeping or dining)
concutiō, -ere, -cussī, -cussum, to strike

condō, -ere, -didī, -ditum, to put, put away; to establish, found; to compose; to bury
congerō, -ere, -gessī, -gestum, to collect, pack; to heap up
cōniciō, -ere, -iēcī, -iectum, to hurl, throw
coniugium, -(i)ī, *n.,* marriage
cōnōpium, -(i)ī, *n.,* mosquito-net
cōnōr, -ārī, -ātus sum, to attempt, try
cōnscendō, -ere, -scendī, -scēnsum, to embark; to mount; to climb to the top
cōnsilium, -(i)ī, *n.,* advice, counsel, discussion
cōnstans, *gen.* **-ntis,** *adj.,* stable, mentally or morally settled, steady
cōnstituō, -ere, -stituī, -stitūtum, to resolve, decide
cōnstō, -āre, -stitī, —, to remain constant; to stand still
cōnsūmō, -ere, -sūmpsī, -sūmptum, to destroy, wear away, consume
contentus, -a, -um, *adj.,* content, satisfied
conterō, -ere, -trīuī, -trītum, to crush, grind; to spend, use up
contexō, -ere, -texuī, -textum, to weave, connect
contingō, -ere, -tigī, -tactum, to touch; to affect; to reach, achieve; to hit

contrā, *adv.,* on the contrary, conversely
contundō, -ere, -tudī, -tūsum, to crush, quell, suppress
contus, -ī, *m.,* pole
conueniō, -īre, -uēnī, -uentum, to meet, agree; to be suitable
conuertō, -ere, -uertī, -uersum, to cause to turn, change the course of
conuīuium, -(i)ī, *n.,* dinner-party, banquet, feast
cornū, -ūs, *n.,* horn, trumpet
corolla, -ae, *f.,* small wreath, garland
corōna, -ae, *f.,* wreath, crown
corōnō (1), to crown
corpus, -oris, *n.,* body
corripiō, -ere, -ripuī, -reptum, to seize, snatch up
corrumpō, -ere, -rūpī, -ruptum, to seduce, corrupt, tempt
corruptus, -a, -um, *adj.,* corrupt, impure
coruus, -ī, *m.,* raven
cōtēs, -is, *f.,* rock, cliff
Cōus, -a, -um, *adj.,* of or belonging to the island of Cos, Coan
Crassus, -ī, *m.,* Crassus
crēber, -bra, -brum, *adj.,* closely set; crowded with, full of
crēdō, -ere, credidī, creditum, to believe, trust (+ dat.)
crēdulus, -a, -um, *adj.,* trustful, credulous

crepitō (1), to rattle, rustle; to chatter
Cressa, -ae, *f. adj.,* Cretan
Creūsa, -ae, *f.,* Creusa (betrothed to Jason)
crīmen, -inis, *n.,* charge, accusation, crime
crotalistria, -ae, *f.,* woman who dances to the castanets
cruentō (1), to cause to bleed, wound
cruentus, -a, -um, *adj.,* bloody
crūs, -ūris, *n.,* leg
cubitum, -ī, *n.,* elbow
cubō (1), to recline
culpa, -ae, *f.,* blame, offence
culpō (1), to blame, censure
cultus, -a, -um, *adj.,* well-groomed, elegant
cum, *conj.,* when, since, although, in that; *prep.+abl.,* with (sometimes suffixed to a pron. as in *mēcum* or *tēcum*)
cumba, -ae, *f.,* small boat, skiff
cupīdō, -inis, *f./m.,* passionate desire, longing, lust
cupiō, -ere, -īuī *or* **-iī, -ītum,** to desire, want
cūr, *interr. and rel. adv.,* for what reason, why
cūra, -ae, *f.,* anxiety, worry, care, concern; beloved
Curēs, (-ium), *m./f.,* Cures (an ancient Sabine town)
Curiī, -ōrum, *m. pl.,* the Curiatii
curō (1), to care for
currō, -ere, cucurrī, cursum, to run, hurry
currus, -ūs, *m.,* chariot
Curtius, -(i)ī, *m.,* Curtius
cuspis, -idis, *f.,* sharp point, spear
custōs, -ōdis, *m./f.,* guardian, protector
cyathus, -ī, *m.,* a ladle (used for wine)
cycnus, -ī, *m.,* swan
Cynthia, -ae, *f.,* Cynthia (Propertius's name for his mistress)
Cytaeīnē, -ēs, *f.,* the woman of Cyta or Cytaea, i.e., Medea

damnō (1), to condemn; to doom (to a fate or condition)
damnōsus, -a, -um, *adj.,* causing financial loss, ruinous
Danaē, -ēs, *f.,* Danae
Danaus, -ī, *m.,* Danaus
Danaī, -um, *m. pl.,* the Greeks (especially in reference to the siege of Troy)
dē, *prep.* + *abl.,* from, down from; about
dea, -ae, *f.,* goddess
dēbeō, -ēre, -uī, -itum, to owe, ought, should
dēbilis, -e, *adj.,* enfeebled, crippled
decens, *gen.* **-ntis,** *adj.,* seemly, fitting, appropriate
decet, -ēre, -uit, —, it is right, proper, fitting
dēcipiō, -ere, -cēpī, -ceptum, to deceive, mislead
Decius, -(i)ī, *m.,* Decius

dēclinō (1), to close, droop; to deflect; to bend down

dēcrētum, -ī, *n.*, judgment, verdict, order

dēdūcō, -ere, -duxī, -ductum, to lead away (from), remove; to draw down; to draw out (a thread in spinning)

dēfatiscor, -fatiscī, -fassus sum, to become tired out

dēficiō, -ere, -fēcī, -fectum, to fail, lack

dēfīō, -ierī, —, —, to be lacking; to subside

dēiciō, -ere, -iēcī, -iectum, to throw or cast down, bring down

deinde *or* **dein,** *adv.,* afterwards, then, next

dēligō, -ere, -lēgī, -lectum, to remove by plucking, pick off

dēmens, *gen.* **-ntis,** *adj.,* mad, frenzied

dēmittō, -ere, -mīsī, -missum, to send down

dēmō, -ere, -psī, -ptum, to remove, take away

dēmum, *adv.,* at last, only

dens, -ntis, *m.,* tooth, ivory

dēperditus, -a, -um, *adj.,* abandoned, corrupt

dēperdō, -ere, -idī, -itum, to lose, be deprived of

dēportō (1), bring, convey

dēprendō, -ere, -prendī, -prensum, to find, discover; to catch, seize

descensus, -ūs, *m.,* descent

dēserō, -ere, -seruī, -sertum, to leave, abandon

dēsertus, -a, -um, *adj.,* deserted, lonely

dēsiliō, -īre, -uī (-īuī, -iī), —, to leap or jump down

dētondeō, -ēre, -tondī, -tonsum, to shear, clip

dētrahō, -ere, -traxī, -tractum, to deprive

Deucaliōn, -ōnis, *m.,* Deucalion (king who survived the flood)

dēuius, -a, -um, *adj.,* remote

dēuoueō, -ēre, -uōuī, -uōtum, to vow as an offering; to devote, dedicate oneself

deus, deī, *m.,* god

dexter, -(e)ra, -(e)rum, *adj.,* favorable

Diāna, -ae, *f.,* Diana

dīcō, -ere, dixī, dictum, to speak, say

diēs, -ēī *m.* (*f.*), day

dīgerō, -ere, -gessī, -gestum, to lay out, arrange

digitus, -ī, *m.,* finger

dīripiō, -ere, -ripuī, -reptum, to pull, tear

dīruō, -ere, -ī, -itum, to demolish, wreck

discō, -ere, didicī, —, to learn

dīuersus, -a, -um, *adj.,* turned, pointed, or facing in different directions; differing in identity, distinct, separate

dīues, *gen.* **-itis,** *adj.,* wealthy, rich

diurnus, -a, -um, *adj.,* daily
dīuus, -ī, *m.,* god
dō, dare, dedī, datum, to give, grant
doceō, -ere, -uī, -tum, to instruct, teach
doctus, -a, -um, *adj.,* learned, wise
dōlium, -(i)ī, *n.,* earthenware vessel
dolor, -ōris, *m.,* anguish, grief
dolus, -ī, *m.,* trick, cunning, plot
domina, -ae, *f.,* female head of a household, mistress (used as a title of respect or affection)
domō, -āre, -uī, -itum, to subdue, subjugate, tame
domus, -ūs (-ī), *f.,* home
dōnec, *conj.,* until, as long as, while
dōnum, -ī, *n.,* present, gift
dracō, -ōnis, *m.,* snake
dubius, -a, -um, *adj.,* uncertain, doubtful
dūcō, -ere, duxī, ductum, to lead, guide
dum, *conj.,* as long as, while; until, provided that
duo, -ae, -o, *adj.,* two
duplex, *gen.* **-icis,** *adj.,* double
dūrus, -a, -um, *adj.,* hard, firm, harsh, heavy
dux, ducis, *m.,* leader, commander

ē. *See* **ex**
ēbrius, -a, -um, *adj.,* intoxicated, drunk
eburnus, -a, -um, *adj.,* ivory

Ēdōnus, -a, -um, *adj.,* of the Edoni, Edonian
efferō, -ferre, extulī, ēlātum, to carry out
effūsus, -a, -um, *adj.,* loose; unrestrained, wildly impetuous, headlong
egeō, -ēre, -uī, —, to need
ego, meī, *pers. pron.,* I, me, myself
ei, *interj.,* an exclamation expressing anguish
ēn, *interj.,* see! behold!
Enceladus (-os), -ī, *m.,* Enceladus (a giant defeated by Jupiter)
enim, *particle,* for
Ennius, -(i)ī, *m.,* Ennius (poet who wrote an epic about Roman history)
ēnumerō (1), to count out
eō, īre, iī *or* **īuī, itum,** to go
Epidaurius, -a, -um, *adj.,* Epidaurian
eques, -itis, *m.,* horseman, rider
equidem, *particle,* truly, indeed
equus, -ī, *m.,* horse
ērādō, -ere, ērāsī, ērāsum, to scrape clean or smooth
ergō, *particle,* therefore, then
Eriphȳla, -ae, *f.,* Eriphyla (wife of Amphiaraus)
ēripiō, -ere, ēripuī, ēreptum, to seize, snatch away
errō (1), to wander, roam, go astray
ēruō, -ere, ēruī, ērutum, to remove forcibly

Erythēa, -ae, *f.,* Erythea (the island home of Geryon)
esca, -ae, *f.,* food
Esquiliae, -ārum, *f. pl.,* Esquiline Hill
essedum, -ī, *n.,* Gallic war-chariot
et, *conj., adv.,* and; even, also
etiam, *particle,* still, yet, even now, also
Etruscus, -a, -um, *adj.,* Etruscan
ēuehō, -ere, ēuexī, ēuectum, to carry away; (pass.) to pass beyond
ēuertō, -ere, ēuertī, ēuersum, to overthrow, ruin
Euphrātēs, -ī *or* **-ae,** *m.,* Euphrates River
ex, *prep.* + *abl.,* out of, from, as a result of
exactus, -a, -um, *adj.,* exact, precise
exāmen, -inis, *n.,* multitude, swarm; weighing, consideration, examination
excantō (1), to charm out or away
excipiō, -ere, -cēpī, -ceptum, to gather, catch; to accept, receive
exclūdō, -ere, -clūsī, -clūsum, to exclude, hinder
exemplum, -ī, *n.,* example
exerceō, -ēre, -uī, -itum, to train, exercise, keep busy
exhauriō, -īre, -hausī, -haustum, to drink up, drain

exiguus, -a, -um, *adj.,* small
expellō, -ere, -pulī, -pulsum, to drive out, expel
expertus, -a, -um, *adj.,* well-proved, tested
expleō, -ēre, -plēuī, -plētum, to fill up
ex(s)pectō (1), to wait for, await
exstinguō, -ere, -stinxī, -stinctum, to kill; (pass.) die
externus, -a, -um, *adj.,* external, foreign
extrēmus, -a, -um, *adj.,* situated at the end, uttermost, extreme
exuuiae, -ārum, *f. pl.,* spoils

Fabius, -(i)ī, *m.,* Fabius
faciēs, -iēī, *f.,* appearance; shape; beauty
facilis, -e, *adj.,* easy
faciō, -ere, fēcī, factum, to make, do, compose
factum, -ī, *n.,* deed, action
fallax, *gen.* **-ācis,** *adj.,* deceitful, treacherous, false
fallō, -ere, fefellī, falsum, to deceive, mislead
fāma, -ae, *f.,* rumor, reputation
famulus, -ī, *m.,* servant, attendant
fānum, -ī, *n.,* shrine, temple
fascia, -ae, *f.,* ribbon, band (for a woman's breasts)
fascis, -is, *m.,* fasces (bundle of rods carried by lictors [as symbol of power]); power or office of a magistrate
fastīgium, -(i)ī, *n.,* roof

fastus, -ūs, *m.,* pride, haughtiness, arrogance
fātum, -ī, *n.,* destiny, fate
faueō, -ēre, fāuī, -tum, to show favor to (with dat.), be favorable
fauilla, -ae, *f.,* ash
fax, -cis, *f.,* torch
fēlix, *gen.* **-īcis,** *adj.,* lucky, fortunate; rich
fēmina, -ae, *f.,* woman
fēmineus, -a, -um, *adj.,* of a woman, female
fenestra, -ae, *f.,* window
fera, -ae, *f.,* wild animal, beast
feriō, -īre, —, —, to strike
ferō, ferre, tulī, lātum, to carry, bear; to endure; to tell
ferox, *gen.* **-ōcis,** *adj.,* fierce, warlike
ferrum, -ī, *n.,* iron, sword
fertilis, -e, *adj.,* fruitful, fertile
ferus, -a, -um, *adj.,* wild, fierce
fessus, -a, -um, *adj.,* tired, weary, exhausted
fētus, -a, -um, *adj.,* fruitful
fictilis, -e, *adj.,* of terracotta
fidēlis, -e, *adj.,* faithful, loyal
fīgō, -ere, fixī, fixum (fictum), to drive in, transfix, fix
fingō, -ere, finxī, fictum, to devise, contrive
fīō, fīerī, —, —, to come about, happen (that)
flagrans, *gen.* **-ntis,** *adj.,* flaming, blazing
flamma, -ae, *f.,* flame, fire
flāuus, -a, -um, yellow

fleō, -ēre, -uī, -ētum, to weep, cry
flētus, -ūs, *m.,* weeping, tears
flō (1), to blow, play on
fluctus, -ūs, *m.,* wave
flūmen, -inis, *n.,* river
fluō, -ere, fluxī, fluxum, to flow
focus, -ī, *m.,* hearth
foedus, -a, -um, *adj.,* foul, loathsome, hideous
foedus, -eris, *n.,* formal agreement, compact
fons, -ntis, *m.,* a spring, source
foris, -is, *f.,* door, double doors
forma, -ae, *f.,* form, appearance
formō (1), to mold, fashion
formōsus, -a, -um, *adj.,* beautiful, handsome
formula, -ae, *f.,* terms, provisions
forte, *adv.,* by chance
fortis, -e, *adj.,* strong, hardy
fortiter, *adv.,* vigorously, powerfully, firmly
forum, -ī, *n.,* forum
frangō, -ere, frēgī, fractum, to break, shatter
frāter, -tris, *m.,* brother
fremitus, -ūs, *m.,* roar, rumble, growl
frēnum, -ī, *n.,* bridle, reins
frons, -ndis, *f.,* foliage, bough
frons, -ntis, *f.,* forehead
fruor, -ī, fructus *or* **fruitus sum** (+ abl. or acc.), to enjoy, derive pleasure from
fuga, -ae, *f.,* flight, fleeing

fugiō, -ere, fūgī, —, to flee, avoid
fugō (1), to cause to flee, put to flight
fulcrum, -ī, *n.,* head- or back-support of a couch
fulgens, *gen.* **-ntis,** *adj.,* flashing, gleaming
fulmen, -inis, *n.,* lightning, thunderbolt
fulminō (1), to flash fiercely
fundō, -ere, fūdī, fūsum, to extend, spread
fūnus, -eris, *n.,* funeral rites; corpse; death
fūr, -ris, *m./f.,* thief
furibundus, -a, -um, *adj.,* maddened, distraught, frenzied
furor, -ōris, *m.,* violent madness, delirium, passionate desire
furtīuus, -a, -um, *adj.,* stolen
furtum, -ī, *n.,* deception, trick; secret love, stolen pleasure

Gallus, -ī, *m.,* a Gaul
gaudeō, -ēre, —, gāuīsus, to be glad, rejoice
gemma, -ae, *f.,* jewel, gem
gena, -ae, *f.,* cheek
genius, -(i)ī, *m.,* genius, male spirit of a **gens**
gens, -tis, *f.,* race, nation, people
glōria, -ae, *f.,* praise, honor, glory
Gorgō(n), -onis *or* **-onos,** *f.,* Gorgon

Gorgoneus, -a, -um, *adj.,* of the Gorgon; *with* **lacus,** the spring Hippocrene
Graecus, -a, -um, *adj.,* Greek
Grāius, -a, -um, *adj.,* Greek
grāmen, -inis, *n.,* grass; plant, herb
grātus, -a, -um, *adj.,* pleasant, charming
grauis, -e, *adj.,* heavy, serious
grauō (1), to weigh down, oppress
grex, -egis, *m.* (*f.*), herd
Gȳgaeus, -a, -um, *adj.,* of Gyges of Lydia
gȳrus, -ī, *m.,* circular course

habeō, -ēre, -uī, -itum, to have, hold
habitō (1), to live in, inhabit
hāc, *adv.,* in this manner; **hāc ... hāc,** on this side ... on that
Haemonius, -a, -um, *adj.,* Haemonian, Thessalian
haereō, -ēre, haesī, haesum, to adhere, cling, hold on tightly
Hamadryas, -ados, *f.,* wood nymph
(H)annibal, -alis, *m.,* Hannibal (Carthaginian leader in the Second Punic War)
(h)arēna, -ae, *f.,* sand
hedera, -ae, *f.,* ivy
Helena, -ae, *f.,* Helen
Helicōn, -ōnis, *m.,* Helicon, a mountain in Boeotia
herba, -ae, *f.,* plant, herb
herbōsus, -a, -um, *adj.,* covered with grass, grassy

Herculēs, -eī (-ī) *or* **-is,** *m.,* Hercules
Herculeus, -a, -um, *adj.,* Herculean
hērōus, -a, -um, *adj.,* heroic
heu, *interj.,* alas
hiātus, -ūs, *m.,* crevice, chasm
hic, haec, hoc, *pron.* and *adj.,* this
hīc, *adv.,* in this place, here
hiō (1), to have mouth wide open, gape
hirsūtus, -a, -um, *adj.,* hairy, shaggy
hiscō, -ere, —, —, to utter
historia, -ae, *f.,* inquiry; history (as a written account); story
Homērus (-os), -ī, *m.,* Homer
homō, -inis, *m.,* human being
honestus, -a, -um, *adj.,* honorable, of good repute; well-born, of high rank
honor (-ōs), -ōris, *f.,* honor; that which confers honor
hōra, -ae, *f.,* hour
Horātius, -a, -um, *adj.,* Horatian
hospes, -itis, *m.,* guest, host
hospes, *gen.* **-itis,** *adj.,* of the relationship of guest and host; foreign, alien
hūc, *adv.,* to this place, hither
hūmānus, -a, -um, *adj.,* human
humilis, -e, *adj.,* low, humble
humus, -ī, *f.,* earth, ground
Hȳlaeus, -a, -um, *adj.,* of Hylaeus

iaciō, -ere, iēcī, iactum, to throw, cast; to utter words
iactō (1), to throw, hurl
iactūra, -ae, *f.,* loss
iam, *adv.,* now, already, at last
iānua, -ae, *f.,* door, doorway
Īasis, -idos, *f.,* daughter of Iasius, Atalanta
Īda, -ae, *f.,* Ida (a mountain range in Phrygia)
Īdaeus, -a, -um, *adj.,* of or belonging to the Phrygian Mt. Ida
īdem, eadem, idem, *pron.* and *adj.,* the same
iēiūnus, -a, -um, *adj.,* hungry
igitur, *conj.,* in that case, then, therefore
ignāuus, -a, -um, *adj.,* indolent, slothful; cowardly, spiritless
ignis, -is, *m.,* fire
ignoscō, -ere, -nōuī, -nōtum, to forgive
ignōtus, -a, -um, *adj.,* unknown, unfamiliar, strange
Īlias, -adis (-ados), *f.,* the *Iliad*
illacrimō (1), to shed tears, weep
ille, -a, -ud, *pron.* and *adj.,* he, she, it; that
Illyria, -ae, *f.,* Illyria
Illyricus, -a, -um, *adj.,* Illyrian
imāgō, -inis, *f.,* likeness, image
imitor, -ārī, -ātus sum, to copy, imitate
immundus, -a, -um, *adj.,* unclean

impellō, -ere, -pulī, -pulsum, to strike, push
imperium, -(i)ī, *n.,* power, authority
imperō (1), to demand, command
implacidus, -a, -um, *adj.,* restless, unquiet; ungentle, savage
impōnō, -ere, -posuī, -positum, to place on; to inflict (wounds, blows)
improbus, -a, -um, *adj.,* shameless, wanton; improper, morally unsound
impūne, *adv.,* without punishment, with impunity
impūrus, -a, -um, *adj.,* dirty, muddy; morally foul
īmus, -a, -um, *adj.,* lowest, bottom
in, *prep. + acc.,* into, onto, to, on, against, for the purpose of; *+ abl.,* in, on
Īnachis, -idos, *f.,* a female descendant of Inachus, Io
inānis, -e, *adj.,* empty, hollow; vain, futile
incēdō, -ere, -cessī, —, to proceed, walk
incestus, -a, -um, *adj.,* unclean, incestuous
inclūdō, -ere, -clūsī, -clūsum, to shut up, surround
incola, -ae, *m./f.,* inhabitant
incolumis, -e, *adj.,* unharmed, safe
India, -ae, *f.,* India

indīcō, -ere, -dīxī, -dictum, to impose
indignus, -a, -um, *adj.,* unworthy
iners, *gen.* **-rtis,** *adj.,* inactive, idle, clumsy
infāmis, -e, *adj.,* notorious, infamous
infāmō (1), to give a bad name to, bring into disrepute
infernus, -a, -um, *adj.,* lower, of the underworld
infīdus, -a, -um, *adj.,* faithless, treacherous
inflectō, -ere, -flexī, -flexum, to bend
ingemō, -ere, —, —, to groan, moan
ingenium, -(i)ī, *n.,* innate quality, talent
ingrātus, -a, -um, *adj.,* ungrateful, thankless
iniūria, -ae, *f.,* unlawful conduct, a wrong, injustice
inops, *gen.,* **-pis,** *adj.,* powerless, unable
inquam, —, —, —, to say
insānus, -a, -um, *adj.,* demented, mad
insidiae, -ārum, *f. pl.,* plot, trap, snare
insolitus, -a, -um, *adj.,* unusual, unfamiliar
insum, inesse, infuī, —, to be in
intactus, -a, -um, *adj.,* untouched
intentus, -a, -um, *adj.,* intent, attentive

inter, *prep.* + *acc.,* among, amid, between
interdictus, -a, -um, *adj.,* forbidden, prohibited
interdum, *adv.,* from time to time, now and then, meanwhile
intonō (1), to thunder
inueniō, -īre, -uēnī, -uentum, to meet, find; to discover
inuictus, -a, -um, *adj.,* unconquered, undefeated
inuidiōsus, -a, -um, *adj.,* arousing envy, enviable; unpopular, odious
inuītus, -a, -um, *adj.,* unwilling, reluctant
inultus, -a, -um, *adj.,* unpunished, unavenged
Iolciacus, -a, -um, *adj.,* of or belonging to Iolcus
Īonius, -a, -um, *adj.,* Ionian
ipse, -a, -um, *pron.* and *adj.,* himself, herself, itself; (emphasizing the exceptional)
īra, -ae, *f.,* anger, rage
īrātus, -a, -um, *adj.,* angry, enraged
irritus, -a, -um, *adj.,* ineffectual
is, ea, id, *pron.* and *pronominal adj.,* he, she, it; this, that
iste, -a, -ud, *pron.* and *pronominal adj.,* that, that of yours
ita, *adv.,* accordingly, therefore
iter, -ineris, *n.,* journey, route, path
iterum, *adv.,* again, once more

iubeō, -ēre, iussī, iussum, to order, command, enjoin; to bid, entreat
iūcundus, -a, -um, *adj.,* pleasant, agreeable
iūdicium, -(i)ī, *n.,* judgement
iugum, -ī, *n.,* yoke
Iūnō, -ōnis, *f.,* Juno
Iuppiter, Iouis, *m.,* Jupiter, Jove
iurgium, -(i)ī, *n.,* quarrel, dispute
iūs, iūris, *n.,* law; authority, jurisdiction
iustus, -a, -um, *adj.,* rightful, proper
iuuencus, -ī, *m.,* young bull or ox
iuuenis, -is, *m.,* youth, young man
iuuenta, -ae, *f.,* youth
iuuō, -āre, iūuī, iūtum, to benefit, help; to delight, gratify
Ixīonidēs, -ae, *m.,* a son of Ixion, (applied especially to Pirithous)

lābēs, -is, *f.,* disgrace, dishonor
lābor, lābī, lapsus sum, to glide, slip, slide
labor (-ōs), -ōris, *m.,* work, labor, toil
labrum, -ī, *n.,* lip
lacertus, -ī, *m.,* arm, shoulder
lacrima, -ae, *f.,* a tear, weeping
lacūna, -ae, *f.,* pit
lacus, -ūs, *m.,* lake
laedō, -ere, laesī, laesum, to injure, harm

lāna, -ae, *f.,* wool
languidus, -a, -um, *adj.,* exhausted, weary, inert
Lānuuium, -(i)ī, *n.,* Lanuvium (a town in the Alban Hills)
lapillus, -ī, *m.,* small stone, ornamental stone
Lar, -ris, *m.,* a household god
largior, -īrī, -ītus sum, to bestow, lavish
lascīuus, -a, -um, *adj.,* playful, frisky, wanton
lassō (1), to make tired, weary
lateō, -ēre, -uī, —, to hide
Latīnus, -a, -um, *adj.,* Latin
lātrō (1), to bark
latus, -eris, *n.,* side
laudātus, -a, -um, *adj.,* esteemed, valued
laudō (1), to praise, extol
lauō, -āre *or* **-ere, lāuī, -ātum** *or* **lautum,** to wash
laus, -dis, *f.,* praise
lectīca, -ae, *f.,* litter
lectulus, -ī, *m.,* couch, bed
lectus, -ī, *m.,* bed, couch
legō, -ere, lēgī, lectum, to gather, collect; to read, peruse
lēniō, -īre, -īuī *or* **-iī, -ītum,** to pass pleasantly, beguile
leō, -ōnis, *m.,* lion
Lesbia, -ae, *f.,* Lesbia (fictitious name of Catullus's mistress)
Leucadius, -a, -um, *adj.,* of or belonging to Leucas
leuis, -e, *adj.,* light, trivial, fickle, inconstant
lēuitās, -ātis, *f.,* lightness, fickleness
leuiter, *adv.,* lightly, gently
lex, lēgis, *f.,* law, settlement
libellus, -ī, *m.,* little book
līber, -era, -erum, *adj.,* free
Līber, -erī, *m.,* Dionysus, Bacchus
liber, -brī, *m.,* book
lībertās, -ātis, *f.,* freedom
libet, -ēre, libuit *or* **libitum est,** it is pleasing or agreeable
libīdō, -inis, *f.,* desire, longing; lust
Liburnus, -a, -um, *adj.,* Liburnian
Libycus, -a, -um, *adj.,* African
līmen, -inis, *n.,* threshold
līmes, -itis, *m.,* channel
lingua, -ae, *f.,* tongue
linquō, -ere, līquī, —, to go away, leave
lītus, -oris, *n.,* seashore, coast
locus, -ī, *m.,* or **locum, -ī,** *n.,* place
longus, -a, -um, *adj.,* long
loquor, -ī, locūtus sum, to speak, talk
lūceō, -ēre, luxī, —, to shine
lucerna, -ae, *f.,* oil lamp
luctor, -ārī, -ātus sum, to wrestle
lūcus, -ī, *m.,* sacred grove, wood
lūdō, -ere, lūsī, lūsum, to play, make merry
lumbus, -ī, *m.,* (in pl.) the loins (as the seat of sexual excitement)

lūmen, -inis, *n.,* light, radiance, eye
lūna, -ae, *f.,* moon
lustrō (1), to purify, expiate; to move round; to traverse
lūsus, -ūs, *m.,* sport, game
Lȳdius, -a, -um, *adj.,* Lydian
Lȳdus, -a, -um, *adj.,* Lydian
Lygdamus, -ī, *m.,* Lygdamus (Propertius's slave)
lympha, -ae, *f.,* water-nymph, water
lyra, -ae, *f.,* lyre

Machāōn, -onos, *m.,* Machaon (a Greek physician)
Maecēnās, -ātis, *m.,* Maecenas (a patron of Propertius)
Maenalius, -a, -um, *adj.,* of Mt. Maenalus, Arcadian
Maeōtis, *gen.* **-idos, -idis,** *or* **-is,** *adj.,* of Maeotis
maereō, -ēre, —, —, to mourn, grieve
mage. *See* **magis**
magicus, -a, -um, *adj.,* magic, magical
magis, *adv.,* more, rather
magnus, -a, -um, *adj.,* great
malum, -i, *n.,* pain, hardship, woe; wickedness; evil
malus, -a, -um, *adj.,* unpleasant, wicked, evil, bad
maneō, -ēre, -sī, -sum, to remain
manifestus, -a, -um, *adj.,* obvious, conspicuous
mannus, -ī, *m.,* pony

manus, -ūs, *f.,* hand; band (of soldiers)
mare, -is, *n.,* sea
Mariānus, -a, -um, *adj.,* of C. Marius, Marian
marīnus, -a, -um, *adj.,* of the sea, marine
Marius, -(i)ī, *m.,* Marius
marmor, -oris, *n.,* marble
marmoreus, -a, -um, *adj.,* marble
Marō, -ōnis, *m.,* Maro
Mars, -tis, *m.,* Mars
māter, -tris, *f.,* mother
maximus, -a, -um, *adj.,* greatest
medicīna, -ae, *f.,* practice of healing, medicine
medius, -a, -um, *adj.,* central, in the middle of
melius, *compar. adv.,* better; more profitably
membrum, -ī, *n.,* limb; penis
meminī, -inisse, —, to remember
memor, *gen.* **-oris,** *adj.,* mindful
memorō (1), utter, speak of; to remind of, recall to mind
Memphis, -is, *f.,* Memphis (a city in Lower Egypt)
Menoetiadēs, -ae, *m.,* son of Menoetius, Patroclus
mens, -tis, *f.,* mind
mensa, -ae, *f.,* table
mercor, -ārī, -ātus sum, to buy, purchase
mereō, -ēre, -uī, -itum *or* **mereor, -ērī, -itus sum,** to earn, merit, deserve

meretrix, -īcis, *f.,* prostitute, whore
merum, -ī, *n.,* unmixed wine
merx, -cis, *f.,* wares, merchandise
messis, -is, *f.,* crop, harvest
Mēthymnaeus, -a, -um, *adj.,* of Methymna (a city on Lesbos)
metuō, -ere, -ī, metūtum, to fear, be afraid of
metus, -ūs, *m.,* fear
meus, -a, -um, *poss. adj.,* my
Mīlaniōn, -ōnis *or* **-ōnos,** *m.,* Milanion (successful suitor of Atalanta)
mīles, -itis, *m.,* soldier
mille, *indecl. n. and adj.,* a thousand
minae, -ārum, *f. pl.,* threats, menaces
ministrō (1), to furnish, supply
minor, -us, *adj.,* smaller; falling short; appropriate to those of lower rank
Mīnōs, -ōis (-ōnis), *m.,* Minos (king of Crete)
minus, *compar. adv.,* less, to a smaller extent; fewer, less (by so many)
mīror, -ārī, -ātus sum, *also* **mīrō** (1), to be surprised, marvel at
miser, -era, -erum, *adj.,* wretched, unfortunate, pitiful
mittō, -ere, mīsī, missum, to send
modo, *adv.,* only, if only; just now; sometimes

moenia, -ium, *n.,* walls of a town
mollis, -e, *adj.,* soft, tender; effeminate; amorous
molliter, *adv.,* softly, gently
Molossus, -a, -um, *adj.,* Molossian
moneō, -ēre, -uī, -itum, to remind, warn
mons, -tis, *m.,* mountain, hill
monstrō (1), to point out, show
monumentum, -ī, *n.,* statue, monument
mora, -ae, *f.,* delay; lingering; that which creates delay
morbus, -ī, *m.,* disease, sickness
morior, -ī, mortuus sum, to die
moror, -ārī, -ātus sum, to delay, detain
mors, -tis, *f.,* death
morsus, -ūs, *m.,* bite
mortālis, -e, *adj.,* mortal
mōs, mōris, *m.,* custom; (pl.) habits, morals
mōtus, -ūs, *m.,* motion, movement
moueō, -ēre, mōuī, mōtum, to move
mūgītus, -ūs, *m.,* lowing, bellowing
mulier, -eris, *f.,* woman
multus, -a, -um, *adj.,* many, much
mundus, -a, -um, *adj.,* elegant
mundus, -ī, *m.,* world
mūnus, -eris, *n.,* gift
murmur, -uris, *n.,* rumble; murmur, indistinct sound
mūrus, -ī, *m.,* wall

Mūsa, -ae, *f.,* Muse
muscōsus, -a, -um, *adj.,* mossy
Mutina, -ae, *f.,* Mutina (a town in Cisalpine Gaul)
mūtō (1), to change
mūtus, -a, -um, *adj.,* silent
Myrō(n), -ōnis, Myron (Greek sculptor)
Mȳsus, -a, -um, Mysian

Nāis, -idis *or* **-idos,** *f.,* Naiad (river nymph)
nam, *particle,* for, moreover
namque, *conj.,* certainly, to be sure
nānus, -ī, *m.,* dwarf
narrō (1), to relate, tell, say
nascor, -ī, -nātus sum, to be born
nāuigō (1), to sail
nāuita, -ae, *m.,* sailor
nauta, -ae, *m.,* sailor
nē, *negative adv. and conj.,* not; in order that . . . not
-ne, *interr. particle, attached to emphatic word*
nec. *See* **neque**
neglegō, -ere, -glexī, -glectum, to disregard, ignore
negō, (1), to deny (that), to say (that . . . not) (with acc. and inf.); to refuse (with inf.)
nēmō, -inis, *m.* (*f.*), nobody, no one
nemus, -oris, *n.,* wood, sacred grove
nepōs, -ōtis, *m.,* descendant; spendthrift, playboy
Neptūnus, -ī, *m.,* Neptune

neque, *conj. adv.,* not; and not, nor; not even
nequeō, -īre, -quīuī *or* **-quiī, —,** to be unable
neruus (-os), -ī, *m.,* string, cord, sinew
nesciō, -īre, -scīuī *or* **sciī, -scītum,** to not know (how)
nihil, *n. indecl.,* nothing
nihilum, -ī, *n.,* nothing
nīl. *See* **nihil**
Nīlus, -ī, *m.,* Nile River
nimium, *adv.,* too much, excessively
nisi, *conj.,* except if, unless
nītor, -ī, nixus sum *or* **nīsus sum,** to rest, lean (on), be supported by (+ abl.)
niueus, -a, -um, snow-white, snowy
nōbilis, -e, *adj.,* famous, remarkable, outstanding
noceō, -ēre, -uī, -itum, to injure, hurt
nocturnus, -a, -um, *adj.,* nocturnal
nōlō, nolle, nōluī, —, to be unwilling, not want to
nōmen, -inis, *n.,* name; fame, repute
nōn, *adv.,* not
nōndum, *adv.,* not yet
nōs, nostrī *or* **nostrum,** *pron.,* we
noscō, -ere, nōuī, nōtum, to get to know, find out; (in pf.) know, be familiar with
noster, -tra, -trum, *poss. adj.,* ours
nota, -ae, *f.,* mark, stain

notō (1), to mark, identify
nōtus, -a, -um, *adj.*, known, accustomed, familiar
nouem, *indecl. adj.*, nine
nouerca, -ae, *f.*, stepmother
nouō (1), to refresh, renew
nouus, -a, -um, *adj.*, new
nox, noctis, *f.*, night
noxius, -a, -um, *adj.*, delinquent, harmful
nūbilus, -a, -um, *adj.*, cloudy
nūbō, -ere, nupsī, nuptum, to marry
nudō (1), to strip bare, uncover
nūdus, -a, -um, *adj.*, naked, bare
nullus, -a, -um, *adj.*, not any, no; no one, nobody (as substantive)
numerus, -ī, *m.*, number
numquam, *adv.*, at no time, never
nunc, *adv.*, now
nūper, *adv.*, recently, just now
nympha, -ae, *f.*, nymph

ō, *interj.*, O
oblīquus, -a, -um, *adj.*, slanting, at an angle
obscēnus, -a, -um, *adj.*, filthy, loathsome, indecent
obscūrus, -a, -um, *adj.*, dim, dark
obstupescō, -ere, -uī, —, to be struck dumb, be stunned
occultus, -a, -um, *adj.*, concealed, unknown
Ōceanus, -ī, *m.*, Oceanus, the ocean

ocellus, -ī, *m.*, (little) eye
oculus, -ī, *m.*, eye
ōdī, -isse, ōsum, to hate, dislike
odōrātus, -a, -um, *adj.*, fragrant
offerō, -ferre, obtulī *or* **optulī, oblātum,** to offer
officium, -(i)ī, *n.*, duty, job
Olympus (-os), -ī, *m.*, Olympus
omnis, -e, *adj.*, entire, all
Omphalē, -ēs, *f.*, Omphale (queen of Lydia)
opācus, -a, -um, *adj.*, shady, dark
operōsus, -a, -um, *adj.*, diligent, painstaking
oppōnō, -ere, -posuī, -positum, to place in front, set against
opprobrium, -(i)ī, *n.*, reproach, shame
oppugnō (1), to attack, assault
ops, opis, *f.*, aid, power, strength; (in pl.) military resources
opus, -eris, *n.*, work, task; effort; literary or artistic work
ōra, -ae, *f.*, coast, shore
orbis, -is, *m.*, circle, ring; world
ordō, -inis, *m.*, row
orgia, -ōrum, *n. pl.*, secret rites
Ōrīōn, -ōnis (-ōnos), *m.*, Orion
ornō (1), to adorn, decorate
Orphēus, -a, -um, *adj.*, of or belonging to Orpheus
Ortygia, -ae, *f.*, Ortygia (an old name for Delos)
ōs, ōris, *n.*, mouth; face; *in ōra venīre,* to become famous or notorious

osculum, -ī, *n.,* kiss
Ossa, -ae, *f.,* Ossa (a mountain in Thessaly)
ouis, -is, *f.,* sheep

pābulum, -ī, *n.,* food
pācātus, -a, -um, *adj.,* peaceful, tranquil
pāgina, -ae, *f.,* column or page of writing
Palātium, -(i)ī, *n.,* Palatine Hill
palātum, -ī, *n.,* roof of the mouth, palate
palla, -ae, *f.,* mantle, worn by women
Pallas, -adis *or* **-ados,** *f.,* Pallas Athene (Minerva)
palleō, -ēre, (-uī), —, to be pale, become pale
pallium, -(i)ī, *n.,* bed-cover, sheet
palma, -ae, *f.,* palm
Pān, Pānos, *m.,* Pan
pandō, -ere, —, passum *or* **pansum,** to extend, open
pār, *gen.* **paris,** *adj.,* balanced, even, equal
parcō, -ere, pepercī (parcuī, parsī), —, to refrain from using (+ dat.)
pārens, -ntis, *m./f.,* parent
Paris, -idis, *m.,* Paris
pariter, *adv.,* evenly, uniformly; side by side
Parnāsus (-os, -ass-), -ī, *m.,* Parnassus (a mountain by Delphi)
Parthī, -ōrum, *m. pl.,* Parthians

Parthenius, -a, -um, *adj.,* of or connected with Mt. Parthenius in Arcadia
partiō, -īre, -īuī, -ītum, to divide, distribute
parum, *n. indecl. adv.,* insufficiently, too little
paruus, -a, -um, *adj.,* small
pascuum, -ī, *n.,* pasture
pastor, -ōris, *m.,* shepherd
patefaciō, -ere, -fēcī, -factum, to make visible, reveal, open
pateō, -ēre, -uī, —, to open
pater, -tris, *m.,* father; *pl.,* senators
patior, -ī, passus sum, to experience, undergo, suffer
patria, -ae, *f.,* one's native land, homeland
patrius, -a, -um, *adj.,* paternal
pauper, *gen.,* **-eris,** *adj.,* poor, meagre
pax, pācis, *f.,* peace
peccō (1), to make a mistake, do wrong
pecorōsus, -a, -um, *adj.,* marked by large numbers of cattle
pectus, -oris, *n.,* chest, breast
pecus, -oris, *n.,* livestock, sheep
pecus, -dis, *f.,* animal, livestock
Pēlion, -(i)ī, *n.,* Pelion (a mountain in Magnesia)
pellō, -ere, pepulī, pulsum, to push, strike
pendeō, -ēre, pependī, —, to hang

penetrō (1), to penetrate
pensum, -ī, *n.,* an allotment of spinning or weaving
Penthesilēa, -ae, *f.,* Penthesilea (queen of the Amazons)
per, *prep.* + *acc.,* through, across
percurrō, -ere, -(cu)currī, -cursum, to move quickly through
percutiō, -ere, -cussī, -cussum, to strike, hit
perdūcō, -ere, -duxī, -ductum, to conduct, bring, lead; to pass (a period of time)
pereō, -īre, -iī (-īuī), -itum, to perish, die
perfundō, -ere, -fūdī, -fūsum, to wet, drench
Pergama, -ōrum, *n. pl.,* Troy
periūrus, -a, -um, *adj.,* perjured
Permessus, -ī, *m.,* Permessus (a river on Mount Helicon)
Persēs, -ae, *m.,* a Persian
peruersus, -a, -um, *adj.,* facing the wrong way, reversed
perūrō, -ere, -ussī, -ustum, to burn, scorch
pēs, pedis, *m.,* foot
petō, -ere, -īuī *or* **-iī (-ī), -ītum,** to seek, fetch
Phaedra, -ae, *f.,* Phaedra
Pharos (-us), -ī, *f.* (*m.*), Pharos (an island off Alexandria)
Philippēus, -a, -um, *adj.,* of Philip II of Macedon
Philippī, -ōrum, *m. pl.,* Philippi (a town in Macedonia)

Philītēus, -a, -um, *adj.,* of Philitas (poet from Cos)
Phillyridēs, -is, *m.,* a son of Philyra, i.e., Chiron
Philoctēta (-ēs), -ae, *m.,* Philoctetes
Phlegraeus, -a, -um, *adj.,* of or associated with Phlegra
Phoebus, -ī, *m.,* Phoebus, Apollo
Phoenix, -īcis (-icos), *m.,* Phoenix
Phrygius, -a, -um, *adj.,* Phrygian, Trojan
Phyllis, -idis (-idos), *f.,* Phyllis
Pīeris, -idos, *f.,* a daughter of Pierus, Muse
pīlum, -ī, *n.,* spear, javelin
piō (1), to propitiate; avert by expiation; expiate (an offense)
pius, -a, -um, *adj.,* faithful, dutiful
placidus, -a, -um, *adj.,* calm, tranquil
plāga, -ae, *f.,* blow
platanus, -ī, *f.,* plane-tree
plectrum, -ī, *n.,* plectrum, used to strike a lyre's strings
Plēïas, -adis (-ados), *f.,* Pleiades
plēnus, -a, -um, *adj.,* full, replete
pluteus, -ī, *m.,* upright board forming the back, or far side, of a couch
pōculum, -ī, *n.,* cup, bowl
Poenus, -a, -um, *adj.,* Phoenician, Carthaginian
poēta, -ae, *m.,* poet

polluō, -ere, -uī, -utum, to dirty, pollute
Pompēius, -(i)ī, *m.,* Sextus Pompeius, Pompey
Pompēius, -a, -um, *adj.,* Pompeian
pōmum, -ī, *n.,* fruit
ponderō (1), to weigh
pōnō, -ere, posuī, positum, to place, set, put or lay down
pons, pontis, *m.,* bridge
pōpulus, -ī, *f.,* poplar
porta, -ae, *f.,* gate
porticus, -ūs, *f.* (*m.*), portico, colonnade
portō (1), transport, carry
portus, -ūs, *m.,* harbor, port
poscō, -ere, poposcī, —, to demand, call for
possum, posse, potuī, —, to be able, can
post, *prep.* + *acc.,* behind
postis, -is, *m.,* door post, jamb
postmodo, *adv.,* later, presently
postquam, *conj.,* after
pote. *See* **potis**
potis, *adv.,* able
pōtō, -āre, -āuī, -ātum *or* **-um,** to drink
praebeō, -ēre, -uī, -itum, to put forward, present, offer
praecipuē, *adv.,* especially, above all
praecōnium, -(i)ī, *n.,* public announcement, declaration
praecordia, -ōrum, *n. pl.,* vitals; diaphragm; chest, breast

praecurrō, -ere, -(cu)currī, -cursum, to run in front of others, hurry on ahead; to run past the front of
praeda, -ae, *f.,* plunder, spoil; prey, game (of a hunter); prize
praedor, -ārī, -ātus sum, to plunder, pillage
Praeneste, -is, *n.,* Praeneste (a town in Latium)
praesāgiō, -īre, -īuī, —, to have a foreboding of, portend
praescrībō, -ere, -scrīpsī, -scriptum, to prescribe, appoint
praesideō, -ēre, -sēdī, —, to watch over, govern, control
praetereō, -īre, -iī *or* **-īuī, -itum,** to go by, pass
praetor, -ōris, *m.,* praetor, leader
prātum, -ī, *n.,* meadow
precor, -ārī, -ātus sum, to pray for, implore
premō, -ere, pressī, pressum, to press
pretium, -(i)ī, *n.,* price; reward; recompense
prex, -ecis, *f.,* entreaty, prayer
prīmus, -a, -um, *adj.,* foremost, first
prīuignus, -ī, *m.,* stepson
prius, *adv.,* earlier, previously, before
probō (1), approve of, commend
prōcēdō, -ere, -cessī, -cessum, to go forward, advance
procella, -ae, *f.,* storm, gale

procul, *adv.,* apart; some way off; far away
proelium, -(i)ī, *n.,* battle
Promētheus, -eī *or* **-eos,** *m.,* Prometheus
prōnus, -a, -um, *adj.,* leaning or bending forward; sloping
Propertius, -(i)ī, *m.,* Propertius
prōtrahō, -ere, -traxī, -tractum, to drag forward or out
proximus, -a, -um, *adj.,* nearest, adjacent
Ptolomaeēus (Ptolem-), -a, -um, *adj.,* of the Ptolemies
pudendus, -a, -um, *adj.,* shameful, disgraceful
pudeō, -ēre, -uī *or* **-itum est,** —, to make ashamed; to feel shame, be ashamed
pudīcus, -a, -um, *adj.,* sexually pure, chaste
puella, -ae, *f.,* girl; girlfriend
puer, -erī, *m.,* boy; slave-boy
pugna, -ae, *f.,* fight, battle
pulcher, -chra, -chrum, *adj.,* beautiful, lovely
puluis, -eris, *m.,* dust
pūmex, -icis, *m.* (*f.*), pumice
pūniceus, -a, -um, *adj.,* bright red, scarlet
pūnicus, -a, -um, *adj.,* bright red, scarlet
pūniō, -īre, -īuī *or* **-iī, -ītum,** to punish
purgō (1), to purify; to rid (a place) of pests and undesirable persons
purpureus, -a, -um, *adj.,* purple
pūrus, -a, -um, *adj.,* clean, pure
putris (puter), -tre, *adj.,* putrid, crumbling
Pyrr(h)us, -ī, *m.,* Pyrrhus (king of Epirus)
Pȳthius, -a, -um, *adj.,* Delphic, Pythian

quā, *interr., rel.,* and *indef. adv.,* in which part, where
quaerō, -ere, quaes(i)ī *or* **quaesīuī, quaesītum,** to search for, seek
quaesō, (-ere), —, —, ask
quālis, -e, *interr.* and *rel. adj.,* of what sort, such as (correlative with **tālis**)
quamuīs, *rel. adv.,* to any degree you like, however, although
quandō, *rel.* and *indef. adv.,* when; seeing that, since
quandōcumque, *rel.* and *indef. adv.,* at whatever time, whenever
quantum, *interr.* and *rel. adv.,* how much?, to what extent, degree
quantus, -a, -um, *adj.,* of what size, how great
quārē, *interr.* and *rel. adv.,* in what way; for what reason, why
quatiō, -ere, —, **quassum,** to shake, rock
quattuor, *indecl. adj.,* four
-que, *conj.,* and
querēla, -ae, *f.,* grievance, complaint

queror, -ī, questus sum, to complain, grumble, protest
quī, quae, quod, *pron.* and *adj.,* who, which, what
quia, *conj.,* because
quīcumque, quaecumque, quodcumque, *rel.* and *indef. pron., adj.,* whoever, whatever
quīdam, quaedam, quoddam, *adj.,* a certain
quiēs, -ētis, *f.,* sleep, rest, repose
quīn, *adv.,* indeed, in fact; *conj.* (+ subjunctive), so that ... not
quippe, *particle,* for, indeed
Quirītēs, -ītium, *m.,* citizens of Rome
quis, quid, *interr., indef. pron. (adj.),* who?, which?, what?; someone, something
quisquam, quicquam (quidquam), *pron., (adj.),* anyone, anything
quisque, quaeque, quidque (quicque) *or* **quodque,** *pron., adj.,* each, each one
quisquis, quidquid (quicquid), *indef. pron. and adj.,* whoever, whatever
quīuīs, quaeuīs, quiduīs, *pron.,* whatever person you please, whatever thing, anyone, anything
quod, *rel. adv.,* as to which, wherefore; (+ *si*) in view of which; wherefore; and yet; *conj.* that, because

quodsi, *rel. adv. and conj.,* as to which, wherefore, now
quondam, *adv.,* before, formerly
quoniam, *conj.,* as soon as; now that; since
quoque, *adv.,* besides, as well, too
quotiens (-iēs), *interr. and rel. adv.,* as often as, whenever

radius, -(i)ī, *m.,* ray of light
rādō, -ere, rāsī, rāsum, to scrape, graze, brush
rāmus, -ī, *m.,* branch, club
rapidus, -a, -um, *adj.,* rapid, quick
rapīna, -ae, *f.,* plunder
raptō (1), to carry away forcibly; to hale off (to court)
raptor, -ōris, *m.,* robber
rārus, -a, -um, *adj.,* sparse, infrequent, rare
ratis, -is, *f.,* boat, ship
raucus, -a, -um, *adj.,* harsh, noisy, raucous
recidō (recc-), -ere, -c(c)idī, (-cāsum), to fall back
recipiō, -ere, -cēpī, -ceptum, to receive
recondō, -ere, -didī, -ditum, to put away, hide away
recubō, -āre, —, —, to lie back, recline
recurrō, -ere, -currī, -cursum, to run back, return
redeō, -īre, -iī, -itum, to come back, return

redūcō, -ere, -duxī, -ductum, to lead back, bring back
referō, -ferre, rettulī, relātum, to bring back, return, report
refringō, -ere, -frēgī, -fractum, to break
rēgius, -a, -um, *adj.,* royal
regnum, -ī, *n.,* realm
remaneō, -ēre, -sī, —, to remain, stay
remittō, -ere, -mīsī, -missum, to relax
Remus, -ī, *m.,* Remus (the brother of Romulus)
reor, rērī, ratus sum, to think, suppose
reperiō, -īre, repperī, repertum, to find
repleō, -ēre, -plēuī, -plētum, to fill up
reposcō, -ere, —, —, to demand back; to claim
rēs, reī, *f.,* thing, matter; in *pl.* deeds, exploits
respondeō, -ēre, -dī, -sum, to reply
restituō, -ere, -uī, -ūtum, to restore, revive
restō, stare, stitī, to be left, remain
resupīnō (1), to knock flat; to cause to lie flat
rēte, -is, *n.,* net
retegō, -ere, -texī, -tectum, to make visible, reveal
reuocō (1), to call back, recall
rex, rēgis, *m.,* king
Rhēnus, -ī, *m.,* Rhine River
rīdeō, -ēre, rīsī, rīsum, to laugh, smile
rigō (1), to make wet
rixa, -ae, *f.,* altercation, brawl
Rōma, -ae, *f.,* Rome
Rōmānus, -a, -um, *adj.,* Roman
Rōmulus, -a, -um, *adj.,* of Romulus, Roman
rosa, -ae, *f.,* rose
rostrum, -ī, *n.,* beak, the beak of a ship
rota, -ae, *f.,* wheel
rūmor, -ōris, *m.,* rumor, gossip
rumpō, -ere, rūpī, ruptum, to break
ruō, -ere, -ī, —, to rush headlong; to charge; to come to ruin
rūpēs, -is, *f.,* rocky cliff, crag
rursus, -um, *adv.,* backwards, once again

Sabīnī, -ōrum, *m. pl.,* the Sabines
sacer, -cra, -crum, *adj.,* sacred
sacerdōs, -ōtis, *m./f.,* priest
sacrum, -ī, *n.,* sacred object; religious ceremony or rite
saepe, *adv.,* often, frequently
saeta, -ae, *f.,* hair of animal
saeuiō, -īre, -iī, -ītum, to rage
saeuitia, -ae, *f.,* savageness, cruelty, violence
saeuus, -a, -um, *adj.,* harsh, savage, ferocious
sagīna, -ae, *f.,* the diet of gladiators and athletes
sagitta, -ae, *f.,* arrow
salīua, -ae, *f.,* flavor

saluē, *imperative,* hello, hail
saluus, -a, -um, *adj.,* safe, secure
sanciō, -īre, sanxī, sanctum, to ratify, confirm; to consecrate; to hallow
sanctus, -a, -um, *adj.,* holy, sacred
sanguis, -inis, *m.,* blood
sānō (1), to heal, restore to health
sānus, -a, -um, *adj.,* sound, healthy
sapiō, -ere, -īuī (-iī), —, to know, understand
sat. *See* **satis**
satis, *adv.,* enough, sufficient
Sāturnus, -ī, *m.,* Saturn
sauciō (1), to wound, cut
saucius, -a, -um, *adj.,* wounded, suffering
saxum, -ī, *n.,* rock, boulder
scamnum, -ī, *n.,* stool, bench
scīlicet, *particle,* naturally, it is obvious
sciō, -īre, -iī *or* **-īuī, -ītum,** to know
Scīpiadās, -ae, *m.,* one of the Scipiones
scrībō, -ere, scripsī, scriptum, to write
sē, *reflex. pron.,* himself, herself, itself
sēcrētus, -a, -um, *adj.,* secluded
secundus, -a, -um, *adj.,* next in order, following; favorable
secūris, -is, *f.,* axe
sed, *conj.,* but

sedeō, -ēre, sēdī, sessum, to sit, be seated
sēdēs, -is, *f.,* seat
sēdō (1), to mitigate, relieve
sēdulus, -a, -um, *adj.,* attentive, sedulous
sēiunctus, -a, -um, *adj.,* separate, detached
Semīramis, -idis, *f.,* Semiramis (queen of Assyria)
sēmita, -ae, *f.,* side-path, course, track
semper, *adv.,* always
senex, *gen.* **-is,** *adj.,* old
sensus, -ūs, *m.,* sense, sensation
sentiō, -īre, sensī, sensum, to feel, sense
sepeliō, -īre, -pelīuī *or* **-peliī, -pultum,** to bury; to submerge; to overcome
septem, *indecl. adj.,* seven
septēnī, -ae, -a, *adj.,* seven
sequor, -ī, secūtus sum, to follow
sēricus, -a, -um, *adj.,* made of silk, silken
serō, -ere, sēuī, satum, to plant, sow
sērō, *adv.,* late, tardily, too late
serpens, -ntis, *f./m.,* snake, serpent
seruīlis, -e, *adj.,* of a slave, servile
seruō (1), to preserve, keep
sērus, -a, -um, *adj.,* belated, slow, tardy
seu. *See* **sīue**
sī, *conj.,* if
sībilum, -ī, *n.,* hissing

sīc, *adv.,* thus, so
siccō (1), to dry
siccus, -a, -um, *adj.,* dry
Siculus, -a, -um, *adj.,* Sicilian
Sīdonius, -a, -um, *adj.,* Sidonian
sīdus, -eris, *n.,* heavenly body, star, planet
signum, -ī, *n.,* sign, standard, statue
Sīlēnus, -ī, *m.,* Silenus (tutor of Bacchus)
similis, -e, *adj.,* similar, like
sīn, *conj.,* if however, but if
sine, *prep. + abl.,* without
singulī, -ae, -a, *adj.,* individual, single
sinister, -tra, -trum, *adj.,* adverse, harmful; left
sinus, -ūs, *m.,* breast; lap; garment fold; purse; harbor
sistō, -ere, stetī *or* **stitī, statum,** to halt, stop
sistrum, -ī, *n.,* sistrum, rattle used in the worship of Isis
sitiens, *gen.* **-ntis,** *adj.,* thirsty
sitis, -is, *f.,* thirst
sīue, *conj.,* or if
smaragdus (-os), -ī, *m.,* a green gem, emerald
sōbrius, -ia, -ium, *adj.,* sober
socer, -erī, *m.,* father-in-law
sōl, sōlis, *m.,* the sun
soleō, -ēre, -itus, —, to be accustomed
solidus, -a, -um, *adj.,* solid
solum, -ī, *n.,* soil, earth
soluō, -ere, -uī, -ūtum, to loosen, untie; slacken, relax
sōlus, -a, -um, *adj.,* alone

somnus, -ī, *m.,* sleep
sonans, *gen.* **-ntis,** *adj.,* noisy
sonitus, -ūs, *m.,* sound, noise
sonō, -āre (-ere), -uī, -itum, to sound, celebrate in speech
sonus, -ī, *m.,* sound, noise
sōpiō, -īre, -īuī *or* **-iī, -ītum,** to cause to sleep, overcome with sleep
sopor, -ōris, *m.,* a deep or overpowering sleep
sordeō, -ēre, —, —, to seem unworthy, mean, not good enough
soror, -ōris, *f.,* sister
sors, -rtis, *f.,* lot, oracular response
sortior, -īrī, -ītus sum, to obtain by lot, have allotted
spargō, -ere, sparsī, sparsum, to scatter, spread
spatior, -ārī, -ātus sum, to walk about, stroll
speciēs, -ēī, *f.,* sight, display
spectāclum, -ī, *n.,* a sight, spectacle
spectō (1), to look at, observe
speculor, -ārī, -ātus sum, to observe
spēlunca, -ae, *f.,* cave
spērō (1), to hope
spēs, -eī, *f.,* hope, expectation
spīrō (1), to breathe, exhale
spolium, -(i)ī, *n.,* spoils, booty
stabulum, -ī, *n.,* stable
stagnō (1), to be covered with pools, be under water
stāmen, -inis, *n.,* the warp, thread

statua, -ae, *f.,* statue
statuō, -ere, -uī, -ūtum, to erect, build
sternō, -ere, strāuī, strātum, to scatter, strew
stō, -āre, stetī, statum, to stand
stolidus, -a, -um, *adj.,* stupid, brutish
strāmineus, -a, -um, *adj.,* made of straw
stringō, -ere, strinxī, strictum, to graze, scratch
stuprum, -ī, *n.,* dishonor, illicit sexual intercourse
Stygius, -a, -um, *adj.,* Stygian
sub, *prep. + acc.,* to a position below; *prep. + abl.,* under
subdō, -ere, -didī, -ditum, to subject, make subordinate to
subdūcō, -ere, -duxī, -ductum, to draw up, raise
sūbiciō, -ere, -iēcī, -iectum, to place underneath, cast beneath
subitō, *adv.,* suddenly
subsiliō, -īre, -uī, —, to jump up, spring up
subtrahō, -ere, -traxī, -tractum, to drag away, remove; withdraw
succipiō, -ere, -cēpī, -ceptum, to catch from below; to take up
succurrō, -ere, -currī, -cursum, to run or move quickly
Suēuus, -a, -um, *adj.,* of the Suebi

suffiō, -īre, -īuī *or* **-iī, -ītum,** to fumigate
sulpur, -uris, *n.,* sulphur
sum, esse, fuī, —, to be, exist
summoueō, -ēre, -mōuī, -mōtum, to move out of the way; to keep at a distance, seclude; to prohibit
summus, -a, -um, *adj.,* highest, topmost, farthest
sūmō, -ere, sumpsī (sumsī), sumptum (sumtum), to take up, seize
supellex, -ectilis, *f.,* furnishings; paraphernalia
superbus, -a, -um, *adj.,* proud, haughty
superus, -a, -um, *adj.,* upper, of the upper world
supīnus, -a, -um, *adj.,* flat on one's back, upturned
suppleō, -ēre, -ēuī, -ētum, to fill up
supplex, *gen.* **-icis,** *adj.,* suppliant
suppōnō, -ere, -posuī, -positum, to place under or beneath
suprā, *prep. + acc.,* on top of
surdus, -a, -um, *adj.,* deaf, unhearing
surgō, -ere, surrexī, surrectum, to get up, rise
suspīrium, -(i)ī, *n.,* sigh
suus (-os), -a, -um (-om), *poss. adj.,* his, her, its,
Syphax, -ācis, *m.,* Syphax (Numidian prince during the Second Punic War)

taberna, -ae, *f.,* shop
taceō, -ēre, -uī, -itum, to be silent, say nothing
tacitus, -a, -um, *adj.,* silent, quiet
taeda, -ae, *f.,* torch
tālis, -e, *adj.,* of such a kind, of such a kind as/that (with **quālis**)
tam, *adv.,* to such a degree, so much
tamen, *adv.,* nevertheless
tandem, *adv.,* at last
tangō, -ere, tetigī, tactum, to touch
Tantaleus, -a, -um, *adj.,* of or belonging to Tantalus
Tantalis, -idos, *f.,* a female descendent of Tantalus
tantum, *adv.,* to such an extent or degree
tantus, -a, -um, *adj.,* of such magnitude, so great
tardus, -a, -um, *adj.,* slow
Tarpēius, -a, -um, *adj.,* Tarpeian
Tarquinius, -(i)ī, *m.,* Tarquin (name of Roman kings)
Tatius, -(i)ī, *m.,* Tatius (a Sabine king of Cures)
Tatius, -a, -um, *adj.,* of Tatius
taurus, -ī, *m.,* bull
Tegeaeus, -a, -um, *adj.,* of Tegea, Tegean
tegō, -ere, texī, tectum, to cover
Tēia, -ae, *f.,* Teia
Tēlegonus, -ī, *m.,* Telegonus (son of Odysseus and Circe)
tellūs, -ūris, *f.,* ground, earth
tēlum, -ī, *n.,* weapon

temere, *adv.,* heedlessly, recklessly
tēmō, -ōnis, *m.,* pole or yoke-beam of a cart or chariot
tempestās, -ātis, *f.,* time
templum, -ī, *n.,* temple
temptō (1), to test, try out; to make an assault on
tempus, -oris, *n.,* time, season
tempus, -oris, *n.,* the side of the forehead, temple
tendō, -ere, tetendī, tentum *or* **tensum,** to extend, stretch out
tenebrae, -ārum, *f. pl.,* darkness
teneō, -ēre, -uī, -tum, to hold, grasp
tener, -ra, -rum, *adj.,* soft, tender
ter, *adv.,* three times, thrice
tergeō, -ēre, tersī, tersum, to rub clean, wipe
tergum, -ī, *n.,* back, the rear
terō, -ere, trīuī, trītum, to wear down, wear away
terra, -ae, *f.,* land
terreō, -ēre, -uī, -itum, to terrify
testis, -is, *m.,* witness
testor, -ārī, -ātus sum, to invoke as a witness; testify to
Teutonicus, -a, -um, *adj.,* of the Teutoni
texō, -ere, -uī, -tum, to weave
theātrum, -ī, *n.,* theatre
Thēbae, -ārum, *f. pl.,* Thebes
Thēseus, -ei *or* **-eos,** *m.,* Theseus
Thēsēus, -a, -um, *adj.,* of Theseus

thyrsus, -ī, *m.,* thyrsus (wand carried by worshippers of Bacchus)
Tiberis, -is, *m.,* Tiber River
tībīcen, -inis, *m.,* one who plays the *tibia*, piper
Tībur, -ris, *n.,* Tibur (a town on the Anio)
timeō, -ēre, -uī, —, to be afraid
timidus, -a, -um, *adj.,* fearful
timor, -ōris, *m.,* fear
tingō, -ere, tinxī, tinctum, to wet, dip; to imbue; to color, stain
Tīresiās, -ae, *m.,* Tiresias
Tītān, -nos, *m.,* one of the Titans
tollō, -ere, sustulī, sublātum, to pick up, raise; to take away, carry off; to remove
torqueō, -ēre, -quesī, -quetum, to twist
torus, -ī, *m.,* the bed as the place of conjugal union
toruus, -a, -um, *adj.,* fierce, savage
tot, *indecl. adj.,* so many
totiē(n)s, *adv.,* so often
tōtus, -a, -um, *adj.,* whole, all, entire
trādō, -ere, -didī, -ditum, to deliver, hand over
trahō, -ere, traxī, tractum, to drag, carry along, haul; to draw (into one's body); to draw out (of spinning thread)
tremō, -ere, -uī, —, to tremble, show fright at
trēs, tria, *adj.,* three
tristis, -e, *adj.,* stern
Trītōn, -ōnis, *m.,* Triton
trītus, -a, -um, *adj.,* worn
triuius, -a, -um, *adj.,* of or belonging to a *triuium*, meeting of three roads, "the public gutter"
triumphus, -ī, *m.,* triumph
tropaeum, -ī, *n.,* trophy
truncus, -a, -um, *adj.,* stunted in growth
tū, tuī, *pers. pron.,* you, yourself (sing.)
tueor, -ērī, tuitus (tūtus) sum, to keep safe, protect
Tullus, -ī, *m.,* Tullus
tum, *adv.,* at that moment or date, then
tumultus, -ūs, *m.,* commotion, uproar, turmoil
tunc, *adv.,* then
tunica, -ae, *f.,* tunic
turba, -ae, *f.,* commotion, turmoil, crowd
turbō (1), to agitate, stir up, disturb
turma, -ae, *f.,* troop, squadron
turpis, -e, *adj.,* ugly, shameful
tūs, tūris, *n.,* frankincense
tūtēla, -ae, *f.,* guardianship, protection; source of protection; charge or object of a guardian
tūtus, -a, -um, *adj.,* protected, safe, secure
tuus (-os), -a, -um (-um), *poss. adj.,* your (sing.)
tympanum, -ī, *n.,* small drum

Tyndaris, -idis *or* **-idos,** *f.*, a daughter of Tyndareus, Helen
Tyros *or* **Tyrus, -ī,** *f.*, Tyre

uacō (1), to be vacant, empty
uacuus (uacuos), -a, -um (-om), *adj.*, empty
uadum, -ī, *n.*, water
uagus, -a, -um, *adj.*, wandering
ualeō, -ēre, -uī, -ītum, to be powerful, have strength
ualuae, -ārum, *f. pl.*, double door
uānus, -a, -um, *adj.*, insubstantial, empty, false
uastus, -a, -um, *adj.*, huge, tremendous
uātēs (uātis), -is, *m.*, seer, poet
ubī, *interr., rel.,* and *indef. adv.*, where, when
-ue, *enclitic conj.*, or
uectō (1), to transport, carry
uehō, -ere, uexī, uectum, to convey, carry
Vēlābrum, -ī, *n.*, Velabrum (a low-lying area between the Capitol and Palatine)
uēlificō (1), to sail
uellō, -ere, uellī *or* **uulsī (uolsī), uulsum (uolsum),** to pull, pluck, depilate
uēlō (1), to cover
uēlox, *gen.* **-ōcis,** *adj.*, rapid, swift
uēnālis, -e, *adj.*, for sale
uenēnum, -ī, *n.*, potent herb, poison
uēneō, -īre, -iī, (-itum), to be sold; to be sold as a slave
ueneror, -ārī, -ātus sum, to worship
ueniō, -īre, uēnī, uentum, to come
uentus, -ī, *m.*, wind
Venus, -eris, *f.*, Venus; sexual activity
uerbum, -ī, *n.*, word
uerendus, -a, -um, *adj.*, that is to be regarded with awe or reverence
uereor, -ērī, -itus sum, to regard as a source of fear
uērō, *adv.*, in fact, really, truly
uersō (uorsō) (1), to turn, twist
uersus (uorsus), -ūs, *m.*, line of writing, verse
uertix (uortex), -icis, *m.*, summit, peak
uertō (uortō), -ere, uertī, uersum, to turn
uester, -ra, -trum, *poss. adj.*, your (pl.)
uestīgium, -(i)ī, *n.*, footprint, track, visible trace
uestis, -is, *f.*, attire, clothes
uetō, -āre, -uī, -itum, to forbid, prohibit
uetus, *gen.* **-eris,** *adj.*, old
uexō (1), to harass
uia, -ae, *f.*, road
Via Sacra, Viae Sacrae, *f.*, Sacred Way
uīcīnus, -a, -um, *adj.*, neighboring
uictor, -ōris, *m.*, conqueror
uictrix, *gen.* **-īcis,** *adj.*, victorious

uideō, -ēre, uisī, uisum, to see; *pass.,* to appear, seem
uīlis, -e, *adj.,* cheap
uinciō, -īre, uinxī, uinctum, to fasten, bind
uincō, -ere, uīcī, uictum, to defeat, conquer
uinculum *or* **uinclum, -ī,** *n.,* bond, chain
uindicō (1), to defend, protect
uir, uirī, *m.,* man
uirgineus (-ius), -a, -um, *adj.,* virgin
uirgō, -inis, *f.,* virgin, maiden
uiridis, -e, *adj.,* green
uirtūs, -ūtis, *f.,* manly spirit, valor; virtue
uīs, uis, *f.,* strength
uīta, -ae, *f.,* life
uitium, -(i)ī, *n.,* defect, fault
uītō (1), to avoid, shun
uitrum, -ī, *n.,* glass
uitta, -ae, *f.,* woolen band
uīuidus, -a, -um, *adj.,* lifelike
uīuō, -ere, uixī, uictum, to live
uix, *adv.,* hardly, scarcely, barely
ullus, -a, -um, *adj.,* any
ultimus, -a, -um, *adj.,* final, ultimate, last
umbra, -ae, *f.,* shadow, shade
umbrōsus, -a, -um, *adj.,* shadowy, shady
umerus, -ī, *m.,* shoulder
ūmor (hūm-), -ōris, *m.,* liquid
umquam, *adv.,* at any time, ever
unda, -ae, *f.,* wave
unde, *interr.* and *rel. adv.,* from what place, from where, whence
unguis, -is, *m.,* fingernail
ūnus, -a, -um, *adj.,* one, single
uocō (1), to call, summon
uolō, uelle, uoluī, —, to want, wish
uolucer, -cris, -cre, *adj.,* flying, winged; swift, rapid
uolūmen, -inis, *n.,* roll of papyrus, book
uoluō, -ere, -uī, -ūtum, to roll, roll forward; to cause to fall; to unroll
uōs, uestrum *or* **uestrī,** *pron.,* you (pl.)
uōtum, -ī, *n.,* vow
uox, uōcis, *f.,* voice
urbānus, -a, -um, *adj.,* urban
urbs, urbis, *f.,* city
urna, -ae, *f.,* urn
ūrō, -ere, ussī, ustum, to burn
ut, *adv.,* how, just as; *conj.,* + *indicative* as, when; + *subjunctive* so that, in order that; with the result that
uterque, utraque, utrumque, *adj., pron.,* each; each of two
utinam, *particle,* how I wish that, if only
ūtor, -ī, ūsus sum, to use (+ abl.)
uulgō, *adv.,* commonly, regularly
uulnus, -eris, *n.,* wound
uultus, -ūs, *m.,* countenance, face
uxor, -ōris, *f.,* wife

Xerxēs, -is, *m.,* Xerxes (Persian king)

LATIN Readers

Series Editor: RONNIE ANCONA, HUNTER COLLEGE AND CUNY GRADUATE CENTER

Other Readers Also Now Available

An Apuleius Reader
Selections from the METAMORPHOSES
ELLEN D. FINKELPEARL
(2012) ISBN 978-0-86516-714-8

A Caesar Reader
Selections from BELLUM GALLICUM and BELLUM CIVILE, and from Caesar's Letters, Speeches, and Poetry
W. JEFFREY TATUM
(2012) ISBN 978-0-86515-696-7

A Cicero Reader
Selections from Five Essays and Four Speeches, with Five Letters
JAMES M. MAY
(2012) ISBN 978-0-86515-713-1

A Latin Epic Reader
Selections from Ten Epics
ALISON KEITH
(2012) ISBN 978-0-86515-686-8

A Livy Reader
Selections from AB URBE CONDITA
MARY JAEGER
(2011) ISBN 978-0-86515-680-6

A Lucan Reader
Selections from CIVIL WAR
SUSANNA BRAUND
(2009) ISBN 978-0-86516-661-5

A Martial Reader
Selections from Epigrams
CRAIG WILLIAMS
(2011) ISBN 978-0-86516-704-9

An Ovid Reader
Selections from Seven Works
CAROLE E. NEWLANDS
(2014) ISBN 978-0-86515-722-3

A Plautus Reader
Selections from Eleven Plays
JOHN HENDERSON
(2009) ISBN 978-0-86516-694-3

A Roman Army Reader
Selections from Literary, Epigraphic, and Other Documents
DEXTER HOYOS
(2013) ISBN 978-0-86515-715-5

A Roman Verse Satire Reader
Selections from Lucilius, Horace, Persius, and Juvenal
CATHERINE C. KEANE
(2010) ISBN 978-0-86515-685-1

A Sallust Reader
Selections from BELLUM CATILINAE, BELLUM IUGURTHINUM, and HISTORIAE
VICTORIA E. PAGÁN
(2009) ISBN 978-0-86515-687-5

A Seneca Reader
Selections from Prose and Tragedy
JAMES KER
(2011) ISBN 978-0-86515-758-2

A Suetonius Reader
Selections from the LIVES OF THE CAESARS and the LIFE OF HORACE
JOSIAH OSGOOD
(2011) ISBN 978-0-86515-716-2

A Tacitus Reader
Selections from ANNALES, HISTORIAE, GERMANIA, AGRICOLA, and DIALOGUS
STEVEN H. RUTLEDGE
(2013) ISBN 978-0-86515-697-4

A Terence Reader
Selections from Six Plays
WILLIAM S. ANDERSON
(2009) ISBN 978-0-86515-678-3

A Tibullus Reader
Seven Selected Elegies
PAUL ALLEN MILLER
(2013) ISBN 978-0-86515-724-7

Forthcoming

A Roman Women Reader
SHEILA K. DICKISON and JUDITH P. HALLETT • ISBN 978-0-86515-662-2

**VISIT THE SERIES WEBSITE:
www.bolchazy.com/BCLatinReaders.aspx**